THE
SCANDINAVIAN
Spirit

THE SCANDINAVIAN Spirit

Arland O. Fiske

North American Heritage Press

THE SCANDINAVIAN SPIRIT

International Standard Book Number: 0-942323-08-4

Cover design by
Sheldon Larson of Creative Media, Minot, ND.

Cover photo by
Hruska-Kray-Nauman Photographers, Dubuque, Iowa.

The young girls on the cover are
Anne Marie and Lara Marie Gaylor.

Published by
North American Heritage Press
A DIVISION OF
CREATIVE MEDIA, INC.
P.O. Box 1
Minot, North Dakota 58702
701/852-5552

Printed in the United States of America

811   839.7
          Fis   1/16/90   7.96   Book Club

iv

Dedication

In memory
of my Father
Oscar B. Fiske
(1903-1966)
and
in honor
of my Mother
Anne Thompson Fiske

Thanks

for handing on
the Scandinavian "Spirit"
to your family.

CONTENTS

Foreword
Preface
Chapter   Page

1   "Beowulf" — A Scandinavian Epic Poem   1
2   Early Norse Settlers In The New World   4
3   "Apaurak" In Alaska   9
4   Vitus Bering — Danish Sea Captain   12
5   The "Viking Battalion" In World War II   15
6   The Vikings In The Age Of Charlemagne   18
7   Art In The Viking World   21
8   More Light On The Greenlanders   24
9   Thor Heyerdahl And The "Maldive Mystery"   27
10   Ole Evinrude And The Outboard Motor   30
11   Some Early Norse Settlers In Montana   33
12   The Haugeans At Eidsvoll   36
13   The Scandinavians Meet In Columbus   39
14   "Vesterheim" — The Norwegian-American Museum .   42
15   Lars Skrefsrud — Apostle To The Santals   45
16   Scandinavian Immigrants And The Slavery Issue   . . .   48
17   Scandinavian Immigrants And Public Education   51
18   Abraham Lincoln And The Scandinavian
       Immigrants   54
19   How Finland Got Its Independence   57
20   The "Friends Of Augsburg"   61
21   Racine — City Of "Danish Delight"   65
22   Slesvig — Denmark's Disputed Duchy   69
23   Sten Sture — A Swedish Hero   72
24   "Kalevela" — The Finnish National Epic   75
25   Fredrika Bremer — Early Swedish Visitor To
       America   78
26   General Stuart Barstad — Chief Air Force Padre   81
27   1988 — The Year Of The Swedish-Americans   84
28   The Scandinavian Dedication To Freedom   87

Chapter		Page
29	Edwin T. Denig — Ft. Union Fur Trader	90
30	Norway's Strategic Place In NATO	93
31	Roald Amundsen — Arctic Explorer	96
32	Poulbso, Washington — Norse Home In The West	99
33	Sidney Anders Rand — Ambassador To Norway	102
34	The Danish Immigrant Village — Elk Horn, Iowa	106
35	St. Ansgar — Apostle To the Norse	109
36	The Reformation In Denmark And Norway	112
37	King Olav V And The Church Of Norway	116
38	Sigrid Undset — Norwegian Nobel Laureate	120
39	Knute Rockne — An Untold Story	123
40	The Reformation In Sweden	127
41	Charles Lindbergh And The "Spirit Of St. Louis"	131
42	The Conversion of Iceland	135
43	Nathan Søderblom — Swedish Ecumenical Leader	139
44	The Early Norsemen	143
45	The Mystery Of "Sutton Hoo"	147
46	Alfred The Great And The Vikings	151
47	The Adventures Of Erik "Bloodaxe"	155
48	From Vladimir To "Glastnost" — 1,000 Years Of Christianity in Russia	159
49	M. Falk Gjertsen — A Pastor Under Fire	163
50	Marcus Thrane — Radical Norwegian Social Reformer	167
51	The Mystique Of The Normans	171
52	The Hongs Of Northfield	175
53	The Wisconsin "Birkebeiners"	179
54	The Swedes Of Lindsborg, Kansas	183
55	Vikings In Oklahoma?	186
56	The Swedes In North Dakota	190
57	The Spring Grove Norwegians	193
58	The Swedish-Soviet Relations	197
59	The Adventures Of Svein "Forkbeard"	201
60	The End Of The Viking Age	205
61	The Sons Of Norway "USA Soccer Cup"	209
62	A Tribute To Besta	212
63	The Erickstad Legacy	216

Chapter
Page

64 Norman Borlaug And The "Green Revolution" 220

65 The Genius Of The Sagas 225

66 Paavo Ruotsalainen — Finland's Greatest
Religious Leader 229

x

FOREWORD

I T WAS HENRY WADSWORTH LONGFELLOW who wrote:
> Lives of great men all remind us
> We can make our lives sublime.
> And, departing, leave behind us
> Footprints on the sands of time;
>
> Footprints, that perhaps another,
> Sailing o'ver life's solemn main,
> A forlorn and shipwrecked brother,
> Seeing, shall take heart again.

Our time has become cynical of great men and women unless greatness is determined in terms of wealth and power. The ability to see greatness in the lives of ordinary men and women has been lost. Our times have been unable to see footprints beyond our own personal experience. The price is to lose the rebirth of heart that can come from seeing the footprints. A second loss is to be unable to learn from the stories of the men and women of the past.

Perhaps it was the story of the book "Roots" that has restimulated our interest in our past. I sense that here and there we are finding an interest in our roots and with this the learnings of history and the inspirations gained from seeing the footprints in the sands of time.

Arland Fiske has made a contribution to this new sense of discovery among people of Scandinavian background in his previous volumes, "The Scandinavian Heritage" and "The Scandinavian World." The vignettes have been interesting, easy to read and filled with "footprints." The current volume continues the vignettes of great men and women most often overlooked in history books but nevertheless great. We are invited to read, enjoy, reflect and draw in the learnings for us found in these pages.

In this volume Fiske also includes many tales from Scandinavian history, the wars, the sagas, the Viking Chieftans and their exploits.

Some of them sound crude to us but they are a part of our heritage and offer learnings for us in our time. A couple of learnings that call for reflection are:

• The response of the Scandinavians to the slavery issue. They saw slavery as wrong but felt little kinship with the impatience of William Lloyd Garrison and the radical abolitionists. They felt slavery would die of its own poison. Could more of this kind of thinking have tempered the movements leading to the Civil War? With more of this kind of thinking perhaps the slaves could have been liberated without the deep, enduring hatreds coming out of a long, bloody war?

• The spirit of liberty and the strength of the local "Things." What impact has this had on the populists movements in North Dakota, Minnesota and Wisconsin? What impact has this had on church polity tensions in the Evangelical Lutheran Church in America between the midwestern Lutherans and the eastern Lutherans?

You will find your own seeds of reflection.

The chapters are brief and can be read in little snatches of time or all in one sitting. With many different stories and many different themes the reader will find some more significant than others. However, there will be ample occasion both for enjoyment and the learnings from these stories of our forebeaers. With a little care you will see many "footprints in the sands of time" if need be to take heart again.

Richard D. Vangerud
St. Paul, MN

PREFACE

THIS VOLUME JOINS "The Scandinavian Heritage" (1987) and "The Scandinavian World" (1988) in attempting to tell some stories about the people of Europe's far North, both in their native lands and in diaspora around the world. There aren't many of us (only one percent of the world's population), so our story needs to be told, both to our own generations and to the world.

Three purposes have motivated the writing of these stories. The first is to offer an information basis for pride in the heritage. The second is to provide ethnic entertainment, like the old sagas. The third is to encourage the readers to preserve the best of the heritage and hand it on to future generations. So I'm a protagonist, you might say, if not a propagandist, eager to keep the Scandinavian "spirit" alive.

In America, we're all taken up with the "Vikings." There are the Minnesota Vikings, plus the many colleges and high schools which are named after those buccaneers who used to move across the waters in their longboats to terrorize unsuspecting people.

But there was much more to those people than just "Vikings," however much they may intrigue us today. There were also many good people among them who had a code of honor, a democratic system of government, and a respect for women that was advanced for their time. The "sea pirates" undoubtedly deserved the bad press that their enemies gave them, but their descendants today are among the most dedicated people to "peacemaking" in the world.

If there is any one characteristic about the Scandinavian spirit that deserves mention it is dedication to freedom. They have not only sacrificed to maintain their own freedom, but work for peace among other nations. Yet they stand up for human rights of the oppressed when more powerful nations ignore those who suffer.

THE SCANDINAVIAN SPIRIT

Our cousins across the sea take good care of their own people. They haven't invented the perfect society yet (neither has anyone else), but there is concern for children, families, the handicapped, the infirm and the aged among them. They are highly literate, have a passion for education and a safe environment. In less than half a century they've developed one of the highest standards of living in the world.

Few of us Scandinavian-Americans would give up our citizenship in the New World to return to the lands of our ancestors. Yet we cherish a deep love for those places and people, and we count them as dear friends. It's a special day when we visit back and forth. In other words, we're quite comfortable with each other.

It's been gratifying to note the high acceptance of these writings both in the New World and in the Old. In some places the books are used for classroom reading, including a high school in Norway. Thanks to the many people who have shared their interests in these stories by offering new information, corrections and the inspiration to keep on writing.

I continue to owe deepest appreciation to my wife, Gerda, for her encouragement, proofreading and suggestions. Our children and grandchildren have also been highly supportive. My many friends involved in the Norsk Høstfest have vindicated my belief that the Scandinavian spirit always rises to the big tasks and has fun doing them. Thanks to Allen O. Larson and the North American Heritage Press for making this third book possible. Thanks to Tammy Wolf for her preparation of the manuscript for publication; to Sheldon Larson for designing the cover; and to my daughter, Lisa Gaylor, for drawing the illustrations and dressing up her daughters, Anne (Ah-neh) and Lara, to appear on the cover.

I owe special thanks to Dr. William H. Halverson, Ohio State University (retired), Columbus, OH; Dr. Art Lee, Bemidji State University, Bemidji, MN; Dr. Todd Nichols, Luther Northwestern Seminary, St. Paul, MN; and Rev. Richard Vangerud, St. Paul, MN, for their critical reading of the manuscript and suggestions, as well as their commendations.

—Arland O. Fiske
Minot, ND
July 29, 1989 — The Festival of St. Olaf

CHAPTER 1

'Beowulf' —
A Scandinavian Epic Poem

THE WORLD NEVER TIRES of heroes or hero worship. The best known "hero" story in the Western world was told by an ancient Greek writer, Homer, in the "Iliad" and the "Odyssey." "Beowulf" is also such a story — an epic poem about a Scandinavian warrior from Sweden who, according to legend, rescued Denmark from two great monsters and fought a duel unto death with a dragon in his own land. It's the oldest story in existence in a modern European language.

Written in Anglo Saxon England in about the seventh century, it reflects life among the Danes and Geats from a century earlier. The invasions of Britain by the Angles and Jutes from Denmark, and Saxons from northwest Germany, during the fifth and sixth centuries, provided the setting for this story. When the Roman legions left this island early in the fifth century, waves of Teutons poured in as settlers and conquerors. They remembered their homelands just as the Icelandic sagas recorded the deeds of the Norse kings five centuries later, or as modern Scandinavians in America still search for the heroes of their homelands.

"Beowulf" is a story of crisis and heroism in Denmark. Grendel, a man-eating monster who lived at the bottom of a stench-filled lake, together with his equally dangerous mother, was supposedly a descendant of Cain in the biblical story. Each night the dreaded beast broke into the castle and carried off warriors for its midnight meal. For 12 years the castle stood empty and in shambles, awaiting its final destruction.

Deliverance came from a young Gothic warrior named Beowulf who lived in a region of southwest Sweden called "Geatland." He was said to be "stronger than anyone anywhere in this world." With 14 warriors, he rowed to Denmark to face the dreaded enemy.

Every victory has its price. Grendel devoured one of the great Geats before the mighty Beowulf seized and fought him, bare-handed and

1

without a sword, until the terrible beast, minus an arm, returned to his murky lake abode, mortally wounded. As always, a big feast was held to celebrate the victory and the castle was repaired. Great gifts were lavished upon Beowulf.

Then another terror appeared. Grendel's mother, bent on revenge, came in the dark of night to work havoc on the castle of the Danes. She smashed their weapons and took the king's closest friend as victim for her supper. His head was displayed on a rock for all to see. Beowulf was summoned to the grief-filled castle.

The brave warrior tracked Grendel's mother to her lair in the foul lake and descended with full armor to do battle. As always before such battles, a full array of speeches was made, boasting of victory before the fight began. Beowulf's sword proved useless against the beast, however, for his strength was greater than that of the iron blade and it shattered with the blow. For a moment he was down and about to be struck by the monster's powerful claw. With mighty effort, he arose and took from Grendel's wall a heavy sword, forged by giants. Its maker's magic proved adequate: Grendel's mother fell dead. Then our hero finished off Grendel as well.

After rounds of banquets, the Geats returned to their own land, laden with gifts. Years later, another enemy appeared. A mighty dragon flew through the night bringing destruction to the land. Beowulf was now an old man, having ruled for 50 winters, but still was strong and courageous. He advanced with his warriors to the dragon's lair, but at first sight of the beast, they all fled, leaving only Beowulf and Wiglaf, his loyal companion, to face the terror.

The dragon's fire melted his shield and his sword shattered upon striking the beast's scaly coat. Its poisoned tusks found their mark in Beowulf's neck. Then Wiglaf struck a mighty blow that felled the dragon and brought it to its death. Dying, Beowulf gave Wiglaf the kingdom and the treasure from the dragon's den.

A giant funeral pyre was built to burn Beowulf's body. Wiglaf added the dragon's treasure to the fire, since none was worthy to claim it. Difficult days were ahead. News of the king's death would bring war with the Uppsala Swedes, the Frisians and Germans. There was no great warrior to protect their borders and homes.

The fact that cremation, instead of burial, was used is clear evidence that this story was pagan Anglo-Saxon in origin. The minstrel who carried the song is unknown, but language was no barrier then. The people of northern Europe spoke a common tongue. The poet who first told the story several centuries later was evidently Christian. The frequent references to "Almighty God" are clearly Christian and give the impression that Beowulf was such himself. But this can hardly have been the case.

Is this history or romantic fiction? Higlac, who was supposed to be an uncle of Beowulf and king of the Geats, is mentioned by Gregory of Tours in his "History of the Franks." Beowulf was a mythical person who embodied the ancient ideal warrior, like St. George, who fought with the enemies of mankind to make the world safe. A delightful translation of Beowulf was printed by Alan Sutton Publishing, Wolfboro, NH.

Our age does not glorify warriors nor approve the ways of violence. Yet violence has increased. Times may change, however, and the warrior-hero may again return to receive his due.

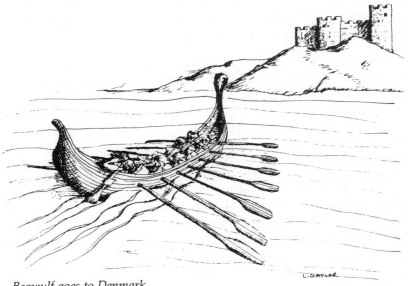

Beowulf goes to Denmark.

CHAPTER 2

Early Norse Settlers
In The New World

I'VE HAD AN AWARENESS of my Scandinavian heritage since earliest childhood and was probably five years old before realizing that I lived in America. That was when my father told me that Franklin Roosevelt, a Democrat, was going to be President of the United States. Since the picture of the Norwegian royalty hung in our living room, I wondered, "What will happen to the king?" That was the beginning of my education as an "American." After that, I decided Norway must be the same thing as "heaven," from the way everybody talked about it, and I was sure that's where I'd go when I died.

Since that time I've been curious about every Scandinavian who settled in America. Some time ago, there came into my possession a book entitled "Normaendene i Amerika" ("Norsemen in America") through the courtesy of Larry Anderson, a fellow member of the Sons of Norway. It was published by Martin Ulvestad in 1907. It's printed in Gothic script and has no statistics after 1900.

Of special interest is Ulvestad's map, "Norge i Amerika" ("Norway in America"). The principal concentration of Norwegians at the time was in Wisconsin, Minnesota, northeast Iowa, northeast Illinois, eastern South Dakota, and eastern and northern North Dakota. If his research had occurred a little later, he would have colored in most of North Dakota plus eastern Montana. He does, however, include western Washington, parts of Oregon, Utah, Boston, New York and Philadelphia as heavy concentrations.

Norwegians who fought in the Civil War are listed. Special recognition was given to Colonel Hans Heg (1829-1863), commander of the 15th Wisconsin Regiment made up of Scandinavians, who died at the Battle of Chickamauga. Ulvestad listed 3 colonels, 27 majors, 52 captains, 76 lieutenants, 154 sergeants, 219 corporals, and 4,042 enlisted men. Their places of birth and where they lived after the war are also given.

4

I was surprised to learn that Pembina County was the home of the first Norwegian settler in North Dakota. R. E. Nelson was the first homesteader in the state, according to Ulvestad. He noted that Burlington was the earliest site of Norse settlers in Ward County. Among these were Ole Ingesen from Skien, Ole Spokkeli from Telemark, John Jacobsen from Kongsberg, Sivert Anderson from Sogn and H. Gasmann from Gjerpen. They had come from Wisconsin. Among those coming shortly thereafter, he listed the Ramstads from Sigdal, Watnes from Sogn, and Johnsons from Nordland. I had a special interest in reading about the first settlers in Richland County, my home community.

Kendall, in New York state, founded by Cleng Peerson and the "Sloopers" in 1825, was the earliest Norwegian settlement in America. The first colony to have continuity was the Fox River settlement in LaSalle County, IL (1834). The main center of Norwegian immigrants in Illinois was Chicago. The first settler in Cook County was Halstein Torrisen who arrived in September, 1836. Among these immigrants were some outstanding community leaders among those immigrants.

Jefferson Prairie was the first Norwegian settlement in Wisconsin: Ole Nattestad arrived there from Nummedal in 1838. Muskego, about 25 miles southwest of Milwaukee, was settled in 1839. Racine was the first city in the state to attract Norwegian settlers. The Johnsons, a famous family in that city, were the first Norwegians to set foot on Wisconsin soil. Racine later became the favorite city of Danish immigrants. Koshkonong, near Madison, was settled in 1839-1840. Situated on the Great Lakes, Milwaukee had an early settlement of Norsemen.

Keokok, in southeast Iowa, became that state's first Norse settlement (1840). Winneshiek County, however, in northeast Iowa, became the main settlement of Norwegians in the state. Decorah is still a major center for Iowa Norwegians, having been settled in 1852. The first Norsk settler was Erik Anderson Rude from Voss.

Minnesota's earliest Norwegian settlement was in Fillmore County ("Little House on the Prairie" country) in 1851. The Minneapolis area began to attract Norwegians about 1855 and it developed into the "most Norwegian" metropolis in America. The St. Anthony Park community of St. Paul, near the Minnesota State Fair Grounds, became a favorite place for these immigrants. It's the location of a seminary built by

Norwegians, now called Luther Northwestern Theological Seminary. It's the largest Lutheran seminary in the New World.

South Dakota's first Norwegian settlement was in the Yankton area in 1859. Settlers came from Hallingdal, Ulvik, Voss and the Sogn area while it was still "Indian Territory." The South Dakota settlements in the Canton and Sioux Falls area were made famous by Ole Rolvaag's writings.

Not enough is known in the Midwest about the large number of Norwegians who settled on the West Coast, the largest concentration being in Washington. The earliest known "hvid Mand" ("white man") to settle in the state, according to Ulvestad, was Martin Zakarias Tosteson who landed at Dak Harbor in 1847. Seattle still has a very active Norwegian community. The fishing and lumber industries were a natural attraction to them. Besides that, there were mountains. What could be a more natural habitat for a Norseman?

It's easy for many of us to assume that all Norse settlements in America are in the Upper Midwest. Martin Ulvestad's map of "Norway in America" shows that by 1900 Norse settlements were in every U.S. state except Arkansas and Nevada, as well as in the Canadian provinces of Quebec, British Columbia, Ontario, Alberta, Manitoba, Saskatchewan and "Assiniboia" (Indian territory north of Montana). The availability of free land from Wisconsin to Montana after the Civil War is the main reason why this region became the Scandinavian "heartland" of America. The New World wanted settlers — and Scandinavians have always been hungry for tillable land.

The seacoast cities were the natural places for Scandinavians to settle. The first Norwegian settler in Massachusetts was Ole Haugen, who came to Lowell County from Bergen in 1815. New England was considered to be "Leif Erikson" land. Since New York City was a port of immigration, a large number settled there. Brooklyn still has a distinct Norwegian population with its own newspaper - "Nordisk Tidende." (In 1970, while attending a national youth convention in the Big Apple, I was interviewed by one of their reporters. My North Dakota background interested them, even though I was living in Chicago at the time.) The first Norwegian congregation in New York was in Brooklyn (1860).

Some of the most interesting Norse settlements were in Texas. John Nordboe from Ringebo in Gudbrandsdal was the first Norwegian to settle in the state. He took land in Dallas County in 1838. Cleng Peerson, who started the Norwegian immigration to America in 1825, founded the best-known Norse colony in Bosque County (1854). King Olav V visited this community on one of his recent trips to America.

A look at the Salt Lake City phone book shows that many Scandinavians settled in Utah, largely as a result of recruitment by Mormon missionaries. My mother-in-law remembers the activity of the Mormons in Denmark when she was a little girl. The first Norwegian in Utah was Augusta Sondrason Bakke from Tinn in Telemark, who joined the Mormon trek to Utah from Nauvoo, IL, in 1847.

It has surprised me to learn how many Norwegians settled in Michigan. There is a strong Scandinavian center in Detroit with its own Symphony Orchestra. The first Norwegian settlement in the state was at Muskegon County in 1848. One of my good Academy of Parish Clergy colleagues from Michigan is Rev. John Sorensen, a "Norwegian Methodist" pastor who is active in the Sons of Norway (though being Danish!). Since his retirement, he's lived in Florida.

Nebraska had its first Norwegian settlement in 1857 at Newman Grove. A strong Hauge Synod congregation was started there in 1873. The first Norwegian settlement in Kansas was also in 1857.

California had an early attraction for Norwegians (and still does). Sailors and gold seekers were the first to arrive. The "I Remember Mama" television series featured these immigrants in San Francisco. Portland, OR, got its first Norwegian congregation in 1876.

The story of Norwegians in Montana deserves special attention. Chris Boe of Billings is gathering this material and has shared some information with me about such men as Martin Grande, pioneer of the sheep industry in the state; Anton Holter, a leader in the lumber industry; and J. Hugo Aronson of Sweden, who was governor from 1952-1960. I hope he publishes his discoveries. It's an exciting story.

We could count many more settlements: New Hampshire (1854), Oklahoma (1869), Idaho (1876), Colorado (1878), Tennessee (1887) and Georgia (1898). Individual Norwegians found their way to all the states,

7

but because they were often a small segment of society they were not identified as ethnic sub-groups as in the Upper Midwest.

One of the colorful, though ill-fated, Norwegian colonizing attempts was by Ole Bull (1810-1880), who bought 120,000 acres of infertile, title-flawed land in Pennsylvania. The world famous violinist set up the "Oleana" colony in Potter County in 1852. About 1,000 people tied their hopes to his community, but it turned out to be a money-losing disaster. If music could have maintained a settlement, "Oleana" would have become the paradise of which he dreamed. Now it's only a song at which people laugh and perhaps wipe a tear or two.

British Columbia had a Norse settlement by 1860. Quebec, a point of entry for many immigrants, had Norwegians by 1857. The Norwegian settlements in Canada are in Alberta, Saskatchewan, Manitoba and British Columbia. Travelling with the Concordia College Choir by boat from Seattle to Vancouver in 1946, I visited with a man from Saskatchewan who told me about the "Norwegians" north of Saskatoon. In typical English style, he spoke of them as "foreigners." The first Norse settlement in Alberta was in Calgary (1886). Manitoba followed in 1887 and Saskatchewan in the 1890s. Saskatoon is a Norwegian center. Another significant location of Norsemen is in the Peace River country, the home of the Ronning family which has given distinguished service to church and state in Canada, China and the United States. Busloads of Norwegian-Canadians attend the Norsk Høstfest each year.

It continues to amaze me that 100 years after immigrating, Norsemen continue to cherish their ethnic roots while being strongly committed to their new lands. It's inevitable, I suppose, that some day, like Scandinavians in England and Ireland, the New World Norse will just be called Americans and Canadians.

CHAPTER 3

'Apaurak' In Alaska

I READ HER OBITUARY with special interest: "Alaska missionary dies at age 90." It referred to Dagny Brevig Nimmo who died Jan. 19, 1987, in Maine. My mind flashed back to my freshman year at Concordia College in Moorhead, MN, 42 years earlier.

Concordia's Professor J. Walter Johnshoy had just written a book entitled "Apaurak In Alaska: Social Pioneering Among the Eskimos." It describes the work of Rev. Tollef Brevig (1857-1935) among the Eskimos above the Arctic Circle in the areas of Teller, Igloo and Shishmareff from 1894 to 1917. I bought the book because of my high regard for the author who was my academic advisor in a philosophy major as well as my Hebrew instructor. I've had many outstanding teachers, but few have inspired me to study as much as Johnshoy. I felt a deep loss when he died suddenly at the beginning of my senior year in 1947.

Who or what was "Apaurak?" It's an Eskimo name for "Father of All" and was given to Brevig by the Eskimos in a special ceremony. He was the only pioneer white missionary and social worker in Alaska who was adopted into an Eskimo tribe. Born in Sigdal, Norway, Brevig emigrated to America at age 10 with his parents. After graduating from Luther College in Decorah, IA, he taught school for 11 years in Minnesota. Then he enrolled at Luther Theological Seminary in St. Paul, graduating in 1891. During March, 1894, while serving as a pastor in Crookston, MN, Brevig received a letter from Rev. Herman A. Preus, president of the Norwegian Lutheran Synod, asking him to consider going to Alaska.

The United States government wanted to help the Eskimos get started in raising reindeer. Siberians had been employed for two years but they were cruel to both Eskimos and reindeer. The government wanted to import Lapps (Sami) from Norway, known to be the finest reindeer herdsmen in the world, to come to Alaska. The Lapps, however, agreed to come only if a Norwegian Lutheran pastor lived among them to minister the Gospel. Brevig arrived in Alaska, Aug. 1, 1894, accompanied by his wife, Julia. He didn't know that he'd also be the manager of the reindeer herds and Teller's first postmaster.

Brevig was the first school teacher in the area. He found that the Eskimo children quick to grasp concrete concepts but they had difficulty with abstract reasoning. Because they counted on their toes and fingers, numbers over 20 gave them trouble. Brevig quickly learned the Eskimo ways and the people felt a strong sense of trust towards him because his word was always good.

The fur traders and whalers tried to keep missionaries away. Knowing that the missionaries would protect the Eskimos from exploitation, they said, "Next spring men will come with a book which they say cannot lie and which is given by God. These men who bring the book are liars and the book itself is full of lies." It didn't take the Eskimos long to figure out who the real liars were.

Some of the early encounters of the Eskimos with foreigners had been a disaster. Many of the Russian government officials were extremely cruel. The U.S. purchase of Alaska in 1867 eventually brought better times. The Eskimos were, for the most part, a trusting people with a strong sense of justice. Their religion, however, was centered in spirit worship, controlled by the "shamans" (witch doctors). Their living conditions were anything but sanitary, with poorly ventilated homes and lice everywhere. Bathing was not one of their virtues. They thought water was only for boats and had no appreciation for soap.

Christmas became a high point among Eskimos in Teller after Brevig's arrival. They journeyed 70 miles into the interior to fetch the first Christmas trees. The annual Reindeer Fair brought people together for competition. The U.S. Commissioners and Marshalls were busy protecting the herds from poachers. In the early days, ships with supplies and mail were scarce. Sometimes it took a whole year to get news from home.

Professor Johnshoy, as a little boy in his father's parsonage, had known Brevig. When Brevig died, his journals were given to Johnshoy for editing and publishing. A highly qualified linguist and a master of style, he put together an exciting story. It tells of Brevig's experiences during the "Gold Rush" days (described in Rex Beach's books), of intense cold, treacherous travel across the snow and ice, disease and death, struggles with those who wanted the missionaries out, competition from some later missionaries and the satisfaction of seeing the Christian faith as well as better living conditions take root in an aboriginal people.

Brevig's wife and two children died in Alaska. He returned to mainland USA several times to promote the mission's work. At age 56, he returned again to take over the work when no one else would go. Later missionaries included Bertha Stedje of Hettinger, ND, who went out in 1945, and Pastor Albert Tastad of Rolette, ND, from 1953 to 1956. Dagny "Alaska" Brevig, to whom the book is dedicated, worked with her father as a school teacher and helped with the mission orphanage until 1917. With her recent death, the last of the original missionaries to that far corner of America has come to an end.

Great work is usually done by a few dedicated people, not the masses. Brevig and his family dared to be those kind of people. He well earned their title, "Apaurak, Father of All."

"Apaurak" — Missionary Brevik.

11

CHAPTER 4

Vitus Bering —
Danish Sea Captain

WHAT IN THE WORLD was a Danish sea captain doing in the Russian navy? It was a time of colonial expansion. The British, French, Spanish and Portuguese were building empires in the New World. The Russian Czar, Peter the Great (1672-1725), was committed to bringing his nation out of the Dark Ages into the modern world. He ruled Russia for 36 years and built its navy, brought in experts from other countries to modernize industry and helped establish the Russian Academy of Sciences. He also left a legacy of ruthlessness and cruelty.

One of Peter's goals was to find an outlet for Russia to the sea. As early as 1648 there had been reports that a people rich in ivory lived in the eastern parts of Siberia. At that time, geographers were debating whether Alaska and Siberia were connected. Rumors circulated about a land possessing fabulous wealth and yet populated by giants and enormous beasts. Czar Peter resolved to send an expedition to find out if the rumors were true.

The man selected as commander for the exploration was Vitus Jonassen Bering, a tall 44-year-old Danish sea captain from Horsens on the west coast of Jutland. He had been recommended by Admiral Cruys, the Norwegian commanding officer of the new Russian navy. Another Dane, Martin Spanberg, was chosen as a lieutenant, together with two Russian officers, to accompany Bering on this journey. Bering's forebears on his mother's side had been clergy and judicial officers for two centuries. He had entered the Czar's service in 1704 during a war against Sweden. On Dec. 23, 1724, just five weeks before he died, Czar Peter gave orders for the expedition. The Empress Catherine continued to support the work.

The destination was Kamchatka, a peninsula at the eastern edge of Siberia, 6,000 miles away. Just travelling across such a barren land was a challenge filled with unusual hazards. Winters were deadly and during the summer there were swarms of bloodsucking insects to contend with

12

and large rivers to cross. Leaving his home in the Scandinavian colony in St. Petersburg, Bering set out to solve the mystery of geography and to seek riches for the empire and fame for himself. (He had just returned from a trip to the East Indies.)

Preparations for the trip required assembling carpenters, blacksmiths and other craftsmen. Two ships were to be built with which to do the exploring from the Kamchatka base. In addition to a hostile nature, there was also danger from the dreaded Chukchi tribesmen whom not even the Cossacks had been able to conquer. Bering's party travelled with 13 barges and 204 men carrying 26 tons of flour. Conditions became so bad that the crew became mutinous; the mutiny was checked only by threatening the leaders with hanging and turning other offenders over to the Cossacks. Although Bering sailed the seas east of Siberia, heavy fog prevented him from sighting Alaska. He returned to St. Petersburg on Feb. 28, 1730. The body of water between Siberia and Alaska was later named "Bering Straits." It is recognized as one of the most difficult seas to sail in with waves as high as 40 feet, ice five feet thick and wind-blown ice bergs with peaks up to 100 feet.

Bering did not receive the fame he had hoped for. Summoned before government officials and the Russian Academy of Sciences, he was charged with failure. He defended his return from further northern explorations on the grounds that to have stayed longer in the stormy and fog-bound waters would have endangered the lives of the crew and resulted in their being frozen in by winter without provisions. In 1734, the Academy of Sciences published maps based on traditional knowledge. They rejected his findings, including the St. Lawrence and Diomede Islands.

After suffering humiliation and the feeling that he had failed, Bering proposed a second expedition which was approved by the Empress in 1733. It took until 1740, however, for the ships — the "St. Peter" and the "St. Paul" — to be built. They embarked June 4, 1741, and sighted Mount St. Elias in Alaska (18,000 feet) in July. It was believed to be the highest point in North America until Mt. McKinley (23,000 feet) was discovered in 1897.

Unfortunately, there was dissension among the expedition members. Among them were "drunkards, bankrupt aristocrats, gamblers, and adventurers who could not tolerate strict discipline." They had joined the expedition to gain wealth. Bering wanted to return to the Kamchatka base before the weather turned bad, but they would hear nothing of it. The result was that the two ships were separated and the "St. Peter," on which Bering sailed, was shipwrecked. Captain Bering died at age 60 from scurvy on Dec. 8, 1741, and was buried on a bleak island named after him. Despite great sufferings, the survivors brought home about $3,000 worth of furs per person, a tidy fortune in those days.

Bering gave 16 years of his life to the exploration that eventually made Alaska a Russian colony. He made mistakes under extreme difficulties, but had the reputation of being considerate of those who worked under him. He had the respect of those whom he commanded as well as the native peoples he encountered. He had urged that a younger man lead the expedition but those who knew the dangers were agreed that no one else could have done it.

In 1867, Russia needed money and sold Alaska to the United States for $7,200,000 (two cents an acre). Many considered it a foolish buy at the time and derided the purchase as "Seward's folly." James Michener incorporates the story of Vitus Bering into his novel, "Alaska." The next time you think of Alaska, remember the Danish sea captain who gave his life to discover it.

Captain Vitus J. Bering.

14

CHAPTER 5

The 'Viking Battalion'
In World War II

A SECRET MEMO WAS SENT from the Headquarters of the Army Ground Forces at the Army War College in Washington, DC, to the Commanding General of the Second Army on July 10, 1942. It directed that a Norwegian battalion was to be organized from Norwegian nationals in the United States Army, or from Norwegian-Americans in the armed forces. It was to be called the 99th Infantry Battalion (Special).

Olaf Haaland of Carpio, ND, for many years sheriff of Ward County, was one of the first dozen men to arrive at Camp Ripley, MN, on Aug. 15 when the battalion was activated. It was the beginning of an exciting military career. Apart from combat ability, the main requirement for this group was the ability to speak and act like a Norwegian.

Originally, the battalion called for 931 men to be recruited from other army units for a secret mission. Though loyal Americans, these men had a special reason for interest in this assignment: they all felt a special love for Norway. I remember that day, April 9, 1940, when the Nazis invaded Norway and Denmark. Tensions ran high in many communities. The unthinkable act of Hitler's madness had happened. He had violated the neutrality of two peace-loving nations who had no hostile intent towards their neighbors. Now the Norwegian-Americans had a double reason for entering military service.

Already many Norwegians had found their way to America and were given automatic dual citizenship by joining the armed forces. Many had jumped ship since the merchant marine could not return to its homeland. Among them were shipbuilders, seamen, carpenters and cabinet makers. Joining them were farmers, cooks, college students and factory workers from the Middle West. They were transferred to Ft. Snelling in St. Paul, MN, on Oct. 1. From there they went to Camp Hale, CO, on Dec. 19 where they underwent rigorous mountain training until Aug. 24, 1943. They learned to live on skis, carrying a 97-pound load.

Everything they needed for survival was with them. Here they learned the value of "jeeps."

Their first overseas assignment was to Perham Downs, Wiltshire, in England, arriving on Sept. 16. They kept waiting for the command to be dropped by parachute into Norway. The Allied High Command decided that the planned attack on Norway would cost too many lives, so after spending some time in England and Wales, they suddenly shipped off for Normandy and the invasion of Europe on June 6, 1944, arriving five days later. There they joined other army units and fought in five major campaigns: Normandy, Northern France, Ardennes, Rhineland and Central Europe.

They were the first American troops to enter Belgium and fought valiantly in the Battle of the Bulge. Olaf Haaland was in charge of his platoon which included five tanks. Early one morning, while boarding his tank, he looked up at the GI giving him a hand and instantly recognized a neighbor from Carpio, Woodrow Anderson (now his wife's cousin). Woodrow had fought his way with the Army all the way up from North Africa. It was a good day! They spearheaded the advance of the troops and in a very short time took 1,200 prisoners. Later Olaf made contact with his brother, John, and joined him in Paris for three days of rest and recreation. These soldiers were so thoroughly Norwegian, Olaf told me, that they even gave battlefield commands in the Norwegian language.

On March 24, 1945, members of the 99th Battalion parachuted into Norway for sabotage missions and joined the underground for the liberation of the nation. Olaf, however, didn't make the jump because he had broken his leg playing volleyball. After the Nazis surrendered, the 99th Battalion was headquartered at Smestad, near Oslo, and served as Honor Guard for King Haakon and Crown Prince Olav. The men of the 99th Battalion also visited relatives and made new friends: by mid-September they had won the hearts of 87 young Norwegian girls who returned with them to America as their wives. They were deactivated at Camp Miles Standish in Boston on Nov. 11, 1945. A major with the 2nd Armored Division said of these men, "This Viking battalion is the only infantry that the tanks have trouble keeping up with."

The 99th wasn't the only force recruited for service in Norway. Wilfred Winters, a long time friend in Webster Groves (St. Louis), MO, was at an Army camp in Abilene, TX, when he was recruited because of his Danish heritage for secret training that was to lead him to Norway. His assignment was to be a part of the group that was to destroy the heavy water plant in Rjukan, where Hitler was manufacturing deuterium-oxide for making the atomic bomb. Wil was sent to the University of Wisconsin in Madison for language study for six months. The group was suddenly disbanded as the Allied war planners decided to send Knut Haukelid and a detachment of Norwegians from England to do the job. Wil never made it to Norway, but he did get to Europe and after the war he visited his relatives in Denmark.

Forty-two years after the war ended, Olaf Haaland finally got to Norway. He and his wife visited their daughter, Joan, who was completing a doctoral disseration in music in Norway for a degree at the University of Indiana. While there, they had an audience with Crown Prince Harald. Among the gifts they brought to the Royal Family was a copy of my book, "The Scandinavian Heritage."

Scandinavian-Americans have retained a deep love for the lands of their ancestors while being loyal Americans. A strong spirit of comradery brings the 99th back for annual reunions. Of the 1,002 men who went to Europe, only 487 returned.

The 1989 Norsk Høstfest honored the "Viking Batallion" by inducting them into the Scandinavian-American Hall of Fame. A special medallion was struck for them. Long may they live!

CHAPTER 6

The Vikings In The
Age Of Charlemagne

KARL DER GROSSE, known to the world as "Charlemagne" ("Charles the Great"), ruled over a powerful kingdom in western Europe from 768 to 814. He came from a long line of Frankish (German) rulers whose power became the ideal for Christian kings in future generations. His grandfather, Charles Martel ("The Hammer"), had defeated the Saracens at the Battle of Poiters in 732 — the decisive battle that saved western Christendom from the Islamic invaders.

In his 46 years of rule, Charlemagne ordered 60 military expeditions, leading over half of them in person. This unusually gifted man promoted learning and employed the greatest scholar of the time, Alcuin of Northumbria in England, though he himself never learned to write more than his name. He was feared by his neighbors and admired by those at a distance. While he ruled, the kingdom was safe.

It was the time of the Viking "breakout." The North Sea was infested with pirates. In June, 793, a band of Norwegian sea bandits attacked the holy island of Lindisfarne off the northeast coast of England, stealing the wealth and killing most of the monks. Lindisfarne was a famous center of Christian learning. When the English scholar, Alcuin, told the king about the tragedy, Charlemagne burst into tears because of the violence done to Christians. He also feared that his kingdom would be the next to feel the wrath of the pagan Vikings.

On Christmas Day, 800, Charlemagne was worshipping in St. Peter's church in Rome. As he was rising from communion, Pope Leo III placed a crown on his head and declared him to be Emperor and Augustus of the "Holy Roman Empire." He became successor to the Caesars in a kingdom later called the "First Reich" (Kingdom) which lasted until July 12, 1806. (Hitler declared his rule over Germany to be the "Third Reich" that was also to last for 1,000 years). This made Charlemagne the protector of the church, and he took his missionary work seriously. One of his first goals was to convert the heathen Saxons. When they wouldn't listen to his preachers, he sent the sword.

The Vikings kept a sharp eye on the horizons, looking for weaknesses in neighboring defenses. They gave shelter to Widukind, a Saxon king defeated by the mighty Charles. Godfred, who ruled over southern Denmark, began the building of the "Danevirke," a heavy earthen rampart, in 808 as a defense against the Franks. It was the only large-scale fortification ever built on Scandinavian soil.

By 810, Godfred felt strong enough to attack Aachen, the capital of the Frankish kingdom. He boasted that he would occupy the royal palace. The Danish fleet attacked the coasts of France and Germany, looting wherever they went. Viking warriors in Frisia and Saxony threatened the empire. Charlemagne decided that he had to deal with this threat from the north. Though 68 years old, he led his forces to attack the Danes. On the way to battle, King Godfred was murdered by one of his own sons. The new king came to terms with Charlemagne. It was Charlemagne's last military expedition.

When Charlemagne died in 814, the Vikings broke into France and Germany wherever they wished. His grandson, Lewis the "German," showed courage in their presence. Standing before them in a suit of iron, he threw their tributes of gold and silver on the ground as if they were dirt and bent their swords until they snapped. Then he ordered them to be baptized.

Lewis gave a new suit of clothes to the Scandinavian soldiers who accepted baptism. Notker (840-912), one of the royal biographers, wrote that "the nobles of the royal palace adopted these Northmen, almost as if they had been children: each received a white robe from the Emperor's wardrobe, and from his sponsors a full set of Frankish garments, with arms, costly robes and other adornments."

One Easter, more than 50 Vikings appeared before Lewis for baptism. After they had confessed their sins and been sprinkled with holy water, it was discovered that there were not enough royal garments to go around, so some make-do baptismal clothes were offered. One of the Vikings was incensed with anger and told the Emperor: "Look here! I've gone through this ablution (baptism) business about twenty times already, and I've always been rigged out before with a splendid white

19

suit; but this old sack makes me feel more like a pig-farmer than a soldier! If it weren't for the fact that you've pinched my own clothes and not given me any new ones, with the result that I should feel a right fool if I walked out of here naked, you could keep your Christ and your suit of reach-me-downs, too." So much for the attempt to evangelize that Viking!

When the Christian faith finally conquered the Northmen, it was chiefly through the leadership of King Olaf Haraldsson ("Saint Olaf"). He thought of himself as the "Charlemagne of the North." His sword was always reaching out together with the cross to convert his enemies. If they accepted baptism, they were rewarded with gifts. If they refused, they had to flee or to fight him in battle. Both Olaf and Charlemagne faithfully attended worship services several times a day.

Isn't it surprising that those Norsemen have in our day become champions of peace?

Strange things continue to happen. Many of mankind's enemies have been won over to become the champions of all that is humane and good. Think of that before you write off any nation as an enemy of the world. Time and patience may still be on our side.

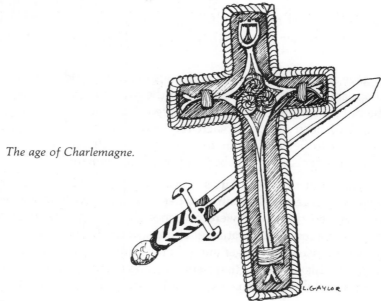

The age of Charlemagne.

CHAPTER 7

Art In The Viking World

MY FRIEND HARLEY REFSAL from Decorah, IA, appeared on one of Garrison Keillor's "Prairie Home Companion" shows carving a Norwegian bachelor farmer. Harley, a faculty member at Luther College, annually displays his woodcarvings at the Høstfest in Minot. Woodcarving is one of the oldest art forms of Scandinavia.

The "Viking World" lasted for about 250 years, from 800-1050 A.D. Though the age began in violence, the Vikings have left us a legacy in art which still remains a wonder. From Ireland to Russia and from North Cape to Sicily, Viking skills have influenced some of the finest European works of art.

Those were brutal times all over the world. The most civilized culture among Christians was perhaps in Ireland, known as a land of scholars, saints and kings. Islam, at that time, was developing a very high level of culture in art and philosophy. The Vikings, despite their reputation for cruelty, were to some extent victims of a bad press. The only contemporary writings about them were done by enemies who pictured them as "savages." They were, however, also a highly skilled people who had their own indigenous art forms. A helpful book on this subject is "Viking Art" by David M. Wilson of the British Museum and Ole Klindt-Jensen from the Institute of Archaeology in Moesgaard in Denmark. The book was published by the University of Minnesota Press.

Animal ornamentation was known as early as the fourth century A.D. in Scandinavia. Naturalistic art with plant ornamentation was introduced from other parts of Europe. Lions, snakes, horses, deer, dogs and human masks were common to early Scandinavian art. The finest example of pre-Viking art is the Oseberg ship found near Tonsberg, south of Oslo in 1904. It was covered by a mound 20 feet high and 130 feet long. Hidden beneath it was a royal burial site . You can see the artifacts at the Viking Ship Museum at Bygdøy Park in Oslo. In addition to the well-preserved longship there was a four-wheeled cart, four sledges and a number of utensils. The woman buried in the boat was possibly the mother of King Halfdan the Black. Buried with her was a slave girl sacrificed for the burial. Skeletons of 14 horses, three dogs and an ox were also found.

The most impressive art works from this source are the carvings on the prow and stern-post of the ship. Built of oak, the 66-foot boat had oar-locks for 30 oarsmen. Wood carvings decorated even the bedposts. The Oseberg must have been one of the finest ships of its time. It reveals a treasure of wood carving, the finest from any Scandinavian period.

In the Viking period, five styles of art are identified. Each was named from the place where examples were found. In the early part of this period, two styles dominated, the "Borre" and the "Jellinge." The Borre style came from a few miles north of Oseberg. As a successor to the art of the famed burial ground, it also included metal work and is identified with a ribbon plait on the borders. The art designs were not limited to the place from which they are named. It is possible to find the Borre style in Sweden, Russia and Denmark. In this style, the animal head often has a triangular shape and wears a mask.

The Jellinge style takes its name from the most famous burial ground in Denmark. Jelling, northwest of Vejle in Jutland, has two large burial mounds built by King Harald "Bluetooth" for his parents, Gorm and Thyra. The style, however, is found in various places. Harald led Denmark into Christianity and these art forms have representations of the crucifixion together with the lion, horse and snake ribbon forms. It has many similarities to the Borre style.

Closely related to the Jellinge style is the "Mammen" style from Mammen in Jutland. Strangely, the most famous art pieces at Jelling are claimed to be in the Mammen style. These are the two runestones erected by King Harald. Stone art must have been learned in England by the Danes. They then applied their wood carving patterns to stone. As a result, Anglo-Saxon and Viking motifs are sometimes combined. The Danes occupied a large area in eastern England (Derby, Stamford, Nottingham, Lincoln, Leicester and Yorkshire) called "Danelaw." Norwegians from Ireland occupied a large part of northwest England (Cumberland, Westmorland, Cheshire, Lancashire, Dumfries, West Yorkshire and North Wales). Christian influences are found in art from these regions. England, being a Viking country, produced a great deal of Viking art.

The "Ringerike" style comes from a few miles north of Oslo. It features animals with double contours, spiral hips and acanthus-like tendrils. It seems to have drawn a great deal from the Jellinge style.

The "Urnes" style takes its name from a stave church in the Sogn region of western Norway. It frequently features a "combat" motif where the animals bite each other. It is thought that this style may have had its origins in Sweden. It dominated the whole of Scandinavia in the late Viking period and seems to have been promoted by the Normans after their conquest of England in 1066. Its latest development was in Ireland during the 12th century, when it was dying in Scandinavia.

Viking art was at its best in the use of wood and often found its expression in furniture making. This art affected all levels of society, from the king to the peasant. At the next Høstfest, look for Harley and the other woodcarvers displaying their wares.

Norse woodcarving —
"The Fiddler."

CHAPTER 8

More Light On The Greenlanders

WHATEVER HAPPENED TO the original Norsemen who settled Greenland just before the year 1,000? I wrote about this puzzling question in my book "The Scandinavian Heritage" and continue to wonder about it. The Vikings were always a people on the go. They lived for adventure.

We know that in the year 1,000 Norsemen accidently discovered America, even though permanent settlements were not established. How far they travelled into the continent is still a matter of debate. When Danes came to Greenland in the 18th century, the Norsemen were all gone. The settlements were found, but there was no trace of the people. (See "The Scandinavian Heritage," chapter 25.)

Prof. T. J. Oleson of the University of Manitoba gave a lecture in the Spring of 1963 at the University of Minnesota entitled "Viking-Tunnit-Eskimo." It's published in a book entitled "Life and Thought in the Early Middle Ages" (University of Minnesota Press, 1967). He traced what is known about this hardy race of people and offered some interesting ideas based on archaeological evidence.

According to Oleson, during the 500 years in which the Norsemen lived in Greenland, Labrador, Hudson Bay and the islands of northern Canada they "gradually lost their language, their religion, and to a considerable extent their physical identity." How did this happen? He combines evidence and conjecture for his theories.

Greenland was an independent nation from 984 to 1261, when it came under the control of the Norwegian king. It had been Christian from its founding by Leif Erikson in 984. Iceland's shipping declined in the 13th century as Norway's monopolistic policies controlled much of the trade. Greenland's ties to the outside world were in religion and trade. Its population is thought to have varied from 3,000 to 10,000. That's not a lot of people, but there are only two small regions in the entire island of 840,000 square miles that can support life. In 1124, a bishop was appointed and a cathedral built. The tithes to Rome were paid mainly in walrus tusks and ropes made of walrus hides. Wheat and barley had to be imported from Europe while lumber was probably gotten from Labrador.

The ivory from the walrus tusks was much in demand among wealthy Europeans. The leather ropes were used on the riggings of ships. White falcons from the Baffin Islands in northern Canada, as well as polar bears, were also highly prized. King Haakon Haakonson (1217-1263) is known to have made presents of these New World creatures to the kings of England and Germany. One of the polar bears even found its way to a Muslim Sultan.

Oleson claims that these frontier Norsemen adopted the Eskimo way of life to survive in the New World, abandoning farming and animal husbandry to become hunters. He identifies them as the "Tunnit" people described in the Eskimo legends. They were "a gigantic race formerly inhabiting the northeastern coast of Labrador, Hudson Strait, and southern Baffin Islands." Ruins of their stone houses and graves have been found in those areas. In these legends, the Tunnit are distinguished from both Eskimos and Indians.

The theory advanced by Oleson contends that these Vikings intermarried with the Dorset Eskimos, advancing their culture while losing most of their own. In the course of a few generations, they lost their knowledge of iron-making while improving on the stone and bone tools of the natives. Oleson believes that the mixture of the two races began about 1300 in Greenland and that this new race started to move westward in 1342.

Oleson rejects the idea that the "Skraelings" (natives) destroyed the much larger Vikings in battle as well as the theory that "little ice age" destroyed them. He also claims that there is no evidence that they were wiped out by disease.

One result of this cultural blending was that the Norse language was lost. (That would not be strange. Few third-generation descendants of immigrants to America, know the language of their grandparents.) With the language, they also lost the Christian religion — which many "modern Vikings" have also lost in recent times. The Vikings have always blended into the lands where they settled and become the champions of their newly adopted cultures. This has been true in France, Italy and Sicily, England, Ireland and Russia. We should not expect that it was different among the Eskimos.

Oleson theorizes that this "Thule Culture" moved westward and includes the present-day Eskimos of Greenland, the eastern Canadian Arctic and can even be traced to Alaska. He pays this race a high tribute, writing "the end product was a people who have no peers in geniality, good humor, cheerfulness in adversity, and lack of bellicosity (war-like nature). The world could do with more of them."

Most of the Greenland Eskimos have today been converted to the Christian faith through the work of Danish missionaries. The first of these was Hans Egede (1684-1758), who arrived in 1719. To the credit of the Danes, it must be said that they treated the Eskimos with kindness, in contrast to the exploitation of most Europeans.

We still don't know for sure what happened to the earliest Scandinavian Greenlanders. Oleson's research has a lot of merit. Perhaps new evidence will come to light as we learn more about the many cultures that make up our society. I hope so.

If you'd like to learn more about the people on that lonely, rugged island, read Jan Smiley's novel, "The Greenlanders." It will leave you with a taste for more.

CHAPTER 9

Thor Heyerdahl And
The 'Maldive Mystery'

THOR HEYERDAHL IS the most exciting archaeologist of our century. I have written about him in my book "The Scandinavian Heritage" (see chapter 32). His adventure, "The Maldive Mystery," is the most fascinating of all.

I first learned of this scientific expedition in the Maldive Islands while visiting with Knut Haugland, Director of the Kon Tiki Museum in Oslo, in October, 1983. Haugland was on the Kon Tiki expedition in 1947. Heyerdahl refers to him as "my closest collaborator ever since we waded ashore together in Polynesia." He told me about the Maldive explorations then in progress and indicated that the results would require a lot of history books to be re-written.

The "Maldive Mystery" began for Heyerdahl with an airmail letter in 1982 from Sri Lanka (formerly called Ceylon) south of India. Enclosed was a photograph of a Buddha statue that the President of the Maldives wanted Heyerdahl to examine. They had hoped that his "Tigris Expedition" raft would have landed in the Maldives instead of in Djibouti on the east coast of Africa. The Maldives are a string of islands running 600 miles north and south, to the southwest of India and west of Sri Lanka. There are an estimated 1,200 islands of which only 202 are inhabited by a total of 160,000 people. None of the islands rises more than six feet above sea level. They are protected from the sea by coral reefs and sand bars. Navigation is treacherous.

The Maldivians have been Moslems since 1153 and were ruled by a sultan until 1968, when the islands became a democracy. Many archaeological artifacts had been uncovered, but Moslem intolerance of idols (statues) caused most of them to be destroyed upon discovery. The Maldivians have been reluctant to admit that they had a history before the arrival of Islam. The new government wanted a professional archaeologist of Heyerdahl's stature to visit them.

The famous Norwegian arrived in 1982 to examine the statue. Unfortunately, fanatical Moslems had already destroyed it. All that remained of value was the head. There was no denying that there had been a pre-Moslem culture, in fact several successive cultures. Who had created these cultures? From where had they come? The photographs in Heyerdahl's book show a variety of physical types, indicating that they had come from more than one place. One of the interesting features on the statues was that they had large suspended ear lobes. This was a practice of Hindu royalty who perforated their ears and hung large plugs on them (the original earring).

The earliest level of civilization was created by sun worshippers. Their probable origin was in the Indus River Valley, one of three places to which the earliest civilizations have been traced. The others are Mesopotamia at the confluence of the Tigris and Euphrates rivers, and the Nile river valley in Egypt.

Large man-made earth mounds, called "hawittas," are the usual source of treasure hunting in the Maldives. Temples for sun worship were built on them. Later inhabitants believed to have been Hindus from northwest India and Buddhists from Sri Lanka, destroyed these temples and re-used the stones to build their own. The sun-worship temples bear striking similarities to those found in Peru, the Easter Islands, the north coast of Africa, Asia Minor and in Bahrain on the Persian Gulf. Archaeology is an exacting science. Excavation is often done with spoons, brushes and sieves, not bulldozers or spades. Heyerdahl believes that there was sea traffic between these places 2,000 years before Columbus. He believes that those ancient mariners learned how to follow the sea currents and may have used reed boats.

One of Heyerdahl's quests was to identify a people called the "Redins." They were white with brown hair, had big hooked noses and blue eyes, and were tall with long faces. They were among the earliest settlers.

The Maldivians were the money suppliers for many people of the ancient world with their cowrie shells. These reached the Arctic coasts of Norway by 600 A.D. This was prior to the Viking voyages. It is believed that they were carried there by Arab and Finnish merchants.

Heyerdahl's work will keep historians re-examining their theories about the history of world population movements. He has shown us that those early travellers included some highly cultured people who had great talent in art and building. He concludes that "civilized man suddenly appeared 5,000 years ago, when he began to build cities. He was already a seafarer too, building ports along the riverbanks and along the coasts of the Indian Ocean."

It's strange that this famous scientist, who was afraid of water and could not swim as a boy, has spent so much of his life on the sea in daring adventures. Born in Larvik, southwest of Oslo along the sea, he became fascinated with collecting sea shells, butterflies, insects and sea creatures. Before he finished high school, he had his own museum to which teachers would bring their students. Spending a summer in the mountains with a well-educated hermit helped Heyerdahl to learn self-reliance. Since then he has led new adventures which have startled the world.

"The Maldive Mystery."

CHAPTER 10

Ole Evinrude And
The Outboard Motor

NORSEMEN HAVE ALWAYS LOVED the sea. So it isn't surprising that they turned their inventive abilities to design the longship — and, many years later, the first commercially successful outboard motor. Water recreation was revolutionized by the work of Ole Evinrude.

Evinrude, whose name has become well known to everyone in the recreation business, was born on April 19, 1877, 60 miles north of Oslo, the oldest of 11 boys. When Ole was five, the family went to America and obtained a homestead near Cambridge, WI. But farm life was not for this adventurous young Norseman. As a teenager, Ole built a sailboat which was the talk of the community. At age 16, he walked the 20 miles to Madison, where he became an apprentice machinist in a farm machinery factory. From there he went to Pittsburgh and then Chicago, learning everything he could about steel and motors.

In 1900, still only 23 years old, he opened a shop in Milwaukee while serving as the master pattern-maker and consulting engineer for the E. P. Allis Company. He studied internal combustion engines and manufactured portable motors.

On a hot Sunday afternoon in August, 1906, while on a picnic near Milwaukee, Ole's girlfriend, Bess Cary, said she wanted a dish of ice cream. Dutifully attentive to her wishes, Ole rowed five miles round trip to get the ice cream. Even for a big, strong man like Ole, this was a test of emotions. While pulling the oars, he began to think about mounting motors on boats, and thus began a revolution in recreation.

In 1909 he and Bess, now married with a son, started the Evinrude Company. Ole was the inventor and engineer, Bess took care of the office and wrote letters to promote the business. "Throw away the oars," was the slogan she used. Business, however, was tough. People weren't convinced about the new "putt-putts." The letters and circulars finally paid off. A Danish employee of a company with a Scandinavian department saw the Evinrude circular in the general manager's wastebasket. Starting with two motors, the firm increased its orders to thousands as Scandinavian fishermen clamored for the new invention. After three years, Evinrude was employing 300 people and building a new factory.

Both Ole and Bess worked hard and put in long hours. Because of Bess's failing health, Ole sold his share in the Evinrude Company in 1914 to his business partner with the agreement that he was not to start up a new company for five years. The family went off on a trip to the west in a large Packard that Ole had customized. They also cruised on a 42-foot boat over the Great Lakes.

Ole, however, kept on tinkering and designed a two-cylinder motor. Bess's health improved and they started the Elto Outboard Motor Company in 1921, named from "Evinrude Light Twin Outboard." In 1929, a merger of the Evinrude Company with the Elto Company and the Lockwood Motors of Jackson, MI, resulted in the Outboard Motors Corporation with Evinrude as president and the largest stockholder. Competition was tough. Evinrude's company and the Johnson Company competed for the market. Evinrude stressed lightness and was the first to use aluminum in the motors. The Johnson Company stressed speed, up to 16 miles an hour! Then came the Great Depression. Ole offered the best buy. He sold a motor for only $34.50, F.O.B. Milwaukee, and managed to stay in business through the worst of those times.

Again Bess's health weakened and she died in 1933. Ole's spirit failed without her and he died just 14 months later on July 12, 1934, at age 57. His only son, Ralph, gained control of the Johnson Motor Company after it became bankrupt in 1932. It was merged with the Outboard Motors Company in 1936 to become the Outboard, Marine and Manufacturing Company. By the early 1940s they were making 60% of the outboard motors sold. Today the company is known as the Outboard Marine Corporation with headquarters in Milwaukee.

What kind of a person was Ole Evinrude, the boy who emigrated with his parents from Norway? He was remembered as a shy person whose formal education ended with third grade. He didn't care for farming, but was a mechanical genius in everything that required the use of hands. His favorite subject was arithmetic. While in Madison, he went to night school to learn algebra, calculus, trigonometry and engineering.

He even made his own automobile and built a gasoline engine. Hard work and long hours brought on severe rheumatism. It got so bad in the winter that he had to go to bed, but he'd take his drawing board with him to keep on designing.

Two other outboard motors had been built before Evinrude's, but Ole was the first to produce one that was commercially and mechanically successful. The Evinrude product is now used around the world. The James Bond movie, "Live and Let Die," used an Evinrude on the 110-foot boat making its escape in the final scene. They've come a long way since the original single cylinder built in 1909!

Ole's son, Ralph, lives in Jensen Beach, FL, where he is married to Frances Langford, the former actress. He has been associated with the company since 1927, after attending the University of Wisconsin. The next time you go for a ride on a motorized boat, remember the shy Norwegian boy who changed the world of water sports.

The outboard motor.

CHAPTER 11

Some Early Norse Settlers In Montana

WHO IS THE GREATEST Norwegian to have lived in America? Writing at the turn of the last century, Martin Ulvestad pointed to Knute Nelson, the famous senator from Alexandria, MN, as the best known, but he claimed that Anton M. Holter, pioneer of the lumber industry in Montana was the greatest business entrepreneur among Norwegian-Americans. Holter came to Helena, MT, in 1863 at age 32 and was the first of his countrymen to settle in the state. He urged other Norwegians to follow. At that time, most of the settlers in Montana lived in the mountain areas, on both sides of the Great Divide.

Montana wasn't an easy place to live back in those days. Fierce snowstorms took a terrible toll on the cattle and sheep. As late as 1884, bandits were still robbing the mails and rustling horses. (I remember visiting in 1945 with an early Bozeman pioneer who told me about the Gallatin Valley vigilantes.) There was no effective law enforcement, so it was done by the citizens. T. S. Norgaard moved from Minot, ND, to Helena, a city of 25,000, to edit "Montana Folkebladet" (a Norwegian newspaper). Gold mining, real estate, banking, lumber, retail and contracting attracted 1,400 Scandinavians to share in the new wealth. Danish-Americans published the "Montana Statstidende."

Martin T. Grande came to America from the Trondheim area, in 1866 at age 22. Arriving first in Minnesota, he travelled by stagecoach through Salt Lake City to the Helena area in 1877 to pioneer the Montana sheep industry. That was the year of the Nez Perces Indian uprising. When the wool dealers in Helena refused to pay the prevailing six cents per pound, Grande shipped his wool by riverboat to Boston and got 30 cents a pound. In just a few years he owned 12,000 sheep, many horses and cattle, and 17,000 acres of land. Not afraid of hard work, he also labored in mines and hunted wild game, while keeping a sharp eye out for Indians. Grande became so famous back in Norway that some Norwegians thought he must be President of the United States.

THE SCANDINAVIAN SPIRIT

One of the his descendants, Ray Grande, attended Concordia College in the early 1940s where he became a football star.

The first Norwegian congregation in Montana was Melville Lutheran Church in the Big Timber area, established in 1885. Another early one was Our Savior's Congregation in Helena organized by the Norwegian Lutheran Synod in 1890.

Helena was full of Texas steers and cowboys in those early days. Gun fighting took place on a regular basis. The last Indian uprising occurred in 1890. The immigrants fortified themselves when a message came from Camp Crook in South Dakota that Sitting Bull was about to attack. It was only a rumor, however, Sitting Bull was killed the night after the message arrived.

The story of Endre Bergsagel, born near Stavanger in 1890, is quite another tale. He came to the Larb Hills southwest of Malta, MT, in 1913. The Bergsagels were highly respected people in their homeland. His father, Daniel, served on the school board and was a county commissioner. The oldest of seven children, in 1910 he sold some land and, together with his brother Knut, bought a ticket to America.

Bergsagel described the journey in his memoirs published by the Norwegian-American Historical Association. Many immigrants from Norway took a steamer to England and entered the New World through Canadian ports. Bergsagel went on to San Francisco where an aunt helped him get his start in America.

After working in various odd jobs for three years in western United States and Canada, Endre went to the land office in Malta to claim a homestead. Luckily, the first winter was mild and open. He had to travel 35 miles to Malta for lumber to build his first shack (8 x 10 with tar-paper sides fastened with lathes). The furnishings were simple: a cast iron stove, a table, a chair and a folding bed. In the summer of 1914 his fiancee, Gurina, arrived from Norway. She was in for a surprise. It was not just the wide open spaces of prairie land, but mosquitoes! They were married by Pastor Alfred Hendrickson in the Malta parsonage, with a lunch served by the pastor's wife following the ceremony.

It was not an easy life. The war in Europe caused them deep concern. Rationing and other regulations were in effect. Then the flu epidemic of 1918-1919 took many lives. Gurina became ill, but fortunately recovered. In 1919, the Bersagels rented out their farm and returned to Norway for five years.

They returned to the farm, things looked great for a few years. They were active in building both a church and the local schools. Then came the Great Depression. 1932 saw drought, grasshoppers, cutworms and webworms. By 1933, they moved west to Poulsbo, WA. They returned for a last look at the farm in 1941, but were not tempted to stay. They became part of that great throng of midwesterners who crossed the mountains to live nearer the ocean, the natural habitat for Norsemen.

Many more stayed behind. During the summers of 1946-1949, I worked among Scandinavians from Culbertson, Bainville, Fairview, Sidney, Richey, Lambert and down to Glendive. They're good people. I'm glad they stayed in Montana.

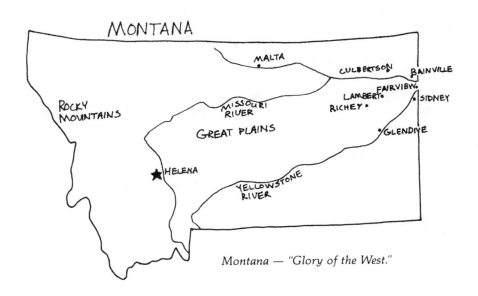

Montana — "Glory of the West."

CHAPTER 12

The Haugeans At Eidsvoll

NO POPULAR MOVEMENT affected Norway more than the one that grew out of the work of Hans Nielsen Hauge (1771-1824). "Haugeanism" played a major role in the tide of events which led to the constitution written at Eidsvoll on May 17 ("Syttende Mai"), 1814. Like most people in Norway, the followers of Hauge were mostly farmers and operators of small businesses. In 1700, the population of Norway was only 500,000, of whom 92% lived on farms. By 1800, the population had grown to almost 900,000 of whom 87% were farmers.

Norway and Sweden were the only two European countries where the common people retained freedom during the Middle Ages. These farmers, called "bonder," were the backbone of the country even before the days of St. Olaf. Between 1770 and 1814, an aristrocracy developed among these farmers, while a poorer class of agricultural laborers ("husmaend" or "crofters") lived in small cottages ("hytter") along the edge of the main farms. By 1807, there were 48,500 such poorer farmers. Despite their dependent financial status, however, they did not lose their rights as free people.

While Haugeanism was essentially a religious movement, emphasizing repentance and personal faith, it also had its political and social significance. In the earlier years of Danish rule (1380-1814), Danes and Germans held the majority of high positions in government. However, by 1814, more Norwegians held official positions in Denmark than Danes did in Norway.

The early 1800s were years of ferment. Napoleon set out to conquer the continent. When Denmark reluctantly entered the war on the Emperor's side, England's Lord Nelson wasted no time in destroying the Danish navy and merchant marine. In 1814, England forced the Danish king to cede Norway to the King of Sweden. This was a signal to the Norwegians to determine their own destiny. Prince Kristian Fredrik of

Denmark almost persuaded the Norwegians to declare their independence and to elect him king. Georg Sverdrup, however, advised him that he had no right to the throne unless the Norwegian people chose him. So the prince invited 21 of Norway's outstanding men to meet at Eidsvoll on Feb. 16, 1814, to formulate a plan of action.

A day of prayer was held throughout the land and delegates were elected from all the parishes. They met at Eidsvoll, 40 miles north of Oslo. Three men from each district were chosen for the assembly, of whom one had to be a farmer. Beginning on Easter Sunday, April 10, the 120 men concluded their work and signed the new constitution on May 17. Several prominent Haugeans were among them.

The farmers were not as well educated as the aristocracy, but the Haugeans had their champions, including Sverdrup. Two groups emerged. The Independence Party, with about 80 members, wanted complete independence. The "Unionists," with about 30 members, favored a union with Sweden in which the Norwegian constitution would be honored. The farmers wanted independence, perhaps in part because of lingering loyalty to the Danish king, but the "Unionists" prevailed. They knew that Norway would be invaded by battle-toughened Swedish soldiers and that their coasts would be blockaded by the British navy. Representatives from Russia and Prussia warned the Norwegians against claiming independence. Austria concurred in this decision.

The new constitution looked back to the ancient laws before Norway was united by King Harald Harfagre in 872. It was an appeal for the freedom of the common people who operated small farms. "Civil liberties" were incorporated into the constitution, which also was patterned in some respects after the new American and French documents. The Norwegians accepted Karl Johan as their new king. He, in turned, agreed to respect their constitution.

The aristocrats in Christiania (Oslo), the new capital, claimed special privileges. They passed a law to draft only rural men for the army, but the officers were to come from the upper classes. Local revolts took place but these were swiftly put down by the central government. By 1833, the farmers started to organize and gained 45 seats in the Storting (Parliament). New leadership emerged as they gained control of the government.

THE SCANDINAVIAN SPIRIT

Among the able Haugeans involved in this agrarian movement was John Gabriel Ueland. It is not by accident that another member of that family, Lars Ueland, later sponsored the "initiative and referendum" in North Dakota, the first of its kind in the nation. John Ueland spent 37 years (1833-1870) in the Storting. He often said that "the Norwegian people's two most precious pearls are their religion and their constitution." Georg Sverdrup entered the Storting in 1851 and also championed the cause of freedom.

The Haugeans were concerned about "true religion." To them, this meant that they acted out their faith in the political and social realms. This influence followed the immigrants to America where they energetically became social reformers and political activists.

The "aristocrats," for the most part, did not migrate to the New World. They stayed in Norway to look after their investments. And while "new aristocracies" have developed among the "new rich" in America, some of the energy that produced their success can be traced to that movement started by Hans Nielsen Hauge, the simple lay preacher, who tirelessly walked the breadth and length of the land to call people to renewal of faith. (For more information on Hauge, see "The Scandinavian Heritage," chapter 49.)

Hans Nielsen Hauge.

CHAPTER 13

The Scandinavians Meet In Columbus

THERE HAVE BEEN MANY Scandinavian organizations in America, but none more influential than the church. Despite warnings and threats from the Lutheran state churches in Scandinavia against going to America, most immigrants looked to their pastors for leadership in the New World.

Because they came from different countries, at different times, and to different places, it was a slow road to unity for the Scandinavian Lutherans in America. When they finally met for their great reunion, it took place in Columbus, OH, where Scandinavians are scarce.

A merger of synods with Danish, Norwegian and German backgrounds had taken place in 1960 to form the American Lutheran Church (ALC). The Lutheran Free Church, also of Norwegian background, joined the ALC in 1963. In 1962, the Lutheran Church in America (LCA) was formed by churches of Danish, Finnish, Swedish and German backgrounds.

The historic gathering of April 30 to May 3, 1987, united the ALC, LCA and AELC (Association of Evangelical Lutheran Congregations) into the Evangelical Lutheran Church in America (ELCA). The seating arrangements for the 1,045 delegates to the constituting convention was alphabetical. This meant that they were integrated from the start and were discouraged from forming power blocks as they voted. (I was fortunately seated at a front row table in the middle of the convention hall. On my left was a delegate of German background from Dayton and a bishop of Swedish background from Seattle was on my right.)

There's paranoia when mergers take place. I had been a delegate to the constituting convention of 1960 and remember the fears of that generation. Rumors were floating among the Norwegians that their leaders had sold out to the Germans and that congregations would lose their freedom. The Germans in Ohio were less than happy with moving to Minneapolis to join the Evangelical Lutheran Church of Norwegian origin. I heard some of the same fears again. This would be the

39

"last hurrah" for the Scandinavians before being swallowed up by the German majority. But when it was all over, the Scandinavians went home with the chief executive offices.

Dr. Herbert W. Chilstrom of Minneapolis was chosen to be the Presiding Bishop. He is of Swedish origin with a degree from Augsburg College in Minneapolis, founded by Norwegians. Mrs. Chilstrom is of Norwegian background and hails from Beresford, SD. The newly elected General Secretary is Dr. Lowell Almen, another Swede. A native of Park River, ND, he is a graduate of Oak Grove Lutheran High School in Fargo, Concordia College, Moorhead, and Luther Theological Seminary, St. Paul, — all institutions founded by Norwegian immigrants.

The headquarters are in Chicago, which has the largest concentration of Scandinavians in America. They are located near O'Hare Airport so that people can fly in for meetings and return the same day to any place in the USA. Just a few miles away is the Lutheran General Medical Center, one of the largest medical facilities in Chicago, founded by Norwegian Deaconesses in 1902.

It shouldn't be assumed, of course, that all Scandinavians are Lutherans. There have been quite a few Norwegian Methodist and Baptist congregations and a significant number of Swedish Covenant congregations. Once they got over to America, many of them joined whatever denomination was convenient or fit their social status. It's a fact of history that the Church of Sweden advised people migrating to America to join the Episcopal Church rather than the Swedish Augustana Synod because the immigrant pastors had not been ordained in the tradition of "apostolic succession." It's also true that as Scandinavians were moving up the social ladder in America, they often joined one of the "American" churches that fit their new social class.

What took the Scandinavian Lutherans so long to get together? There is no difference in teachings that can be traced to ethnic backgrounds. Scandinavian Lutherans are generally conservative in theology and pietistic in their manner of life. Except for the Finns, they've all understood each other from the time they arrived in America, so language was no serious barrier. Some people claim it was stubbornness, and I'll have to admit that there is some basis for this. While no race has a corner on self determination, I wouldn't deny that I've met some headstrong Scandinavians who can test the patience of the most pious saints.

One of the speakers at the constituting convention was Dr. Gunnar Staalsett, General Secretary of the Lutheran World Federation from Geneva, Switzerland. Staalsett is a pastor from northern Norway whose grandparents migrated from Finland. Trained in the pietistic Free Faculty of Theology in Oslo, after studying at the conservative "Little Norwegian" Bethany Lutheran Seminary in Mankato, MN (1957-1959), he studied Greek under Dr. J. A. O. Preus, who was later president of the Lutheran Church - Missouri Synod.

Staalsett took delight in telling us the story of a Norwegian-American woman whom he once met on an airplane. She got right to the point. "I'm opposed to this merger! It's no good," she said. After a pause, she added, "I was also against the last merger (1960), but it worked out all right and I suppose this one will too."

L. GAYLOR

New beginnings in Columbus.

41

CHAPTER 14

'Vesterheim' —
The Norwegian-American Museum

"VESTERHEIM" - "WESTERN HOME" - is one of the oldest and most complete immigrant ethnic museums in America. Located in Decorah, IA, a Norwegian-American center since 1850, Vesterheim began collecting pioneer artifacts in 1877. "Western Home" stands in contrast to Europe as the "Eastern Home." Vesterheim began as a part of Luther College and became an independent corporation with its own national board of trustees in 1972.

Though I had known of this museum for many years, it was not until 1976 that I spent an afternoon viewing its acquisitions. Thirteen buildings make up the Vesterheim complex. The Main Museum Building is an elegant former three-story hotel built in 1877 and renovated in 1975.

Nine original buildings comprise the Outdoor Division of the Museum. The stone mill, important to the early farmers, sits on its original site and dates from 1951. The 17,000-square-foot Vesterheim Center, comparable in size to the Main Museum, was formerly a factory and warehouse built in the 1880s. It houses the Vesterheim offices, libraries, gift shop, classrooms, photographic and conservation laboratories, archives, exhibition galleries, woodworking shop, and volunteers' room. Between the Main Museum and the Vesterheim Center is the small Dayton Building, named after Silas Dayton, a merchant who constructed the building in the 1880s.

About seven miles from Decorah is located the Jacobson Farmstead on a ten-acre site. It was developed in the 1850s by the Jacobsons and remained in the family until donated to Vesterheim in 1977. Six buildings, standing on their original sites, document the culture of those rural immigrants who came to the Midwest almost 140 years ago. When fully restored, it will display Norwegian-American farm life at the turn of the century.

One unusual structure is the Washington Prairie Methodist Church built in the mid 1860s. A stone building that might be mistaken for a country schoolhouse, it stands on its original site near the Jacobson Farmstead in a well-preserved condition. The congregation was formed in 1852 by the Rev. O. P. Peterson, who later returned to Norway to organize the first Methodist congregation in his homeland.

Other buildings of the Vesterheim Complex include the Haugan house, a North Dakota prairie house and pumphouse, a Valdres house, the Tasa Drying house, the Egge-Koren house, a Norwegian Lutheran parochial school, the Norris Mille Stovewood house, the Mikkelson-Skree blacksmith shop and a Norwegian gristmill.

The Museum's collection includes more than 12,500 immigrant artifacts in addition to many books, manuscripts, phonograph records and tapes. The textiles and woodworking exhibits alone make a visit to Vesterheim worthwhile. I was especially impressed with the magnificent collection of trunks built in Norway. These have been restored, complete with beautiful rosemaling decorations.

The materials in the museum are limited to items made by Norwegian immigrants in America that show their ethnic background, objects brought from Norway which show ethnic heritage, and material which documents the early life of these pioneers. What is most impressive about Vesterheim is the quality of the exhibits. It makes one feel that many of the immigrants from Norway were highly skilled artisans who took great pride in their work.

His Majesty King Olav V of Norway serves as Honorary Chairman of Vesterheim's prestigious 74-member board of trustees. Among the board members are Ingrid Semmingsen of Oslo, one of the outstanding authorities on Norwegian immigration history; Gerhard B. Naeseth, the well-known genealogist from Madison, WI; Arthur E. Anderson III of Chicago, from the internationally famous accounting firm; Norman Lorentzsen, formerly Chairman of the Burlington Northern Board of Directors; and Mrs. Leif J. Sverdrup of St. Louis, who has given significant support to the preservation of Norwegian-American culture.

The Vesterheim Board of Directors set a $1,400,000 goal to strengthen Vesterheim's financial base, with $500,000 to be set aside as an endowment. Arley R. Bjella, former Chairman of Lutheran Brotherhood, was Honorary Chairman of the National Campaign, together with Walter F. Mondale, Norman E. Borlaug, David W. Preus, Sidney A. Rand, Eric

THE SCANDINAVIAN SPIRIT

Sevareid, Jan Stenerud and many other nationally known persons of Norwegian-American heritage.

The Museum also publishes a quarterly illustrated newsletter which is sent to its 6,000 members; 24,000 people visit the Museum annually. Vesterheim also serves students from area grade and high schools as well as college and university students from Iowa, Minnesota and Wisconsin. It's open seven days a week.

Vesterheim also has pioneered a Genealogical Center in Madison, WI, directed by Gerhard B. Naeseth, which is planning a new facility to house its work of assisting Norwegian-Americans to trace their family roots. It has been called the "premier Norwegian-American genealogy organization in this country." They need $350,000 to reach their goal.

Naeseth has been the leader behind Vesterheim's most recent development. He was on the staff of the University of Michigan for six years, Oklahoma State University for eight years and the University of Wisconsin for 30 years until his retirement in 1978. Since then, he has volunteered his time in the development of this valuable Vesterheim endeavor. He is preparing a five-volume "Biographical Dictionary of Norwegian Immigrants Prior to 1851." Naeseth has also been awarded the Knight's Cross, First Class and the Royal Order of St. Olaf.

The Vesterheim Board of Directors held its 1987 meeting in Minot during the annual Norsk Høstfest in October. Vesterheim is impressive. It deserves the attention and support of everyone who wishes to keep the best of the Scandinavian spirit alive in the New World. It serves well the 6 million living Americans who claim this ethnic background. For more information, write: Vesterheim, 502 W. Water, Decorah, IA 52101.

CHAPTER 15

Lars Skrefsrud —
Apostle To The Santals

I FIRST HEARD ABOUT Lars Olsen Skrefsrud (1840-1910) from Rev. Bernhard Helland, a veteran missionary to India, when I attended the Red Willow Bible Camp near Binford, ND, in 1943. I was deeply impressed by his missionary stories.

Skrefsrud was born on a small tenant farm not far from Lillehammer in Gudbrandsdal, Norway. The terrain is rough and his mother feared that he'd stumble on a hillside and fall into the river Laagen below. Lars's father was a skilled carpenter and blacksmith who worked hard and was married to the daughter of a large land owner. Though he made good money, he was a poor provider because of his alcohol addiction. His mother, a devout Christian, was influenced by the farmer-preacher, Hans Nielsen Hauge.

Lars attracted attention at a young age by his excellent answers during the catechizing of children during the Sunday services. By the time he was confirmed at age 14, he had memorized the catechism, Bishop Pontoppidan's Explanation and the Bible History. His mother was his main teacher.

At age 16, Lars left home to work. Then his mother died and his life took some bad turns. He was torn between his mother's teachings and the pressure of his pleasure-loving friends. He had promised her that he'd never touch liquor, but when his friends called him "an old woman," it was too much. Trying to prove himself, he fell in with a drinking group and was involved in a series of burglaries in Lillehammer. The policemen caught him while the others got away. Lars refused to divulge their names and went to prison for 32 months.

This was a time of spiritual despair and lonesomeness. The only person who believed in Lars was a young girl named Anna Onsum, who had been brought up in a Haugean home. Her encouragement restored his hope and he returned to his mother's teaching. He memorized the whole New Testament and taught himself English and German in prison. After his release, he learned Greek, Latin and Hebrew.

In 1862, at age 22, Skrefsrud applied for admission to the mission school in Stavanger. Denied acceptance, he set off for Berlin to enroll in the Goszner Mission School. On the way, he met Hans Borreson, an engineer from Denmark, who became his lifelong friend and colleague. Lars finished the school in one year and had the highest grades in the final examination. He left for India in 1863. Anna Onsum came to India to be his bride in 1865. Mission work among the Santals began in the fall of 1867 at a place named "Ebenezer." Anna died in 1870.

Skrefsrud's missionary methods were based on kindness, not argumentation. He did not ridicule the Santal gods. The Santals were intellectually a bright people, but they had been oppressed by their Hindu landlords.

Skrefsrud was more than a religious teacher. He worked for the economic and social improvement of the Santals. Almost single-handed, he broke the power of the landowners, money-lenders and liquor dealers who had been exploiting the people. Several times they tried to assassinate him. He also pressured the British colonial governor to treat the Santals justly and broke the power of the tribal chiefs who opposed his reforms. To support their work, the mission started a tea farm. (I've tasted the tea from this farm and it is of excellent quality.)

In addition to being an evangelist and social reformer, Skrefsrud was an outstanding educator and was elected to the Asiatic Scientific Society of Bengal. He prepared a grammar of 400 pages and a five-volume dictionary of 700 pages each, the first work of its kind in the Santal language. As a scholar in Sanskrit and Persian, he discovered similarities with Old Norse. He also learned Arabic. The King of Denmark once asked him if it was true that he was fluent in 42 languages. He replied, "Your majesty, it does not depend on how many languages a person knows, but what he says in the languages he knows." The king was satisfied. (While speaking at Luther Seminary in St. Paul, he picked up a Hebrew Bible and read from it as though it were written in his native tongue.)

On trips to Norway, Denmark, England, Scotland and the United States, Skrefsrud was a spell-binding preacher who never used notes.

He could speak for two or three hours with hardly a rustle in the audience. He was ordained in 1881 in the Oslo cathedral. On a trip to Minneapolis in 1891, the Santal Mission Committee in America was organized. The first secretary of the society was Prof. John Blegen of Augsburg College, who organized Bethany Lutheran Church in Minot in 1886. That comes very close to home for me, because I served as Senior Pastor of that church from 1974 to 1989.

Anglican Bishop Stephen Neill, a renowned Christian leader in India, called Skrefsrud "one of the most remarkable pioneer evangelists among simple people that India has ever seen." Kenneth Scott Latourette, the dean of American mission historians, called Skrefsrud "an amazing linguist." His work in India bore rich fruit. There are over 56,000 members in the Northern Evangelical Lutheran Church in India today. That may not seem many in a land of over 700 million in which 83% are Hindu, 12% Moslem and only 2.5% Christian. My friends, however, who have visited the Santals, report that Lars Skrefsrud, the boy from Gudbrandsdal, is still revered among the people to whom he gave his life.

Dr. Olav Hodne has written a brief history of the Santal Church entitled "The Seed Bore Fruit." It also lists the names of the missionaries from Norway and America who worked in that area of northern India and Bangladesh. It's an exciting story.

CHAPTER 16

Scandinavian Immigrants
And The Slavery Issue

I HAD ALWAYS WONDERED why the Scandinavians mainly settled north of the Mason-Dixon line. A review of the editorial opinions expressed in the Scandinavian newspapers from the 1840s to 1870s reveals a great deal about the attitudes of those immigrants. One of the most influential early writers was Ole Rynning. His "True Account of America," published in 1838, sparked an outbreak of "America Fever" in Norway. As a Norwegian immigrant and traveler, he predicted that there would be "either a separation between the northern and southern states or bloody civil disputes."

The 19th century saw a great clamor for the freedoms of the common person in the Scandinavian countries and the immigrants were outspoken in their denunciation of slavery. They claimed that Negroes "are redeemed by the same blood and are destined to inherit the same glory as other races." Three Wisconsin counties — Racine, Walworth and Waukesha — voted to approve Negro suffrage in 1847. This was an area where the Norwegians predominated. The state, however, turned down the referendum for fear that Wisconsin would become a haven for runaway slaves.

According to Arlow William Andersen the slavery issue was the main reason why most Scandinavians settled in the northern states. Anderson, formerly a professor at Jamestown College in North Dakota, is the author of "The Immigrant Takes His Stand," published by the Norwegian-American Historical Association (1953).

Until the mid 1850s, Scandinavians tended to vote with the Democratic party. However, as the tension over slavery heightened, most of them became Republicans and were solid supporters of Abraham Lincoln. They were equally pro-Union and anti-slavery. Only a few settled in the South and some of them did own slaves, but not many.

The Scandinavians never did get on the bandwagon with Horace Greeley and the other radical abolitionists. They were also suspicious of America's expansionist foreign policy. They did not support the war with Mexico since they suspected it was a subterfuge to expand the number of slave states. Most Scandinavians expected slavery to die a natural death since it was becoming economically unprofitable. While the number of Scandinavians was not great at the outbreak of the Civil War, they rallied to the cause of the Union with fierce loyalty. The men of the 15th Wisconsin Regiment, commanded by Col. Hans Heg from Racine County, distinguished themselves in battle. Heg was killed at the Battle of Chickamauga (Georgia) in 1863. (See "The Scandinavian Heritage," chapter 26.)

Defenders of slavery claimed constitutional authority and justified it on humanitarian and religious grounds. They pointed to the Ten Commandments which spoke of menservants and maidservants, and to the lack of any prohibition of slavery in the Bible. Some claimed that slavery to Christian masters was a blessing, since many of the Africans had converted to the Faith. The Scandinavian editors of the North did not accept these claims.

The most tragic arguments were in the churches. The Baptist, Methodist, and Presbyterian churches divided over the slavery question. A crisis developed among the Norwegian Synod Lutherans, whose theological students attended Concordia Seminary in St. Louis, MO. Many returned to the North indoctrinated in pro-slavery views. They didn't actually claim so much that slavery was "right," but rather that it was "not wrong," according to the Bible. They also supported the sovereign rights of states and the Dred Scott decision of the Supreme Court in 1857.

When these students returned North, they were challenged by the congregations, and especially by the editors of secular Scandinavian newspapers. There were some heated debates at the Synod conventions in Wisconsin and Iowa in those days. When the Union Army closed Concordia Seminary (1861) for its pro-slavery views, the Norwegian Synod established Luther College in Decorah, IA. In 1876 the Synod took steps to build its own seminary.

Eight decades after the conclusion of the war between the states, I encountered this same pro-slavery position in a college teacher whose background was in the Norwegian Synod. Later, when I enrolled for graduate studies at Concordia Seminary, I found that all traces of pro-slavery views were gone. I was surprised, however, that students commented so openly on the pro-slavery views of Dr. C. F. W. Walther, whom I had held in high esteem.

Tuve Nilsson Hasselquist, a Lutheran pastor and journalist, had great influence in bringing Swedish immigrants into the Republican party over the slavery issue. Claus Clausen, a Danish schoolteacher who became a pastor in the Norwegian Synod, served as a chaplain with the 15th Wisconsin Regiment. He was an anti-slavery leader in the Synod until his resignation in 1868 when the Synod pastors still refused to take a stand against the principle of slavery. Clausen was pastor in my grandmother's congregation of the Norwegian-Danish Conference near Blooming Prairie, MN, after the Civil War.

Now I understand a little better why I was destined to be born in North Dakota and to endure its long winters rather than in the balmy climate of the South where the magnolias and dogwoods grace the countryside.

Breaking the bonds of slavery.

CHAPTER 17

Scandinavian Immigrants
And Public Education

SCANDINAVIANS MAY HAVE BEEN fanatics about education, but they were divided in their opinion about public schools. The earliest immigrants were eager to become assimilated into the American scene. In 1848, however, with the arrival of Rev. H. A. Stub to Muskego, WI, a division occurred. Stub was fearful that the public schools would erode the Norwegian language and pollute the "Lutheran religion."

That set up a battle. In 1850, Knute Langeland, editor of "Democraten," a Norwegian newspaper in Racine, WI, defended the public schools. He wrote, "There is only one remedy for ignorance and that is the common school . . . Countrymen, fathers, mothers! Give your children a good education. Let them not grow up in ignorance." Other editors followed. Charles Wilson, editor of "Fredheds-banneret" ("The Banner of Freedom") in Chicago, urged that parents have their children learn English as soon as possible. He criticized the clergy who wanted to retain Norwegian.

Many Norwegian Synod pastors admired the parochial school system of the Missouri Synod. Rev. Adolph Preus, a "moderate" president of the Norwegian Synod, approved of children attending public schools provided that the instruction was satisfactory and that there was adequate discipline. He suggested that religion should be taught in the homes in the mother tongue, while the public schools should teach English and other practical subjects. Preus expected that parochial schools would eventually replace public schools. He disagreed with Rasmus Sorenson, a Danish schoolteacher from Waupaca County, WI, a champion of the public school system. Preus, having come from a strong educational background in Norway, thought that American public schools were poorly equipped and lacking in discipline. He also charged that children of Norwegian immigrants were discriminated against. He did not want to abandon the public schools, but urged the hiring of highly qualified teachers and administrators.

THE SCANDINAVIAN SPIRIT

One of the problems among the early immigrants was that people were so busy clearing the land, constructing buildings, planting and harvesting that they neglected to educate their children. In 1866, after the Civil War, the Norwegian Synod met in Manitowoc, WI, to take up the issue of education. They urged that parochial schools be established wherever possible, but that public schools, sometimes called "heathen schools," be supported as they were the best for "non-Christians." The Synod concluded that "children of Norwegian stock should learn English after being confirmed in the Lutheran faith."

Rev. Claus Clausen, who left the Norwegian Synod for the Norwegian-Danish Conference, defended the public school and urged young Norwegians to prepare themselves to teach in American colleges. Rasmus B. Anderson, who introduced Scandinavian studies at the University of Wisconsin and was later ambassador to Denmark, was a champion of the immigrant's need for higher education. He regarded opposition to the public school as "treasonable." Victor F. Lawson, a Norwegian immigrant who founded the Chicago Daily News (which existed until recently as one of the city's major daily newspapers), was a strong supporter of public education. Those dissenting from Lutheran doctrine also joined the ranks of public school advocates.

The Norwegians established a goodly number of academies and colleges. There were more than 700 teachers in Norwegian parochial schools by 1890. Among the early schools were Bruflat Academy in Portland, ND; Luther Academy in Albert Lea, MN; Augustana Academy in Canton, SD; Oak Grove High School in Fargo, ND (my Alma Mater); Aaberg Academy in Devils Lake, ND; Park Region Academy in Fergus Falls, MN; academies in Glenwood, MN, and Bode, IA; and many others. Oak Grove is the only one surviving today. Public education finally prevailed among the Scandinavian-Americans.

My parents favored public education. Six white schoolhouses dotted the township where I was reared in North Dakota. I attended Colfax School #5, better known as the "Ista School," where students of German extraction were in the majority. It was a building consisting of two rooms, both of which were in use when my father attended there. So highly was education held that I would never have dared to come home and complain about the teacher. Going off to Oak Grove High School in Fargo for my senior year was not a result of any disaffection with public education. It was simply that our public school couldn't offer adequate preparation for college during the latter years of World War II.

While our home favored public schools at the elementary and secondary levels, college was another matter. The colleges of the church were held in highest regard. St. Olaf in Northfield, MN, was usually thought of as the prestige institution by our pastors. I, however, was "conditioned" by my parents to select Concordia in Moorhead, MN, both because of its solid academic program and because it was a nearby school of the church. Until then, I had not been exposed to the classical education which characterized the Scandinavian-American colleges. I was in for a surprise that was to permanently affect my life.

Though Norwegian-Americans, my family always thought of themselves primarily as "Americans" — even though the picture of King Haakon VII hung in our living room. My parents were eager to learn the ways of the New World and did not join any ethnic organizations. We were also a "Gold Star" family, my father's oldest brother, Olaf, having been killed in France during World War I. Patriotism was strong. In recent years my ethnic heritage has returned to fascinate me and drive me back to my roots so that I might know myself better.

CHAPTER 18

Abraham Lincoln And
The Scandinavian Immigrants

THE EARLY SCANDINAVIAN immigrants were uncommitted to any of the American political parties and distrustful of the new nation's foreign policies. But as Abraham Lincoln moved to the fore among the politicians, they rallied to his support and never wavered. Even when many newspapers attacked the president's leadership, the Scandinavians remained loyal to him. Carl Fredrik Solberg, editor of Emigranten (The Emigrant), hailed Lincoln as "one of the greatest men of our century."

The election of 1860 saw the Democrats hopelessly split. Lincoln was not the best-known presidential aspirant of the new Republican Party, but he had fewer enemies. His "house divided" speech about the nation and slavery won the support of the freedom-loving immigrants. Scandinavians opposed the Fugitive Slave Law, which required that runaway slaves be returned to their owners. Other concerns of the Scandinavians were the Homestead Act and a moderate protective tariff, which benefitted the North and the West.

There was talk of annexing Cuba in those days. This idea was opposed by Solberg because it appeared to be a ruse to extend slavery, as the island would be admitted as a slave state. The "Know-Nothing" movement was directed against immigrants and sought to delay their receiving citizenship and the right to vote. Lincoln opposed this movement. Upon Lincoln's election, Solberg wrote: "A thousand hurrahs for Lincoln!" He wrote of Lincoln's inaugural address that it was "as good as 10,000 men."

When the Confederate forces attacked Ft. Sumpter in the Charleston harbor on April 12, 1861, Solberg wrote, "To arms!" He declared, "Fear not that the cause is not righteous and good. God is on the side of the American soldier." While the number of Scandinavians in the United States was relatively small at the time of the Civil War, their participation was high. One out of six Norwegians of military age volunteered, while only one out of eight "Yankees" were in uniform. Wisconsin sent an estimated 4,000 Norwegians to the Union Army.

The leadership of Col. Hans Heg encouraged the Scandinavians to rally for Lincoln's cause. It was Heg's opinion that the men who conducted the war would be the ones to control postwar affairs. He argued that Norwegians must get into the fight if they hoped to occupy influential positions later. He wrote in a newspaper, "Let us unite in giving to posterity untarnished the old honorable name of Norsemen." In the field balloting of the 15th Wisconsin Regiment under Heg's command, the Scandinavians voted overwhelmingly in the Republican column to support Lincoln. (See "The Scandinavian Heritage," chapter 26.)

When Lincoln issued the Emancipation Proclamation, which was to take effect on New Year's Day, 1863, the full document was published in Norwegian in "Emigranten." The newspaper described Lincoln as "a Christian and a patriotic man." In the election of 1864, most Scandinavians were fully committed to the support of the President against General McClellan, the Democratic candidate. McClellan had pledged a negotiated peace between the North and the South while Lincoln held out for victory to save the Union.

Knud J. Fleischer, editor of "Faedrelandet" (The Fatherland), wrote that if anyone voted for McClellan, people would point to his gravestone and say, "There lies one of those who, blind and confused in party strife, voted for McClellan and immediate peace, thereby fostering eternal war." Fleischer laid the blame for Lincoln's death on the Democratic party. He cited an 1864 Democratic campaign statement which read: "If he in the future as in the past misgoverns the nation, he never will live to complete his term." That seemed all too prophetic for the Scandinavian press. The Scandinavian press reflected the loyalty to Lincoln that characterized the majority of its constituency. ("Emigranten's" Solberg laid the blame for Lincoln's assassination on the Confederates, however.

No Scandinavian has done more to immortalize Lincoln than Carl Sandburg (1878-1967). Born of Swedish parents in Galesburg, IL, he wrote six large volumes on Lincoln's "Prairie Years" (published in 1926) and the "War Years" (published in 1939). He was awarded the Pulitzer prize for history in 1940 for the latter work. Though Sandburg was born 13 years after Lincoln's death, he reported that he came to learn first hand as a boy about Lincoln's times from veterans who had fought under Grant and Sherman.

Sandburg was a newspaper man and became an editorial writer with the "Chicago Daily News," which was founded by a Norwegian, Victor F. Lawson. His fascination with Lincoln was perhaps due in part to the fact that they were both from Illinois. However, I believe that he was also reflecting the general Scandinavian regard for Lincoln as one of the world's greatest heroes. He did solid research on Lincoln history, studying the over one million words written by the President. President Franklin D. Roosevelt personally conducted Sandburg to the Lincoln corners of special interest in the White House in 1937. President Herbert Hoover had done the same in 1930. There seems to be very little about Lincoln that Sandburg didn't uncover.

I don't know how many Scandinavian immigrants Mr. Lincoln might have known, but they certainly held him in highest esteem as the "savior" of the republic.

"The Great Emancipator."

CHAPTER 19

How Finland Got Its Independence

FREEDOM AND INDEPENDENCE have never come easy for any nation. Finland is a case in point. This small nation of fewer than five million people was under Swedish rule from 1216 to 1808, and under Russian rule from 1808 to 1917. The fragile freedom that Finland has enjoyed since 1917 has called for vigilance and sacrifice by this brave and peace-loving people.

Finland has been criticized by the West for appearing to be too friendly with the Soviet Union. In my opinion, this is unfair to the only nation to pay in full its war debt to the United States. Anyone who has visited Finland and seen its clean cities and beautiful countryside, and who has met its delightful people, can't help but admire the Finns for their determination to survive with dignity.

During the long Swedish period, very few Finns would have dreamed of separation from the king in Stockholm. Norway, which was under Danish rule from 1380 to 1814, long felt much the same about the Danish king. The Napoleonic wars changed both political situations.

Sweden's King Gustavus III (reigned 1771-1792) deliberately provoked a war with Russia in which he lost more than he gained. The anti-war leaders in Sweden and Finland even collaborated with the Russian government to bring an end to hostilities. In the end, the king was murdered by a Swedish nobleman.

Sweden's rule over Finland ended in June, 1807, with the Treaty of Tilsit, in which Napoleon promised Finland to Russia. Russian forces moved into Finland in 1808. The Swedish king was compensated by being promised Norway at the Treaty of Kiel in 1814.

The Finns actually made some gains toward freedom under Russian rule. Finland never became a province of Russia; it was elevated to the status of a "Grand Duchy," with the Czar as its guarantor. The purpose of this Russian policy was to wean Finland away from its Swedish political heritage. It remained the Russian policy until the rule of Czar Nicholas II (reigned 1894-1917), who proved to be a treacherous protector.

During the Swedish period, the Finnish language was never used by the educated or ruling classes. Swedish was the official language. The publication of the "Kalevala" by Elias Lonnrot was a great event in the 19th century Finnish history. The Kalevala, written in Finnish, became Finland's national epic and was recognized all over Europe as a work of genius (see chapter 24). Finland was on the way towards national self-consciousness. Music and art followed as expressions of the emerging Finnish culture.

The reign of Czar Nicholas II spurred the immigration of Finns to America. The same was true for Germans and Jews living in Russia. As the Czarist government became more inept and corrupt, some of the empire's finest people came under oppression. "Russification" of conquered people became the official policy. The Russians demanded that Finns serve in the Russian army and that Russians living in Finland be admitted to the Finnish parliament. Fortunately, the Finns appealed the rulings and were spared participation in the disastrous war with Japan (1904-1905).

It is one of the ironies of history that Finland's greatest military war hero, General Karl Mannerheim, was trained for military service by the Russians. He later directed the defense of Finland against the mighty neighbor to the east. As the war with Germany turned to disaster for the Czar's forces, the government fell in the revolution of March 1917. The provisional government headed by Alexander Kerensky was toppled by the Bolsheviks on Nov. 7, 1918.

I became acquainted with one of Kerensky's American advisors when I lived in St. Louis. He gave me a great deal of insight on what actually took place in Leningrad during those days of revolution. I have a Latvian friend who grew up in Leningrad and actually saw the Reds storm the telegraph station. The Reds then sent word out to the Empire that they were in charge of the government when, in fact all they controlled was the telegraph station.

The fall of the Czar brought both relief and dilemma to the Finns. Were they still bound to Russia when there was no Czar? No less a leader than Joseph Stalin went to Finland to urge an independent path to form their own Communist government which could later join the Soviet Union. Finland declared its independence on Dec. 6, 1917, though both "White" and "Red" Russian military forces occupied their land.

Another irony of history occurred on March 3, 1918, at the treaty of Brest-Litovsk between Germany and Russia. This treaty requires that the Russians leave Finland, and to make sure this happened, German troops landed in Finland on April 3, 1918. Together with the Finnish Civil Guards who came out of hiding, Finland was soon liberated. Without foreign intervention, however, Finland would have had a bloody civil war.

The Finnish monarchists wanted a king. They invited Prince Oscar, son of Kaiser Wilhelm II, but he refused. As World War I went against Germany, the republican factions gained control and Finland became a democracy with an elected head of state.

World War II brought a new challenge to Finland's independence. The agreements between Hitler and Stalin made in August, 1939, proposed a new drawing of Europe's maps. Stalin demanded that Finland cede the Karelian Peninsula to provide an approach to Leningrad from the west, offering some Russian land in return. General Mannerheim urged acceptance of the offer but the government refused, believing that France, England and the Scandinavian countries would come to Finland's aid. A disastrous war followed in which the Finnish military displayed great gallantry in the "Winter War" of 1939-1940. (Only the insistence of Churchill and Roosevelt kept Finland from Soviet occupation after the war.)

When I visited Helsinki in 1985, I was impressed by the statue of Czar Alexander II standing in the public square in front of the Lutheran cathedral. The Finns still have high regard for some of the Czars, their former "protectors".

What about Finland's friendliness to the Soviets today? It has its political and economic advantages. The Finnish people, however, are overwhelmingly pro-American, despite their mistrust of our State Department. Are the Communists powerful in Finland? There is no doubt that they have a great deal of influence. One of the participants at a conference I attended was a noted biblical scholar from Finland. He told of leading more than 20 Bible study groups made up of teen-agers whose parents were active Communists. Why would these children of "atheists" join a Bible study group? He explained: "How better could they rebel against their parents?"

I have a special reason for writing this story. I want my Finnish grandsons to appreciate the struggle that brought their maternal grandparents to America. I hope they will always treasure the legacy of freedom and independence that is dear to both Finns and Americans. The struggle took 700 years in Finland, over 20 generations.

CHAPTER 20

The 'Friends Of Augsburg'

MANY PEOPLE ASSUME that the warring spirit of the Norsemen became peaceful when they accepted the Christian gospel. This has been true in military matters of modern times. It is significant that Norway furnished the first Secretary General for the United Nations in the person of Trygve Lie. The Nobel Peace Prize is also awarded in Oslo.

The warrior spirit of the Vikings, however, is not dead. It has taken new directions. Norwegian immigrants always seemed ready for a good fight in politics and religion.

In the late 19th century when the Scandinavians were winning a high percentage of county and state offices in the New World, an intense church struggle occupied the immigrants. As a result, competing Norwegian Lutheran congregations were established in many communities which challenged each other's ministries.

The historic doctrines of the faith were not at stake. It was rather the role of laymen, freedom of congregations, liturgical practices and the emphasis on Christian experience rather than doctrine. The pietistic movement led by Hans Nielsen Hauge was a powerful influence on these people.

The struggle went back to the Old World. The farmers in Norway were rising to assert their rights. The constitution of 1814 encouraged self determination in all areas of life, including the church. What right or competence, for example, did secular authorities have to appoint bishops and pastors?

It was a time of church merger among the immigrants. In 1890, the "United Norwegian Lutheran Church in America" was formed by three groups: The "Conference," the Norwegian Augustana Synod and the "Anti-Missouri Brotherhood." The Hauge Synod was not included in the merger, neither was the Norwegian Synod, which was closely related to the Missouri Synod.

61

THE SCANDINAVIAN SPIRIT

The agreements for merger went well. However, at the last moment it was discovered that St. Olaf, rather than Augsburg, would be the official college of the church. Augsburg was to continue as the official seminary. This posed a threat to Augsburg's integrated educational program to prepare men for the ministry as the seminary included both a college and a high school.

Augsburg's faculty, known as the "New School," was progressive in its educational views. They opposed transplanting a European system for training pastors among the immigrants. Little love was lost between St. Olaf and Augsburg during those days. St. Olaf charged Augsburg with having an inadeqate educational program and Augsburg claimed that St. Olaf was tainted with humanism. Besides, could the church afford two colleges?

As a result, the Augsburg administration, led by Georg Sverdrup and Sven Oftedal, refused to turn Augsburg's property over to the new church. As the situation grew more tense, a group of people calling themselves "Friends of Augsburg" met in June, 1893 to plan their defense. The United Church, led by President Gjermund Hoyme, wanted to force the issue and started Luther Seminary that Fall. Twelve congregations were expelled from the United Church, including Trinity, located near the Augsburg campus.

At their annual conference at Pontoppidan Church in Fargo in June, 1896, the Friends of Augsburg gathered for their last ditch stand. In the meantime, the United Church had started court proceedings to gain control of the Augsburg property. At their annual meeting in June, 1897, the "Friends" met at Trinity Church in Minneapolis to organize the "Lutheran Free Church" (LFC). About 125 congregations with 6,250 members made up the dissenting group. (My mother was confirmed in one of these congregations near Doran, MN, called "Sticklestad" named after the battlefield where St. Olaf was killed). The Minnesota Supreme Court ruled on June 21, 1898, that the United Church had no legal claim to the Augsburg property. Augsburg Publishing House, however, did revert to the United Church. The "Friends" had done their job well.

Bethany Lutheran Church in Minot had been organized by the Augsburg faculty in 1886. When the split took place, Bethany remained in the United Church but its pastor went with the LFC. Shortly afterwards,

Zion Lutheran Church was organized in Minot as a new LFC congregation.

It wasn't until 1963 that the schism was repaired when all but 51 congregations and 6,000 members joined the then American Lutheran Church and today are mainly found in the newly formed "Evangelical Lutheran Church in America" (1988)! The modern day dissenters formed the "Association of Free Lutheran Congregations."

I had frequent contact with the LFC since my high school days. The first Bible camp I attended in 1943 at Red Willow Lake was under LFC auspices. As a result, I attended Oak Grove High School in Fargo for my senior year. Oak Grove had been organized in 1906 as the "Oak Grove Ladies Seminary." My wife, Gerda, attended Augsburg College in 1950-1951 while she was Assistant Health Nurse at the college.

The LFC members later referred to the Norwegian Lutheran Church in America (NLCA) as the "big church." It was organized in 1917 by another merger which included both the Hauge and Norwegian Synods. The LFC and the NLCA drew closer together as a new a generation of leaders led both groups. They cooperated closely in world missions and relief work, evangelism, youth work and in many other areas. In the light of past events, it was significant that the final LFC Annual Conference was held on the St. Olaf College campus in 1962.

A great deal of credit for this reconciliation has to be given to the LFC leadership: Dr. Bernhard Christensen, president of Augsburg from 1938 to 1963; Dr. T. O. Burntvedt, president of the LFC from 1930 to 1958; and Dr. John Stensvaag, president of the LFC from 1958 to 1963. (One of the friends of our family, Dr. Olai Sletten, pastor of St. Olaf Lutheran Church in Minneapolis, was president of the LFC from 1920 to 1923.)

It was Shakespeare who said, "All's well that ends well." We can say that now, but the rift among Norwegian Lutherans was a bitter time for the immigrants. I'm told that my grandfather, Ole Fiske, who immigrated in 1893, strongly opposed the LFC.

In his book, "The Lutheran Free Church," Prof. Eugene Fevold lists among the reasons for the split "Norwegian stubborness." Dr. Edmund Smits, a Latvian professor who came to teach at Luther Seminary after World War II, told me that this "stubborness" can be a valuable asset when rightly directed.

THE SCANDINAVIAN SPIRIT

Like America itself, it has taken the Norwegians in our land a long time to understand their life in the New World. "Freedom" is a priceless possession and should never be surrendered lightly. "Trust," however, is even more priceless and should be cultivated with great patience and even pain. The "Friends of Augsburg" were true to their convictions and were an honorable and gifted people. Their legacy lives on in the Scandinavian heritage today.

Augsburg Seminary — Minneapolis.

CHAPTER 21

Racine — City Of 'Danish Delight'

O
N AUG. 2, 1952, MY LIFE was changed forever. Not only did I begin a journey in life with my wife Gerda (nee Kirkegaard), who had been a surgical nurse at the University of Minnesota, but I became a committed devotee of the best in Danish pastries, chief of which is "kringle."

If you've never seen or tasted kringle, imagine an oval coffee cake with an "out of this world" taste. It was, to be sure, served at our wedding reception at Immanuel Lutheran Church (now Lutheran Church of the Resurrection) together with an assortment of open-faced sandwiches and Danish layer cake. I'm glad that some of my Norwegian relatives were present to experience these Danish delicacies.

Racine, WI, is known for a lot of reasons, including J. I. Case, Horlick's Malted Milk and the S. C. Johnson Company of "Glo-Coat" fame. In the early days, farm wagons were manufactured there and sold all over the Midwest. Norwegians were among the early settlers in the rural areas in Racine County, where the earliest Norwegian Lutheran congregation was organized at Muskego (1843).

It is the Danes, however, who have left the deepest ethnic mark on Racine. They started coming in large numbers during the 1880s and became especially active in the building trades. My father-in-law arrived from Jutland just in time to join the American forces shipping off for France. For this he received automatic American citizenship. My mother-in-law arrived in the early 1920s. When my wife asked her mother why she came to America, she replied: "That's where all the boys went."

Among the Danes who came to America and settled in Racine were some excellent bakers. They were an adventurous lot and soon proved themselves capable of making it in the New World. At one time, Racine was said to be 50% Danish. Today it's a city of about 90,000 people of many ethnic backgrounds.

However, if you should look at the yellow pages of a Racine phone

65

book under "bakeries," you'd conclude that Racine is 100% Danish today. There are at least half a dozen bakeries with 15 retail outlets. Thirteen feature "Danish" as their specialty, besides the many grocery stores selling bakery goods. No other ethnic foods are featured, though one does list "German Chocolate Cake" among its items for sale. Although almost 300 different pastries are offered, "kringle" gets top billing in the ads.

When the Danish booth at the Norsk Høstfest was set up a few years ago, everybody agreed that kringle should be the featured pastry. Rather than try to find local pastry makers, it was decided to have the genuine article shipped to Minot from a bakery in Racine. Despite the high quality of all these bakeries, it was agreed to contact the "O & H Danish Bakery," which had been featured on a TV program called "American Trails." The late Roger J. P. Hansen, as proud a Dane as ever walked the earth, built a classy stand for serving. A folk-dancing group from Dana College in Blair, NE, a school founded by Danish immigrants in 1884, felt right at home by the kringle stand. At the 1984 Høstfest, Victor Borge, the famous Danish musical comedian, stopped by the booth to savor this delicacy.

"O & H" stands for Olesen and Holtz. Christian Olesen, who immigrated from the north tip of Denmark in 1922, worked in several Racine bakeries before opening his own in May, 1949. Holtz was a German-American business partner who helped put up the capital. After a few years, he sold out to Olesen, but the "H" remains in the bakery's name. Christian comes around to visit the bakery these days, but the operation is directed by his son, Ray, and Ray's sons, Dale, Eric and Mike. Ray's wife, Myrna, is also an active partner in the business.

Baking kringle takes special skill and a lot of time. It takes three days to prepare the dough. Ray said, "Making good Danish pastry is an art. You can't take shortcuts, because you sacrifice quality." The dough is rolled 32 times with a layer of butter between each layer of dough. It stands four inches high at the end of the first day. Two days later, it has been compressed to about two milimeters.

Kringle comes in many flavors. O & H ships over 125,000 kringles per year to all parts of the United States. Pecan filling accounts for half of their orders: they use over 12,000 pounds of pecans each year!

Nothing but pure butter from Monroe, WI, is used. Ray believes that this accounts for the excellent quality. Other fillings include cherry, almond, apricot, date, almond macaroon, apple, prune, blueberry and many others.

Although all the Danish bakeries in Racine have a reputation for quality, Michael and Jane Stern wrote in their syndicated column "A Taste of America" that "our favorite in Racine is O & H Danish Bakery." Their culinary report is carried by 146 newspapers, and it resulted in an enormous increase in business for O & H. Letters and phone calls came in from everywhere and their mail order business increased 40%. Ray showed me a copy of the article from the Baltimore Sun. Locally supplied headlines state: "Kringles put Wisconsin town on Map of Great Bakeries"; "Just call Racine 'Kringleville': The Wisconsin city thrives on these delicious Danish delights." A St. Petersburg, FL, paper wrote: "Kringle is Racine's gift to the world."

The Olesens are proud of their products, but humble about themselves. Every time we go to Racine to see Grandma Inger, I make it a point to visit O & H Danish Bakery to buy some bread, rolls and always a kringle. Usually, I visit a few minutes with Ray, telling him about the Høstfest. He's promised to attend some year.

Some unusual orders have been handled by Ray and his crew of 50 employees. The S. C. Johnson Company once ordered a cake six feet long and three and a half feet wide, big enough to feed 12,000. A local bank once ordered a cake that was 15 feet by 30 feet. I asked Ray if there was some special secret for the growth of his business. He reaffirmed that quality was the basis of their good reputation. He told me that he's had lots of suggestions for shortcuts to better profits, but will not sacrifice quality.

O & H is a busy place. I counted over a dozen attendants serving customers at the counter. Then I spotted a beautiful piece of stained glass hanging in the window. It shows a sheaf of wheat and these words, "I Am the Bread of Life."

Each October, the Norsk Høstfest features kringles from Racine at the Danish booth. At least 500 are required to satisfy the demand. They are shipped UPS in boxes of four.

THE SCANDINAVIAN SPIRIT

When attending the Høstfest, visit the Danish booth and sample some of these delights from Racine. But if you can't wait that long for kringle, you can order them by writing: O & H Danish Bakery, 1841 Douglas Avenue, Racine, WI 53402. If you are in a really big hurry, call them at 1-800-227-6665. They'll even ship by air. No one should miss out on this "Danish Delight" from Racine. You can take it from me. I'm a Norwegian-American with 37 years of experience to back up this claim.

CHAPTER 22

Slesvig — Denmark's Disputed Duchy

I N THE SUMMER OF 1977, my wife and I and our children — Christopher and Mark — were returning from Germany to Denmark. As we approached the Danish border, I stopped at a gas station to inquire about the directions. I spoke Danish since we were close to the border and since that area had been under Danish rule for long periods of time. It soon became clear to me that no one understood Danish, so I mustered up the best German I could speak to make sure we were on the right road.

The area through which we were travelling is called Slesvig by the Danes, Schleswig by the Germans. Slesvig and the issue of Denmark's proper border with Germany was a problem for many centuries. When I interned in Chicago, my landlady, Lill Dinnsen, told me that her family had come from Schleswig-Holstein, so she wasn't sure if she should be considered Danish or German. I assured her that she was Danish. She probably was. I've met many people who have claimed to be Danish but were educated in German while growing up in that area between Hamburg and Flensburg.

During the last Ice Age, which began over 30,000 years ago, all of Scandinavia was covered with ice. Denmark did not become ice-free until about 8000 B.C. It took an additional 1,000 years before Norway became a habitable land. The settlers who came to these lands travelled mainly through northwest Germany as they hunted reindeer and other game animals. Large groups of people from Denmark and Germany invaded Britain about 1,500 years ago and those from Slesvig, called "Angles," gave it the name we use today, "Angleland" or "England." A thousand years ago they returned to conquer England again under Kings Svein and Knute.

The border between Denmark and Germany didn't become a big issue until the time of King Valdemar II (1202-1241). His father had built the "Danevirke," a brick wall of fortresses near the city of Slesvig, just north of German Holstein. Slesvig is sometimes called "South Jutland" since it's attached to the main Danish peninsula of Jutland. Hedeby, one of the great trading cities of early times in the northern world, was located there.

It happened that when the Danes were looking for royalty, Christian of Oldenburg (reigned 1448-1481), distantly related to the ancient royal Danish house, was chosen Denmark's king. He was also the ruler of both Slesvig and Holstein. In taking this joint rule, he agreed in 1481 that Slesvig and Holstein should be "forever undivided." This promise proved to be a time bomb that later blew up in the face of the Danish rulers. For generations, control of these "duchies," or provinces, would be a problem.

A Danish prince, Christian Fredrik, was the representative of King Fredrik IV in Norway in 1814 when the Eidsvoll constitution was signed on May 17. King Fredrik urged the young prince to accept the treaty drawn up by the big powers and avoid an inevitable war in Norway. A military threat from England, Russia and the other great powers that defeated Napoleon, forced him to leave Norway. He later became King Christian VII in Denmark and gave them a constitution on June 5, 1849. However, his big worry was the rise of German nationalism in Holstein and southern Slesvig. Holstein had always been German, but now Germans began migrating into southern Slesvig. The Danes won a pitched battle with the Schleswig-Holstein forces at Isted Heath on July 25, 1850, in South Slesvig.

The Danish parliament incorporated Slesvig into Denmark on Nov. 13, 1863. Since this was a violation of the agreement of 1481 that Slesvig and Holstein were "forever undivided," it gave Otto von Bismarck, the prime minister of Prussia, an excuse to attack Denmark. The "Iron Chancellor's" dream was to unite the separated German states and become a great military power. The Danes with 40,000 soldiers using old muzzle-loading rifles were overpowered by the 60,000 Germans with the latest breech-loading rifles and modern artillery. (Seven years later, Bismarck's forces also crushed the French.)

The Danes expected the English and other Scandinavians to come to their rescue. The husband of Queen Victoria, however, was himself German and favored Bismarck's military adventures. Many Scandinavians volunteered for Denmark's cause, but their governments sent no aid.

Henrik Ibsen, Norway's great dramatist from Skien, became bitter towards his homeland for its failure to aid Denmark.

The German occupation of southern Denmark continued until the end of World War I. A vote was taken in Slesvig and it was divided just north of Flensburg. By this time thousands of German settlers had moved into the land. During World War II, during the Nazi occupation, many Germans living in North Slesvig took up the Nazi cause. When the war was over, they pledged their loyalty to Denmark — though under duress, many later claimed.

The Danes of South Slesvig wanted to return to Denmark after World War II. The Allies are said to have offered Denmark the whole of Slesvig on condition that they'd accept German refugees pouring into the land. Based on their past experience, they left the frontier the way it was since 1920. Hopefully, the Slesvig problem has been permanently solved. It is no longer a "duchy." Today, the Danes in South Slesvig receive German sudsidies for their schools, churches and cultural activities. Denmark does the same for Germans in North Slesvig. So, is it "Slesvig" or "Schleswig?" It all depends on which side of the border you happen to be.

Dairy herd in Slesvig.

CHAPTER 23

Sten Sture — A Swedish Hero

FIVE HUNDRED YEARS AGO there lived in Sweden a family named "Sture." They were among the most powerful people of the land from 1470-1520. In fact there were three Stures who governed. Two of them were named "Sten," Sten the Elder and Sten the Younger. Between them, Svante Nilsson Sture ruled. Sten the Younger was Svante's son.

It's easy to idealize the past and think, "How nice it would have been to have lived in the good old days." Reading even a little bit of history can be a good cure for this kind of mistaken nostalgia. When I read about the "good old days," I'm thankful for living today, even with the serious threat of a nuclear holocaust, AIDS and other horrifying dangers to life.

How could it have been so dangerous for people in the "isolated" northlands of Scandinavia? In 1380, Margaret I, a Danish Princess who had become the Queen of Norway, began a rule that gathered Norway, Denmark and Sweden into one kingdom through the Treaty of Kalmar (Sweden) signed on July 13, 1397. Margaret lived for another 15 years and was the virtual ruler even though she was not the official sovereign.

The Norwegians and Danes remained one until 1814, but the Swedes were unhappy with the arrangement. That's where the Stures come into the picture. Among the colorful rulers of Sweden was King Karl Knutsson, who was elected monarch three times — probably a world record. He was caught in a power play between the Kalmar Treaty, the King in Denmark (Christian I), the German merchants who made up the Hanseatic League, the Church representing the influence of Rome, and the Swedish Council which had the power to elect and dispose. The Council members, made up of the wealthy nobility, were always looking out for themselves. It was a cloak-and-dagger political situation in which nobody trusted anyone else.

Sten Sture the Elder, a nephew of King Karl, was a trusted lieutenant of the king and guardian of his son. When the king died in 1470, Sten made his move for power. He threw a big party on Walpurgis Eve 1471 (April 30) for the townsmen and peasants. He served 5,000 pints of strong German beer, after which they acclaimed him "regent" (governor). His rival was Denmark's King Christian, who claimed the right to rule Sweden because of the Kalmar Treaty signed 73 years earlier. The showdown took place on a hill called "Brunkeberg" on Oct. 10, 1471, in what is now downtown Stockholm. The hill has been since levelled for homes and skyscrapers.

Sten Sture won a bloody battle and hired a famous German sculptor named Bernt Notke to make a statue of St. George slaying a dragon which was about to devour the king's daughter (Stockholm). Sten himself posed for the statue as St. George. The dragon represented Denmark and King Christian. The imposing wooden statue stands today in the Stockholm Cathedral (Storkyrkan). (I admit to having been impressed with both the statue and the story.) One of Sten's other significant achievements was the founding (in 1477) of the University of Uppsala, a prestigious center of learning.

The balance of power shifted between the Danish kings and the Swedish dissenters to the Kalmar Treaty. Even without royal lineage or title, Sten Sture was the chief power in Sweden for almost 30 years. Nobody claims that he was virtuous, however. He had no respect for morality or truth. He both supported and plundered churches and was twice excommunicated by the Pope. Still Sweden prospered under him and he was probably no more Machiavellian than other rulers of his time. Vilhelm Moberg, best known for his book "The Emigrants," called Sten the Elder a master of "realpolitik" (the politics of reality) in his book "A History of the Swedish People." Fate finally caught up with him, though. Apparently in good health, he suddenly died — probably from poison slipped into his drink by his successor's fiancee.

His successor, Svante Nilsson, ruled for eight less eventful years. Svante's son, Sten Sture the Younger, was one of Sweden's more interesting rulers. Named a knight at age four, Sten the Younger knew how to appeal to the common people for support. Ruthless like other rulers of his time, he was nonetheless a man of action and knew where he was going. Apart from the Danish kings, his chief opposition came from Bishop Trolle. It was not uncommon in those days for bishops to lead armies and claim political as well as spiritual power.

THE SCANDINAVIAN SPIRIT

The conflict between the regent and the bishop led to the invasion of Sweden by an army of German mercenaries in the service of the Danish King. Sten was cut down at age 27 by a Danish musket ball and died on Feb. 3, 1520. His conflict with the bishop was finally resolved in the infamous Stockholm "Bloodbath" of Nov. 8, 1520. Having been declared a "heretic," his body was exhumed and publicly burned while 82 men were beheaded in the public square beside the castle. The bloodbath travelled to Finland, then ruled by Sweden, where more people, including monks and children, were executed.

The Danish king's position looked safe, but the bloodbath only stirred the Swedish determination to throw out the Danes. This they accomplished under the leadership of Gustav Vasa, who carried out the Sture policies. After the final breakup of their Union, Sweden and Denmark fought 11 wars between 1563 and 1814. One branch of the Sture family — the Oxenstiernas — remains to this day one of Sweden's most famous aristocratic dynasties.

Those are interesting days to read about, but I'm glad I didn't have to live in them. Maybe it's better not to know too much about one's ancient ancestors. You can never tell how many skeletons and ghosts are hidden in the closets.

CHAPTER 24

'Kalevala' — The Finnish National Epic

HENRY WADSWORTH LONGFELLOW was my favorite poet as a young boy. I still remember our country schoolteacher reading his "Hiawatha" aloud to us. What I didn't realize was that his style was influenced by Finland's national epic, the "Kalevala," which he had read in a German translation.

It may seem strange even to young Finns today that for centuries their language was only spoken and not written. Instruction in schools was in Swedish and Latin. The Finnish language bears little resemblance to most other European languages (though it is related to Estonian and Hungarian). The one rule you should know about Finnish is that every word is accented on the first syllable.

Michael Agricola, Bishop of Turku, published a book with the Finnish alphabet in 1548. He had studied in Wittenberg under Martin Luther and Philip Melancthon. Being skilled in languages, he translated the Bible into Finnish. In the national cathedral in Helsinki, there's a beautiful statue of Bishop Agricola. The first Finnish-Latin dictionary was published almost 300 years later in 1826. It was not until Feb. 28, 1835, however, that the Finnish language found popular literary expression in the first edition of the Kalevala.

In 1809, the Russians forced Sweden to give up its claim to Finland. To turn the Finnish people away from their ancient ties with Sweden, they moved the capital from Turku to Helsinki. But the Finnish people started to dream of the day when they would be an independent nation.

A boy named Elias was born to the Lønnrot family on April 9, 1802, one of seven children. The family was so poor that they made bread of pine bark and soup from lichens. Elias's father, a tailor, became an alcoholic in despair over their poverty. Somehow, Elias managed to attend the university in Turku and became a medical doctor.

THE SCANDINAVIAN SPIRIT

While attending the university, Elias did what a lot of other young people do when they go to college: he got caught up in a cause that had little to do with his studies. Though he practiced medicine, his great passion in life was to rescue Finland from obscurity and make it great. He became excited about the old poetry — called "runes" — of the Finnish people which were sung and chanted to simple melodies. These ballads had been preserved in remote villages and the backwoods and especially in the Karelian peninsula, on the Russian side of the border.

The ballads were difficult to find in Finland because the Lutheran Church considered them pagan and discredited their value. The Russian Orthodox priests evidently paid no attention to the stories, however, Lønnrot took 11 extensive trips to listen to the older men and women relate these tales. After collecting them, he wove them into a single story called the "Kalevala." Since all his education had been in Swedish, he had to learn to read and write Finnish to do this work. Lønnrot was not the only one collecting these folk tales, but he is the one who popularized them for the world.

The Kalevala presentation followed a ritual, involving a lead singer, his assistant and a harpist. The two singers sat near the harp, called the "Kantele," and the harpist accompanied the singing. Some people considered these old tales to be "un-Christian." One time, the church where they were gathered was struck by lightning and the singers refused to sing another note.

Lønnrot was influenced by the German philosopher, J. G. Herder (1744-1803), a "cultural historian" who was fired up with nationalism and romanticism. He claimed that a nation could have identity only if it had a national consciousness founded on the language and oral culture of the common people.

The revised Kalevala of 1849 has 50 poems or runes. It's 650 pages long and requires patient reading though it is not difficult in the English translation. After trying for many years to find a Kalevala in America (it was out of print), I purchased my copy in Helsinki. To my surprise, I discovered that it was published by the Athlone Press of Dover, NH.

The Kalevala myths tell of the world's origin, about light and darkness, fertility, fire, animals, plants and the dead. It involves ancient heroes who brought order out of primeval chaos and determined the annual cycles of growth from the beginning of time. It's a story of the struggle between good and evil.

Large sections of the poems concern the efforts of the heroes to find wives. One of them, Ilmarinen, forged a magic mill which produced wealth for its owner. It was meant to be the price for his bride but instead it became a source of strife between two lands, Pohjola and Kaleva. During a furious sea battle, the magic mill was smashed and thrown overboard. The fragments gave wealth to the lands upon which it was washed up. The disappointed maiden, however, wanted revenge for her loss of the magic mill. Vainamoinen, the "eternal sage," used his magic to save the people from diseases sent by her. His skill as a hunter saved them from a gigantic bear sent by the unhappy maiden to destroy the herds. His great knowledge was required to recover the sun and moon after they had been stolen and hidden by her.

What is the value of these stories? The Kalevala is the great epic of Finland's ancient life and it has become the cornerstone of its struggle for a national culture and identity. It is a fascinating story and reveals a great deal of what still lurks in the subconsciousness of the nation. The Kalevala was quickly recognized all over Europe as having a place with the great literature of the world. Musicians, notably Jean Sibelius, have set the Kalevala to music and artists have pictured it in sculpture and paintings. A TV film was made of the story in 1983 which won highest honors at the Naples Film Festival. Lønnrot may have been a good physician, but he will be remembered because he told the story of Finland's mythological origin.

If you lived in Finland, you'd celebrate "Kalevala Day" each Feb. 28. What would you do? You'd probably go skiing, which is what most Finns do whenever they have a day off in the winter.

CHAPTER 25

Fredrika Bremer —
Early Swedish Visitor To America

NOT EVERYONE WHO CAME from Europe to the New World came as an immigrant. There were many distinguished visitors who returned to tell their stories. Among the best known of these were Alexis de Tocqueville of France, Charles Dickens of England and Antonin Dvorak of Czeckoslovakia (then under the Austro-Hungarian monarchy).

But there were many other less famous visitors from Russia, Japan, Argentina, Ireland, Liberia, Poland, Germany, Holland, Cuba, India, Italy and China, just to mention a few. Among these was a delicate woman, Fredrika Bremer (1801-1865), who was born in Finland of a wealthy Swedish family. She did not have to earn her living and showed an early aptitude for writing, publishing her first book in 1828.

The name Fredrika Bremer sounds more German than Swedish. Many German families of lower nobility and wealth moved to Scandinavia to work in government or in business. Many of them adopted their new homelands while retaining their names. The German community in Stockholm at one time had strong influence in government, and even today there is a German section in the city with a German-speaking church. During World War I, Sweden's royalty was partial to Kaiser Wilhelm's cause.

Fredrika turned down an offer of marriage from a dear friend, claiming that her mission in life was to help the distressed, to further women's rights and to continue her writing career. Her domestic novels marked the beginning of the "realistic novel" in Sweden.

She was very knowledgeable about the world's great literature and was attracted to travel stories from the New World. It was popular in those days for young writers to take a trip to America and to gain fame by publishing their stories upon return to Europe. Fredrika was especially influenced by de Tocqueville's "Democracy in America."

Fredrika Bremer — Early Swedish Visitor To America

In 1849, Fredrika went to America (first class!), the only Swede and one of a dozen women aboard the ship. While at sea, she read Longfellow's "Evangeline." Arriving in New York, she was a guest at the Astor House and was feted with many parties. Her fame had preceded her arrival. Soon she met the best-known American writers: George Bancroft, William Cullen Bryant, Washington Irving, Bayard Taylor and John Greenleaf Whittier. Whittier described her as the "Seeress of the misty Northland, daughter of the Vikings bold."

She found the banquet trail in America to be overwhelming and wearisome. She wrote: "It was too much! And that is the way they kill strangers in this country." Nonetheless, she really liked America and developed a love affair with the land and people as the way of the future. Unlike Charles Dickens, she saw the good in this land and after returning to Sweden played a role in encouraging many of her countrymen to seek a new life in America.

New England was regarded as the cultural center of America by many European visitors. Fredrika was a guest of Ralph Waldo Emerson, Henry Wadsworth Longfellow and James Russell Lowell. She had respect for all of them but she regarded Emerson as the "Himalaya of heathenism." Her devout Christian piety did not mesh with the "Transcendentalism" of New England. She did admire Emerson's literature, however, and was the first to translate some of his writings into Swedish.

The institution of slavery in American was repulsive to most European visitors and Fredrika was no exception. But she did not side with the radical abolitionists such as William Lloyd Garrison. She thought they were too violent in their tone of opposition. Most Scandinavians believed that slavery was doomed to die out on its own.

She remained personally open to people of the South and was treated most generously there, despite her known anti-slavery views. After visiting one large plantation, she stated that she would rather live on bread and water than be a slave. She travelled through South Carolina, Georgia, Florida and even Cuba.

Unlike many visitors who remained in the East, Fredrika went west to Chicago, Wisconsin and Minnesota. Of Minnesota, she wrote: "This Minnesota is a glorious country, and just the country for Northern emigrants - just the country for a new Scandinavia." She called St. Paul "one of the youngest infants of the Great West." During her two-year stay in America, she travelled through 27 of the then 31 states by steamboat, train, stagecoach and covered wagon. On her way back to Sweden in the autumn of 1851, she visted some of the famous writers of England. Upon her return, she wrote a 650-page description of her trip entitled "The Homes of the New World: Impressions of America" ("Hemmen in den nya verlden").

Her interest in women's rights was strengthened in America where girls studied foreign languages, mathematics and natural sciences, subjects thought to be too difficult for the female intellect in Sweden. She especially admired Harriet Beecher Stowe for writing "Uncle Tom's Cabin." She wrote: "What will not that people become who can produce such daughters!" Back in Sweden, Fredrika devoted herself to social reform, welfare work and women's rights, much of which she had learned in America. Nathaniel Hawthorne visited with her in Rome and wrote: "She is the most amiable little woman, worthy to be the maiden aunt of the whole human race."

Though she did not remain as an immigrant, Fredrika loved America and her heart bled for her friends during the Civil War. She prayed for the reconciliation of the states and lived to see the end of hostilities. Her overall impression of America was that everyone here was in a hurry and was impatient with imperfection. She believed this was the reason for so much divorce in the New World.

Even today, visitors from Scandinavia and other countries look us over and make the same comments. They still love America as a land moving into the future and not stuck in its past. And they still think we're always in a hurry!

CHAPTER 26

General Stuart Barstad —
Chief Air Force Padre

"SEEK PEACE AND PURSUE IT" was the theme emphasis in the United States Air Force Chaplaincy for 1988. Major General Stuart E. Barstad, Air Force Chief of Chaplains, addressed national Prayer Breakfast observance at Offutt AFB in Nebraska on the theme of "peace," and was asked: "Isn't that something like speaking against hand guns to the National Rifle Association?" "Not at all," he replied, "for peace is our profession."

General Barstad entered the Air Force Chaplaincy in July, 1955, following his graduation from Luther Theological Seminary in St. Paul, MN. Intending to serve only one four-year term, he has seen service in England, Thailand, and twice at Ramstein in Germany. Stateside he has been stationed in New Jersey, Delaware, California, Texas, Colorado and Washington, DC. When the hostages held in Iran were released in January, 1981, Barstad was in Oslo, Norway, for a meeting with U.S. Ambassador Sidney Rand. He promptly flew to Wiesbaden, Germany, to meet the hostages and led a worship service for them. He became Chief of Air Force Chaplains in December, 1985.

A Norwegian-American from Colfax, WI, Barstad attended St. Olaf College where he wrestled and played varsity football. He had seriously considered being an athletic coach until the call of the ministry became too strong. He was given the Distingished Alumnus Award by St. Olaf at the 1989 Commencement.

Barstad believes that a major responsibility of chaplains is to help military personnel and top military leaders understand what the churches are saying. He feels that the issues of war, peace, and nuclear weapons are everybody's business, not just that of the military. He doesn't always agree, however, with what church leaders say about the military, and vice versa.

In November, 1984, Barstad addressed a Lutheran World Federation Consultation on "The Church and the Ideology of National Security" in Geneva, Switzerland. He admitted that he is sometimes embarrassed by the statements of some churchmen when they speak out on national security issues without having adequate information. He also said, "Military people make critical statements about the church or its leaders because they were speaking out on issues or questioning policies or decisions as they related to the moral and spiritual dimension of life." He concluded: "Neither approach enhances communication or speaks effectively to the real issues." In 1986 he participated in another consultation on the subject "The Church and the Struggle for Common Security" in Buckown, East Germany.

As the Chief of Air Force Chaplains, Barstad participated in the regular staff meetings of senior air force leadership at the Pentagon. He supervised 850 active-duty air force chaplains, about 600 reserve and national guard chaplains, 750 active-duty enlisted support personnel, and 250 reserve and national guard enlisted personnel.

The Chief Padre of the Air Force did a lot of preaching too. On Easter Sunday, 1987, Barstad preached to 6,000 people at the sunrise service at Arlington National Cemetery. He has also preached the baccalaureate sermon at the Air Force Academy in Colorado Springs, CO. He is a promoter of Bible study, having taught the "Bethel Bible Series" both at Vandenberg AFB in California and in Germany. He found his confirmation classes in Germany to be exciting because the confirmation service took place at the historic Trinity Church in Worms, the setting of Martin Luther's famous confession, "Here I stand."

While totally committed to the theme "Seek Peace and Pursue It," Barstad proudly wore the Air Force uniform as a military chaplain. He has received the Distinguished Service Medal, the Legion of Merit, the Meritorious Service Medal with three oak leaf clusters and the Air Force Commendation Medal. He also received the Robbe Louis Parris Hall of Heroes Gold Medallion from the Chapel of Four Chaplains in Philadelphia.

I first met Stu Barstad when we were students together at Luther Seminary in 1951-1952. We lived in the same dormitory. I was a senior while he was in his first year. I remember him even then as an examplary person and a diligent student. I was in a position to know as I graded papers for two of the professors. We've renewed our acquaintance during the summers at Kabekona Lake near Walker, MN, where we have both vacationed for many years.

In the early months of 1955, Lutherans were short 28 armed forces chaplains. I had the application forms for the Air Force when a strep throat condition seriously affected my speaking ability for many months. Dr. Gynther Storaasli, the Director of Lutheran Chaplains, advised me to wait with the physical exam until I was completely over the effects of the illness. During the school year 1955-1956, I took a leave of absence from the Mylo Parish to complete a Master of Theology degree. In the spring, the positions were filled and I returned to the parish to resume pastoral work. A year later, when I had begun a new pastorate at New Rockford, another Air Force commission was offered me. But then it was too late: I was committed to my new position. That's how close I came to being an Air Force chaplain. I've often wondered if the strep throat was divine intervention or a demonic obstruction.

Barstad accepted an Air Force commission in 1955 and remained at his post until his retirement in November, 1988. Now that he's retired from the military, Stu tells me that he and his wife, Ruth, want to attend the Norsk Høstfest in Minot.

Barstad sees the chaplain as somebody who stands in both the religious and secular worlds as "one who is deeply committed to the business of peacekeeping and peacemaking." He was responsible for publishing a booklet on the Air Force theme "Seek Peace and Pursue It" with some notable quotes. One from Eli Wiesel reads, "Our lives no longer belong to us alone; they belong to all those who need us." That, together with the quotation from the Sermon on the Mount, "Blessed are the peacemakers for they shall be called the children of God," sums up what Barstad believes about the role of military chaplains. We can be grateful for such noble leadership. The chaplains deserve our appreciation and cooperation.

CHAPTER 27

1988 — The Year Of
The Swedish-Americans

THE SWEDES WERE THE EARLIEST Scandinavians to emigrate to the New World after the age of the Vikings. In 1988, King Carl XVI Gustaf and Queen Silvia spent 17 days in the United States to mark the 350th anniversary of those first Swedes who settled at Wilmington, DE, in 1638. A commemorative postage stamp was issued on March 29 to celebrate "New Sweden '88."

Sweden was a power to be feared in the days of King Gustavus II Adolphus (reigned 1611-1632). After his death at the battle of Lutzen, his daughter Kristina ruled for 22 years (1632-1654). Those were the days when Spain, Portugal, France, Holland and England were looking for places to plant their flags. Sweden also wanted to develop an overseas empire and for a short time had colonies on the Gold Coast of West Africa and along the eastern American seaboard. They did not last long, however. Fort Kristina, which is now Wilmington, DE, was captured by the Dutch in 1655, who later lost it to the English. The English also took control of Sweden's African colony in 1664.

That was the end of the Swedish empire outside of Europe, but Swedish life and influence continued through the churches. It is estimated that there were about 1,500 Swedish settlers and 110 farms in "New Sweden." "Sweden & America," the publication of the Swedish Council of America (Summer, 1987), has identified eight churches that trace their roots back to those days. The most famous of these was Holy Trinity ("Old Swedes") Church in Wilmington. It is still in use and looks much like it did when consecrated in 1699. They still have the original pulpit and silver communion service.

Queen Kristina sent Governor Printz to better organize the colony in 1643 and he moved the seat of government to what is now Essington, PA. Their church was named "Gloria Dei," but also nicknamed "Old Swedes." The Queen sent a bell and baptismal font which are still in use. Other churches are located around Philadelphia and in Delaware and

New Jersey. Originally, these were State Churches of Sweden and Swedish-speaking pastors were sent by the government to minister to the colonists.

About 1770, when a supply of Swedish Lutheran pastors was no longer available, the congregations became Protestant Episcopal (formerly Anglican), which they still are. This seemed to state church clergy to be the most logical solution to their problem of getting clergy since both the Church of Sweden and the Church of England claimed "apostolic succession," a direct line of bishops going back to the church of ancient Rome. Those eight congregations worship in English today but are conscious of their Swedish heritage.

Some famous people lived in "New Sweden." Among them was John Hanson, first president of the American Continental Congress, sometimes called the "first president of the United States." Another was John Morton, one of the signers of the Declaration of Independence.

Perhaps the most famous contribution of the early Swedish community was the log cabin. The Swedes and Finns were experts in the use of wood and had developed an ability to cut logs for building fine houses. From the Delaware valley, the log cabin spread across the whole frontier of America. (There is some debate about the origin of the log cabin in America, but the Swedish claim is well documented.) Seven Swedish log cabins were built on a 25-acre farmstead on the Salem River in New Jersey for the celebration of "New Sweden '88." The craftsmen, using 17th century tools, came from Sweden to supervise the construction. The royal family dedicated the New Sweden Farmstead Museum.

A few years ago when visiting Medora, ND, I met some Finnish carpenters from northern Minnesota building an addition to the Harold Schaefer log home. Their skill with an axe for cutting logs to size for a building was something to see.

Immigration from Sweden to America did not cease after "New Sweden" became a part of "New Holland" and finally "New England." However, those Swedes, like other Scandinavians, tended to melt into the American scene. After the Civil War, however, when large numbers of Swedes settled in America, they started to preserve their heritage.

The Swedish Council of America, located at 2600 Park Avenue in Minneapolis, is made up of 75 member organizations. This group is doing an unusually fine job of promoting their heritage. The founding members of the Council were the American Swedish Historical Foundation, the American Swedish Institute, the Detroit-Swedish Council and the Swedish Pioneer Historical Society.

His Majesty King Carl XVI Gustaf is the "Patron" of the Council and visited 10 major cities in the United States for the celebration of "New Sweden '88." One of the largest celebrations was in Minneapolis. Curtis L. Carlson of Minneapolis, Board Chairman of the Radisson Hotels, was the honorary chairman of the U.S. National Committees for New Sweden '88. Dr. James M. Kaplan, professor at Moorhead State University, was Chairman for the North Dakota Committee. While the royal family was being feted in Minneapolis, Swedes and their friends in Fargo-Moorhead gathered to watch the event on a wide-screen TV.

There were some special events in North Dakota too. The Chautauqua in Devils Lake, ND was dedicated to "New Sweden '88." Money was also raised to bring music students from Sweden to the International Peace Garden Music Camp.

The 1988 Norsk Høstfest had a display of pictures describing the Swedish immigration to America. Swedish musicians on tour of America performed at the Norsk Høstfest.

The North Dakota Heritage Center in Bismarck had special displays on the Swedes in North Dakota. Swedish artists performed at the University of North Dakota and the Fargo-Moorhead Symphony had a concert of Swedish music. So if you're Swedish, even if 1988 is past, stand tall and let the world know that you're proud of your heritage.

CHAPTER 28

The Scandinavian Dedication To Freedom

T HIS STORY WAS TOLD ABOUT the Vikings as they were advancing up-river towards Paris. The Franks sent a messenger to ask, "Who is your leader?" The Vikings replied: "We have no leader. We are all equals."

There may be a lot of folklore to this story, but there's some truth in it too. Since pre-Christian times, the people of Scandinavia have kept the ideal of freedom alive. It's true that they owned foreign slaves, but they were not slaves to each other. During the days of medieval feudalism in Europe, Norway and Sweden escaped the oppressive social structures which denied individual rights.

Inhabitants of the frozen north, Scandinavians have had a feeling for independence and freedom that was unknown in the balmy lands of the Mediterranean. This dedication to freedom seems inbred among them. To this day, if they have any great fault, it would be that they go to great lengths to protect the rights of even convicted criminals. The exception to this was the retribution they dealt to Nazi collaborators after World War II.

The Battle of Sticklestad on July 29, 1030, was fought between Olaf Haraldsson and soldiers in the service of the Danish king of England, Knut the Great. Olaf was greatly outnumbered and was killed, but soon thereafter came to be venerated as "St. Olaf." In his own way, Olaf thought of himself as a serious-minded Christian who was on a missionary crusade. Many opposed him, however — more for his style of leadership than for his religion. While the coming of Christianity to Norway ultimately advanced the cause of individual freedom, it did not happen immediately.

Many early Christian kings, patterning their rule after the Holy Roman Emperors, especially Charlemagne, imagined themselves to be Christian Caesars. It reached its most autocratic stage under Denmark's King Frederick III (1648-1670), who established an "absolute monarchy" over the combined kingdom of Denmark-Norway in 1661. Denmark finally received constitutional law on June 5, 1849, from King Frederick. Norway adopted its constitution on May 17, 1814, in a daring attempt to achieve independence. Norway did not really become independent, however, until 1905.

The ancient Scandinavian form of government was the "T(h)ing," an assembly of free men who made the decisions for the community. They had the power to banish those who broke the law. That's how Leif Erikson and his father were exiled to new lands in the West. Even kings were subject to having their authority ratified by the Tings. There was a constant power struggle between kings and Ting leaders. As kings gained the upper hand, however, the power of these local assemblies diminished. The word "Ting" is found in the names of several modern parliaments: Denmark's "Folketing," Iceland's "Althing," Norway's "Storting," and the "Tynwald" on the Isle of Man off the south coast of England. The Scandinavian commitment to democracy today is an inheritance from ancient times that has been restored in the modern era with encouragement from the American constitution of 1787.

Peter Brent in his book "The Viking Saga," claims that Western civilization's ideal of democracy is more indebted to Scandinavia than to Periclean Athens. He claims that the Vikings, despite their bad reports by church historians, were the principal influence that led to the democratic form of government that came to prevail in both England and America. It is his theory that the democratic ideal derived from the Vikings went underground in England during the oppressive rule of the Normans (Scandinavian-Frenchmen) and the feudalism that they supported.

Brent calls the English Revolution of the 1640s a popular movement that stemmed from the ancient Vikings and Anglo-Saxons (from southern Denmark and northwest Germany). The Anglo-Saxon "Moot" was similar to the Scandinavian "Ting." Brent writes, "Some of the most solidly-established democracies of the modern world can thus trace their direct development back to such Scandinavian and Germanic roots, however much of that development has been modified by the ideas and the vocabulary of ancient Greece." He traces the Common Law and jury system of England to the "Tings" and "Moots."

Brent notes that the trade guilds of the Norsemen were voluntary associations and states that "the very existence of the guilds seems to prove the depth and maturity of Scandinavian liberty, maintained through the centuries when royal power grew, an alternative to the hierarchies of feudalism, founding a tradition kept sinewy and supple even until today." Brent concludes: "It is to the Saxons and above all the Vikings, it seems to me, that the peoples of northwest Europe are truly indebted, and it is their stubborn conviction that the personal liberty of each free man is sacred which underlies our own."

The claim, "we are all equals," exacts a price. The danger is anarchy. The strong nations of the world have always been led by dynamic leaders, for better or for worse. World-wide conquest does not seem to have been the Viking goal. Those Norsemen were more interested in pirating, trading, and colonizing than having a tightly structured world empire. Being "equals," the Vikings would not tolerate a hereditary "Caesar" in their midst. They were crude and their reported cruelty is indefensible by our modern sense of justice. However, by the standards of their own generations, they probably were no more cruel than most of their contemporaries. (Our modern weaponry cannot claim gentility either.)

Whatever else you may wish to think or say about those people from the north, they did prize freedom and managed to preserve it through all sorts of situations. If you should visit their lands today, take note how they still treasure freedom as the highest of human values and watch for the Nobel Peace Prize that is issued each October in Oslo. The Vikings have finally come of age in promoting freedom for all people.

CHAPTER 29

Edwin T. Denig — Ft. Union Fur Trader

EDWIN THOMPSON DENIG, born at Stroudsburg, PA, in 1812, was a fourth generation Danish-American. His great-grandfather immigrated to America in 1748 and settled in the Quaker state. His father was a physician. Having the benefit of a better than average education, no one could have foreseen that he would spend the major part of his life at Ft. Union at the junction of the Missouri and Yellowstone rivers near Williston, ND.

In 1833, Denig joined fellow Pennsylvanian Alexander Culbertson, who has a town named after him in eastern Montana, on a trip to St. Louis, where they began working for the American Fur Company. He earned $400 his first year (not a bad income in those days). People travelling westward normally went to St. Louis and then journeyed up the Missouri into the fur country. One of his fellow travellers on the steamboat was Carl Bodmer, a noted writer and illustrator who became famous for his "Travels in the Interior of North America." Denig was to spend the next 23 years of his life as a fur trader on the Upper Missouri.

Denig spent the winter of 1834-1835 at a small trading post about 60 miles northwest of Ft. Pierre, SD. In the spring of 1837 he became the post bookkeeper at Ft. Union, ND, where he was stationed for 19 years. His letters indicated that he liked his work. Following the custom of white traders, he took an Indian wife. In fact, the record indicates that he had two Assiniboin wives at the same time by whom he had four children. His wives were sisters of chiefs.

He made good use of his Indian family connections to build a strong reputation for the fort with the tribes. His wives dressed like middle class white women and his children were well supplied with toys. Fancy food was always on their table. He did not try to dress or live like the Indians as that would have degraded him in their eyes. His home was also regularly supplied with good books on religion and philosophy as well as newspapers brought up-river from St. Louis. Denig was no mangy "mountain man." He is most remembered for his writings, which are excellent source material for our knowledge of frontier life on the Missouri in western North Dakota almost 50 years before statehood.

Many visitors came to Ft. Union in its early days. John James Audubon, the well-known naturalist, visited the fort in 1843. Denig helped him gather bird and mammal specimens. By that time, he was in charge of the post. Charles Larpenteur, after whom a street is named St. Paul, claimed that Denig was heavily addicted to alcohol. Excessive drinking was not uncommon during the long and cold winters on the desolate prairies. In a letter to Culbertson, Denig once requested five gallons of rye whiskey. Despite the habit, however, he seems to have made a lot of money trading furs with the Indians.

Another of Denig's famous frontier visitors was Father Pierre Jean DeSmet, a Roman Catholic priest who came originally from Belgium and was headquartered out of St. Louis. Fr. DeSmet was well known all over the frontier that branched out from the Missouri River. Because of Denig's great knowledge and sympathy for the Upper Missouri tribes, Fr. DeSmet had him write some sketches describing the Assiniboin and other frontier tribes. He used much of this material in his letters back to Belgium. He described Denig as "an intimate friend." Denig himself was a Swedenborgian, however.

In 1982, I spent some time at the Missouri Historical Society in St. Louis studying the trail of these frontiersmen. The museum under the famed Arch also has helpful background for those who want to know more about America's westward expansion. In 1983, I visited the cemetery in north St. Louis County where Fr. DeSmet is buried together with other Belgian-born clergy. Dr. James Hitchcock, Professor of History at St. Louis University, gave me a guided tour of the grounds to fill me in on the background of this remarkable missionary.

A Swiss artist, Rudolph Friedrich Kurz, went west to sketch "wild Indians" in their native environment. He spent seven months with Denig at Ft. Union. He was not nearly so charitable in his estimate of the fur trader as Fr. DeSmet had been, however. He described Denig as "a hard man, liked by nobody . . . keeps two Indian wives . . . sqauanders all he has on them; begrudges anything paid to employees, oppresses the engagees with too much work, is never satisfied." He spoke of Denig as "a small hard-featured man wearing a straw hat, the brim of which was turned back." Yet he had praise for the fine meals served him at Denig's table. Denig was known as a "bourgeois" or "townman," meaning a middle class shopkeeper.

Despite Kurz's description, Denig reportedly knew how to use authority. John C. Ewers, who edited Denig's writings in the book "Five Indian Tribes of the Upper Missouri," paid high tribute to the master of Ft. Union. He wrote: "Denig exercised an authority over his men that would have been the admiration of his seafaring Danish ancestors." Although he was a fourth-generation Danish-American, Denig's Danish qualities remained: "He insisted on economy and efficiency on the part of his clerks to keep the overhead at a minimum."

Denig left the frontier in 1855 because he wanted his children to have an education. His oldest son was sent to school in Chicago. They moved briefly to Columbus, OH, but found the climate there too warm. In 1856 took his family back to Ft. Union by way of St. Paul and the Red River Valley of Manitoba. Two years later, Denig became ill with an inflammation, believed to have been appendicitis. He died Sept. 4, 1858, and was buried in the Anglican cemetery at Headingly, Manitoba. He was only 46 at the time of death.

Denig performed a significant service for us as his writings are among the best descriptions of Indian history and customs of the Upper Missouri tribes. He was one of the finest friends that the Indians had on the frontier. He was not impressed by George Catlin who only spent 86 days in the summer of 1832 gathering information for his writings. He knew the Indians as human beings rather than as romantic "noble redskins" or "dastardly savages," and they respected him in return. He also issued some prophetic warnings about the coming warfare between the white settlers and the Sioux, but his warnings went unheeded.

I've not met anyone in Denmark who knows anything about this frontier fur trader. They would be well advised to make a statue in Legoland or Tivoli of this Danish-American who has given us so much understanding about the early days in the European settlements on the Upper Missouri.

CHAPTER 30

Norway's Strategic Place In NATO

WORLD WAR II HAD NOT long been finished when the western Allies became uneasy about the intentions of the Russian Bear. The North Atlantic Treaty Organization (NATO) was born as their response to this fear. Fifteen nations signed a pact on April 4, 1949, in Washington, DC. Among them were Denmark, Iceland and Norway. Sweden, which had been neutral during the war, chose not to join. Finland also did not join due to its sensitive relations with the Soviet Union.

Just 70 miles east of northern Norway lies Murmansk, site of a huge Soviet naval base. This makes Norway a critical point in the defense of the North Atlantic. Norway is the only northern NATO nation to actually border the Soviet Union. While travelling a few years ago in Norway, I visited on the train with some Norwegian soldiers who were returning from military exercises on the "Russian Front." I asked them what their job was. They said: "We would have to hold the Russians for one day until NATO troops arrive." I wondered where they were to come from since my son Daniel was stationed with the U.S. Army in Germany at the time.

Since the coming of NATO, Norway has built up a military defense to protect its borders unlike anything in its history. If they would have had this kind of readiness in 1940, Hitler might well have kept over 400,000 troops back on the continent for his invasion of Russia. Despite NATO, I've talked to some Norwegians who really fear that after Afghanistan, the Soviets may then turn their attention to Norway. They claim that the Soviets are spending significant sums of money to neutralize Norway now through propaganda.

Most people in America, including Norwegian-Americans, are quite uninformed about Norway's strategic place in NATO and its significance for the free world. Kenneth K. Robertson, Jr., USAF (retired), has put together a prestigious program called the "Scandinavian Symposium" which is held just prior to the opening of the Norsk Høstfest at Minot

State University (MSU). Robertson is curator of the Gen. David C. Jones Room and Archives at MSU. The programs are planned to better inform the public "about the increasingly important political, strategic and diplomatic role of Scandinavia in today's global environment."

The Symposium has attracted a distinguished roster of speakers. For the 1987 and 1988 Symposiums, Dr. Sidney A. Rand, former president of St. Olaf College and former US Ambassador to Norway, acted as moderator. Appearing with him in 1987 were Dr. Arne Olav Brundtland, husband of Norway's Prime Minister, who discussed the topic "Nordic Balance," describing the unique relationship which the five Scandinavian nations keep with the Soviet Union, with NATO and among themselves. Brig. Gen. Matthew P. Caulfield represented the U.S. Marine Corps. He served as commanding general of the Marines' Atlantic Landing Force Training Command.

Maj. Gen. Richard J. Trzaskoma represented the U.S. Air Force. He worked with global military airlift. Another panel member was James Ford Cooper, director of the Office of Northern European Affairs in the U.S. Department of State. He oversaw the U.S. relations with ten nations, including the five Scandinavian countries.

The Symposium is annually sponsored by the Joint Studies Center at MSU, with support from the Minot Air Force Base, the Norsk Høstfest Association and other individuals and organizations. Admission to the Symposium is free to the public. If you want to get some good information and insights about political and military matters involving Scandinavia, this Symposium is as fine an opportunity as you are likely to find anyplace in the Middle West.

NATO has kept a fairly low military profile in the North Atlantic. There is no desire on the part of the NATO allies to increase the Soviets' apprehension so as to lead to a military encounter. Because the world's attention is directed by the media to the Middle East, to Nicaragua and to South Africa, people are apt to forget about the serious potential danger in northern Europe. The intention of the Symposium is not to be alarmist but informational and to make a contribution to peace.

Norway is the "linchpin" in providing military and political stability to NATO's task in the North Atlantic. When I visited Norway in 1985, it was election time. The anti-NATO forces had posters and chalk-scribbled graffiti written on walls, statues and billboards. The common slogan was "NATO UT" ("NATO OUT"). The conservative coalition won the election by a close margin, but it lasted only a short time. Nonetheless, Norway's membership in NATO seems assured for the foreseeable future.

I talked to a number of people about the anti-NATO propaganda. Everyone with whom I visited wanted Norway to be in NATO and in a close alliance with the United States. I never met anyone from the radical fringe that was protesting, but their posters and graffiti were everywhere. The people of Norway know that the protective umbrella of NATO is necessary for Norway's defense. The memory of the Nazi occupation from 1940-1945 is still vivid in the minds of those who lived through those terrible years. Norway's "Resistance Museum" at Akershus Castle has a sign out in front which says, "Never Again." In both Norway and Denmark I talked to people who expressed concern that their children learn about those trying times so they don't become complacent about their precious freedoms and naive about the need for a strong defense.

The warning given by John Philpot Curran, the Lord Mayor of Dublin, on July 10, 1790, John Philpot Curran, is still worth heeding: "The condition upon which God hath given liberty to man is eternal vigilance; which condition if he break, servitude is at once the consequence of his crime, and the punishment of his guilt."

The NATO flag.

CHAPTER 31

Roald Amundsen — Polar Explorer

WHY WOULD ANYONE TAKE RISKS to accomplish the impossible? Why would anyone be willing to suffer untold dangers and risk life just to be the first to discover the polar regions? In his book, "My Life as an Explorer," Roald Amundsen explained what possessed him to make this great effort.

Amundsen was born July 16, 1872, a short distance from Oslo (then called Christiania). His family moved into the capital city while he was only an infant. When Roald was 14, his father died. The older sons in the family went out to work, but Roald remained home with his mother. In accordance with his mother's wishes, young Roald set out to study medicine. One day, however, he read and was impressed by the story of the British explorer, Sir John Franklin, and his search for the "Northwest Passage." For almost 400 years, explorers had been looking for a way to the Orient over the top of North America. Amundsen became aflame with the passion to be the one to realize this dream.

To get himself into condition, Amundsen played soccer and skied. He slept with his windows open in the winter to get into condition for the cold Arctic air. He studied hard and graduated from college at age 18.

Despite near-sightedness, he managed to get into the military because of his extraordinary physical condition. The medical doctor "forgot" to check his eyes! As one special test of his endurance, he set out with a friend to cross the mountains west of Oslo on skis in the dead of winter. No one had ever done that before. They nearly froze to death trying and at one time went four days without food before turning back.

Amundsen decided that he needed to become a qualified skipper of an ocean vessel in preparation for his attempt to find the Northwest Passage. In 1897, at age 25, he signed on as First Mate with a Belgian ship heading for the South Pole by way of Cape Horn. For 13 months they were caught in an ice field. Everyone got scurvy and two of the crew went insane. As a result, Amundsen became the ranking officer. Finally, they broke free and sailed into open water for home.

The experience on the Belgian ship proved a valuable preparation for Amundsen's later expedition. He and his party left Norway on June 16, 1903. They sailed by way of Godhavn, Greenland, with 20 dogs on a 72-foot converted herring boat named "Gjoa". They survived many perilous dangers along the way. On Aug. 26, 1905, they sighted a ship from San Francisco named the "Charles Hansson." That was the first anyone knew that they had indeed found the Northwest Passage. It was not until Dec. 5, however, that they reached Ft. Egbert, Alaska, a United States military post. From there they sent telegrams out to the world to announce their triumph. From that day on, Amundsen was a world-renowned hero. On his way back to Norway, he gave lectures across the United States and Europe. Many years later — in 1944 — Sgt. Henry A. Larson of the Royal Canadian Mounted Police became the first person to navigate the Northwest Passage in a single season.

Fame fueled the desire in Amundsen for new conquests. He next turned his attention to trying to become the first person to reach the North Pole. For this expedition he used the "Fram," a polar ship made famous by Fridtjof Nansen. At the last moment he learned that Admiral Robert E. Peary, an American, had already reached the North Pole. (That claim has now been challenged, however). Amundsen changed his plans and left with four companions, 52 dogs, and a four-month food supply to reach the South Pole. An English expedition led by Captain Robert F. Scott was already setting out for the same destination.

Some writers have criticized Amundsen on the grounds that he was not fair to Scott in the race to the South Pole. Amundsen's reply was that he had offered to cooperate with Scott and offered him half of his dogs. Scott, however, preferred to use motorized sledges and Shetland ponies. This was Scott's fatal mistake, according to Amundsen.

Amundsen and his men reached the South Pole on Dec. 15, 1911 (mid-summer in the Antarctic). They planted their country's flag and left letters certifying their discovery. Amundsen's success was made possible because he had planted supplies in advance every three days journey. Scott's group reached the Pole and found Amundsen's claims. On the way back, however, Scott and his crew froze to death. Their motorized units were no match for the Antarctic freeze, whereas Amundsen's dogs endured the cold and provided food for their owners. Amundsen complained that the English were reluctant to admit that the Norwegians had won the race.

In 1925, Amundsen and Lincoln Ellsworth, an American, became the first to fly over the North Pole, using a dirigible purchased from the Italian government. In his writings, Amundsen offered appreciation to Benito Mussolini for his support of these explorations. The Italian leader gave all credit to Amundsen for the success of the venture. Such expressions of appreciation for Mussolini were rare a decade later, but Amundsen did not live to learn the political future of Europe. On June 18, 1928, the famous Norwegian left Tromsø with five companions to search for Umberto Nobile, a famous Italian explorer whose dirigible had gone down. He was never heard from again, though Nobile was rescued.

At the Olav Bjaalands Museum in Morgedal (Telemark), Norway, I learned more about the South Pole expedition. An eyewitness account of Amundsen's discovery has been recorded in "Ski og Sudpol" ("Skis and South Pole"), a book published in Skien, Norway (1970). The book contains, among other things, a number of interesting photographs taken on the expedition.

Al Gimse, a noted Minot skiing enthusiast, shared with me some of his recollections of meeting both Fridtjof Nansen and Roald Amundsen in Minot. His father, Peter, knew both of these famous explorers. He had met them while working in a dry cleaning shop at "Seven Corners" near Augsburg College in Minneapolis. Al related to me that in the early 1920s, both Nansen and Amundsen came to Minot and spoke in the high school auditorium. Al's father was proprietor of the Gimse Cleaners, and Amundsen made the Gimse home his Minot headquarters. Though he had talked with both of these noted men, Al mostly remembers what they said about the importance of skis for their success in polar explorations.

What possesses people to take such risks while others stay comfortably at home? That's a mystery that can only be known by those who take such risks. Most of us are content just to read about the daring exploits of others.

CHAPTER 32

Poulsbo, Washington —
Norse Home In The West

I SHOULD HAVE REALIZED when I bought a loaf of "Poulsbo Bread" that it came straight from the heartland of a Norwegian settlement. Not only did it have a Viking ship design on it, but it reflected the tastes of those hardy Northmen.

Poulsbo, WA, a city of about 4,000, is located north of Bremerton on Puget Sound. The very name "Poulsbo" means "the place where Paul lives." There are a couple of theories about how the city got that name. Some say it was named after Iver Moe who had come from Norway. He was one of the town's first settlers. It has been suggested that the postal authorities misspelled the name on the application for a post office, the intended name being "Paul's Bo." Another theory is that it was named after a Paul Wahl. Whatever it was, the city has retained its strong Norwegian character since its founding in 1886.

If you've ever travelled in the Seattle and the Puget Sound area, you can understand why this place attracted Scandinavians. Poulsbo appeared as a Norseman's paradise with the forests and lumber industry, the water and fishing, but without the harsh winters of their homelands. Many of the early settlers wrote back both to Norway and to Minnesota urging their friends and relatives to become a part of this new community.

The idea to write this story was given a boost when I went to give farewell greetings to Betty Rogstad as she retired from the Minot Daily News and prepared to move back to Poulsbo. Betty had grown up in that community and was now returning home. She tried to convince me that Poulsbo is even more Norwegian than Minot and sent me a packet of information to prove it. I am also indebted to a good friend from college and seminary day, Peter Tengesdal, formerly from Maxbass, ND. Peter was pastor of First Lutheran Church in Poulsbo from 1967 to 1987.

The church was one of the first institutions to be planted in Poulsbo. The Norsemen organized "Fordefjord Menighed" in 1887, now known as "First Lutheran." Lutherans in America are fond of calling their congregations "First," something unknown in their homelands. They learned it from their American Protestant neighbors. In 1897, when the "Friends of Augsburg" broke away from the United Norwegian Lutheran Church in America to form the "Lutheran Free Church," emissaries were sent from Minneapolis to Norwegian communities to organize new congregations. Thus a second Norwegian congregation called "Grace Lutheran" was organized. That's also how Zion Lutheran Church in Minot, ND, was started.

Another interesting connection for me to Poulsbo is that Rev. A. M. Lunde, who was pastor of Our Savior's Lutheran Church in Colfax, ND, during my childhood, later located in Poulsbo. My baptismal certificate carries his signature. He died in 1946.

The roster of names in the early days of Poulsbo would make you think you were right back in Norway or North Dakota. Names like Borgen, Eliason, Fatland, Hagen, Iverson, Langeland, Moe, Myrvang, Nilsen, Tallagson, and Vik, not to mention the Andersons, Johnsons and Olsons, reveal the ethnic heritage of the community. The list of men inducted into the military during World War I sounds like the roster of a Norwegian regiment. Several of these men served in France.

During World War II, when Norway suffered under the Nazi occupation, the people of Poulsbo supported the Norwegian relief efforts. They continued doing so after the end of the occupation as Norway began to emerge from the ravages of war. They publicly saluted the courageous people of Finland who sent over $500,000 in cash and supplies within a one-month period to Norway, despite their own hardships resulting from the Soviet invasion. The Finns also sent more than $200,000 worth of medical supplies to Norway which were needed in Helsinki.

In 1905, the people of Poulsbo received with enthusiasm the exciting news that Roald Amundsen and his crew had discovered the "Northwest Passage." They eagerly awaited the arrival of his ship to Seattle the following summer and gave him a tumultous welcome upon his arrival.

The Sons of Norway organization has a strong chapter in Poulsbo. In 1973 they built "Grieg Hall" to preserve their heritage and to serve as a home for their many activities. One of the interests of the townsmen is to have a model Norwegian city built using architecture like that

100

found in the Old Country at the turn of the past century. Poulsboites also celebrate a "Viking Fest" for three days around "Syttende Mai" (17th of May), when Norway remembers its constitution of 1814.

Just to illustrate how "Norwegian" the Poulsbo folks feel themselves to be, a poll was taken in 1969 asking for suggestions for a community theme. Seven hundred fifty-seven residents responded "Little Norway" and 382 said "Scandinavian." So "Little Norway" it has been.

The city is growing too. At the beginning of World War II, Poulsbo had 639 residents. By 1960 it reached 1,505, by 1970 it had 1,856, and by 1980 it had grown to 3,453. And it's still growing.

In 1975, Poulsbo was honored by the visit of His Majesty King Olav V from Norway. The King was in nearby Seattle, the home of a large and active Norwegian-American settlement. People of that area also attend the Norsk Høstfest in Minot. The Viking Fest and the "Little Norway" theme have rallied the people of Poulsbo to take pride in heritage.

Poulsbo, of course, is not exclusively Scandinavian, even though their Chamber of Commerce brochure has the words "Velkommen til Poulsbo" on the front cover and "Welcome to Little Norway" on the inside. In addition to the Viking Fest, annual events include the "Midsommar Fest" (Midsummer Festival), a lutefisk dinner in October and a "Yule Log Lighting Ceremony" in early December. They've also erected a Viking statue on the waterfront. The map of the North Kitsap Peninsula area contains many names that show that this is a Norse home in the West. "Velkommen til Poulsbo" is this town's invitation to the world.

CHAPTER 33

Sidney Anders Rand — Ambassador To Norway

VICE PRESIDENT WALTER MONDALE visited his ancestral home at Mundal in western Norway during Easter, 1979. To his surprise, he found 150 relatives. An idea occurred to him and upon his return to Washington he talked with President Carter about it. His request to the President was that if the post of ambassador to Norway should become vacant that someone from the Middle West with Norwegian roots be appointed to fill it.

Shortly thereafter the ambassador — Louis Lerner, a Chicago newspaper publisher — resigned because of illness. President Carter remembered his conversation with the Vice President and asked for a recommendation. After consulting with friends in Minnesota, Mondale called Dr. Sidney Anders Rand, President of St. Olaf College in Northfield, MN, to ask if he mgiht be interested in the assignment.

On Feb. 14, 1980 — after a security check by the State Department and the FBI, and a two-week briefing in Washington — Rand was sworn in as ambassador to Norway by Vice President Mondale. The ceremony took place at Boe Memorial Chapel on the St. Olaf Campus before an overflowing crowd of faculty and students.

The security check was thorough. Dr. Rand had to submit the names of 20 references plus the names of everyone who had lived within one block of him in Northfield for the past ten years. In addition, the government made up its own special list. Neither the interviewers nor those interviewed had any idea what it was all about, though there were some curious neighbors and townspeople.

The interview with the Senate Foreign Relations Committee was chaired by Sen. Frank Church. Sen. Jacob Javits, the vice chairman, was also present. They asked: "Mr. Rand, what makes you think you have the qualifications to be a U.S. Ambassador?" He answered that he had great confidence in his selectors and that his 25 years as a college president constituted a kind of diplomatic service. Sen. Jesse Helms asked:

"Do you speak the Norwegian language?" He replied: "Not as well as I should and not as well as I expect to speak it." With that brief interview, the Senators approved the appointment.

Three days after the swearing-in ceremony, the Rands were on their way to Oslo via Copenhagen. In his new job, Ambassador Rand reported to Robert Funseth, who was in charge of the State Department's relations with ten north European countries. The Undersecretary of State turned out to be Warren Christopher (originally Christopherson), a Norwegian-American whose roots were from Minnesota.

Once in Norway, there was a protocol for the presentation of Rand's credentials. First, he had to meet with His Majesty King Olav V. Then he called on the Prime Minister, the Foreign Minister, the Defense Minister and the other ministers of state. A call on the dean of foreign ambassadors was next. This was at the Embassy of the Soviet Union. The ambassadors of our NATO allies were visited next, followed by those of the other friendly aligned nations in Europe and then of the countries outside of Europe. The last group to be visited were the Warsaw Pact nations. There were four nations whose representatives the American ambassadors were to avoid except to exchange formal greetings at public functions. They were Cambodia, Cuba, North Korea and Vietnam, the reason being that the U.S. did not have diplomatic relations with them. Protocol specified a 20-30 minute time limit for these visits, with specific directions for seating of both ambassador and spouse.

What does an ambassador do besides attending formal functions? In Oslo, Ambassador Rand supervised a staff of 100. About half of these were Americans and the other half Norwegian nationals. Some Norwegians were advisors in such areas as agriculture and business, others served as chauffeurs, librarians, bookkeepers and photographers.

The Rands had time for private excursions too. They visited Mrs. Rand's relatives in the Trondheim and Hadeland areas. The ambassador found relatives of his mother at Sigdal in Numedal. That especially interested me since it's near Lyngdal, the home of my maternal grandfather. Rand's father's family had come from Surrey in England, though he has always been identified as a "Norwegian-American" during the many years that I have known him.

The Rands also took time to visit fairs, schools and churches. When we visited the American Lutheran Church in Oslo, the members were proud of the fact that the Rands had introduced the new Lutheran Book of Worship to them in 1980. Mrs. Rand was organist in the church during the time the Rands lived in Oslo.

The ambassador's residence is separate from the embassy, which is located on Drammensveien just west of Oslo's business district. The ambassador's residence, located on Nobelsgate, is a building of 24,000 square feet and is located about a mile west of the embassy near Bygdøy Alle. It is near Frogner Park, where the famous Vigeland statues are located. The embassy was secured by seven Marine guards, who carefully screened visitors. During the Rands' ambassadorship, there was one bomb threat and that proved to be false.

The Rands found that public demonstrations in Norway were carefully regulated by the police. Would-be demonstrators had to secure a permit a week in advance. Demonstrations were limited to one hour and had to be conducted across the street from the embassy. From his office window, Rand could watch the events without concern for violence. The demonstrations were generally quite peaceful and usually consisted of protests against nuclear arms or against U.S. policy in Central America.

The life of an ambassador is a busy one, with official duties taking up not only the work day but most evenings as well. Rand regularly met with the Norwegian Foreign Minister, delivering messages from the American President. His office also assisted tourists who had problems. Whenever Americans were jailed in Norway, the embassay had to report this fact to Washington and advise those who were detained as to how to get legal assistance.

Mrs. Rand (Lois) also found herself very busy. She directed the house staff, kept the calendar of events and made sure that groceries and other supplies were on hand for official functions. When there is a change of ambassadors, all perishable items are removed from the embassy residence and all new stock has to be purchased out of the ambassador's own bank account. For the ambassador to be reimbursed for expenses, at least 50% of the guests have to be non-Americans. Financial records had to be kept in both U.S. dollars and Norwegian kroner (crowns).

How did the Rands feel about their term in Oslo? They refer to it as a high point of their lives, although it cost them a considerable amount of their own money. They were amused by the fact that some Norwegians referred to the ambassador by his Norwegian-sounding middle name, "Anders," rather than by his English name, "Sidney."

The Norwegian government has twice given special recognition to Ambassador Rand's services in promoting good relations between our two countries. He has been awarded the Knight First Class - Order of St. Olav and the Commander of the Royal Norwegian Order of Merit. It is unusual for anyone to receive both awards.

I have known Dr. Rand since he was my teacher at Concordia College in 1945. It was my privilege to present him for induction at the Scandinavian-American Hall of Fame at the 1987 Høstfest. Vice President Mondale was also present to be inducted as well as to congratulate Ambassador Rand. It was a proud moment for me and for the Norsk Høstfest.

Ambassador Rand.

CHAPTER 34

The Danish Immigrant Village —
Elk Horn, Iowa

O UT IN SOUTHWEST IOWA, a new village is being built. It's really a museum to remember the immigrants from Denmark who came to seek their fortunes in America.

The earliest known Dane to reach North America was Erik Upsi, appointed in 1112 to be bishop of Greenland and Vinland by Pope Paschal II. Residing in Greenland, he visited Vinland in 1121, probably in Labrador at Christmas time. Another early Dane in America was Brother Jakob, an Augustinian monk who accompanied Cortez in his conquest of Mexico.

The earliest attempt by Danes to cross North America was an expedition led by Captain Jens Munk, who was commissioned by King Christian IV to find the "Northwest Passage" to India in May, 1619. Munk had two ships and 65 men. They camped at the mouth of the Churchill River in Manitoba and named it "Nova Dania" ("New Denmark"). The winter was so fierce that only two men survived to return with Munk to Europe in September, 1620. Among those who perished was Rasmus Jensen, the first Lutheran pastor to die in the New World. He preached his last sermon from his sick bed. The "Northwest Passage" was not discovered until the beginning of the 20th century, when the Norwegian expedition led by Roald Amundsen achieved it (see chapter 31).

In the 17th and 18th centuries, Denmark had a powerful navy and was a nation to be reckoned with in the North Sea. Because the Danes ended up on the wrong side of the Napoleonic wars, their military power faded. The rise to power of Bismarck in Germany removed Slesvig and Holstein from Danish rule. The result led to depression and immigration, and America was the most inviting place. Danes were among the early settlers in New York City when it was called "New Amsterdam" and was under Dutch rule. One of the best known of these Danes was Jonas Bronck, after whom the "Bronx" was named.

The Danish Immigrant Village — Elk Horn, Iowa

In the Middle Ages, Denmark suffered under the feudal system which controlled the working classes and kept them poor. The feudal laws were abolished in 1788 and a constitution was given by the king in 1849.

Thereafter, the working class began to assert itself. As education became available to the common people, ordinary Danes began to look to America as the land of opportunity. The land and businesses were still largely under the control of the middle and upper classes. In America, a hard-working family could soon have a larger farm than a "wealthy" landowner in Denmark. America offered an "escape" to people who could not advance in the Old World.

Since clergymen were government appointees, many common people felt no close kinship to them. I remember how anxious my prospective mother-in-law (an immigrant from Denmark) became when she learned that her daughter was planning to marry a pastor. In Denmark, people bowed to the clergy when leaving church!

The years 1870-1910 saw the largest Danish immigration to America. According to John M. Jensen, former editor of the "Ansgar Lutheran," the majority of these immigrants were receptive to socialism and the influence of George Brandes (1842-1927), an anti-Christian agnostic. The Danes were slow to form new Lutheran congregations and received little help and encouragement from their homeland. No Danish professors of theology came to teach in the Danish seminaries in the New World. Many newcomers formed Danish-speaking Baptist, Methodist, Moravian and Seventh Day Adventist congregations. A significant number of Danes also joined the Mormon trek to Utah. Others joined English-speaking congregations out of a desire to quickly "become American."

Two Danish Lutheran groups were eventually formed. These were known as the "American Evangelical Lutheran Church" (AELC) and the "United Evangelical Lutheran Church" (UELC). The former was identified with N.S.F. Grundtvig, the Danish hymnwriter, and established Grand View College in Des Moines, IA. The latter was associated with Dana College in Blair, NE. They were finally united in the 1987 merger of the Evangelical Lutheran Church in America. (I was a pastor of a former UELC congregation in Webster Groves — St. Louis, MO — from 1961 to 1965.

THE SCANDINAVIAN SPIRIT

The states with the highest number of Danes are California, Illinois, Iowa, Minnesota, New York, Utah and Wisconsin. Until 1910, North Dakota had attracted fewer than 15,000 and Montana only about 5,000 Danes. By 1920, the census statistics listed 210,000 Danish-born people in the United States and another 300,000 who claimed Danish parents. There were many more, of course, but they did not list their ethnic background. They preferred to be called "Americans." Over 300,000 Danes came to America between 1870 and 1930.

The first Danish settlement in America was at Hartland, WI (1845). The first congregation was Emmaus Lutheran Church in Racine (1851) — and it's still going strong. Danes settled in southwestern Iowa at Elk Horn as early as 1856. A folk high school was established there in 1878.

Kenmare, ND, became a Danish community before the turn of the century. Trinity Lutheran Church was organized in 1896 and Brorson folk high school in 1901. In 1912, English was used for the first time at a Danish Church convention in Kenmare. Not until a decade later did English come into common usage in Danish Lutheran congregaions. The switch to English was a traumatic event for many Danes as it was for many other ethnic groups.

A century later, Danish-Americans are building a Danish Immigrant Village near Elk Horn and Kimballton in southwest Iowa. June Sampson, Director of the museum, was at the 1987 Norsk Høstfest in Minot with a model display. Heading up the financial campaign is Lydell L. Christensen, a native of Elk Horn, now a business executive in San Francisco.

The Scandinavin Heritage column salutes this worthy project and urges all Danish-Americans to support it. For information, write: The Danish Immigrant Museum, Box 178, Elk Horn, IA 51331. Or call (712) 764-7001.

CHAPTER 35

St. Ansgar — Apostle To The North

EVERYONE HAS HEARD ABOUT the fearful exploits of the Vikings and the courageous efforts of the English, Irish, French and Germans to defend themselves from their onslaughts. Less well known, however, is the gallant work of a Benedictine monk named Ansgar (Anskar), which sounds suspiciously like "Oscar." With courage and dedication, he did what military might could not achieve, even though his work suffered many reversals.

Ansgar was born of Saxon stock in 801 near Amiens in northwest France. The mighty emperor, Charlemagne, died when Ansgar was only 13 years old. Charlemagne's death had a profound influence on his life. He became deeply religious. Visions and dreams were a part of his growing up. His personality was said to be marked with humility, courage and energetic initiative.

It is not surprising, then, that he entered a monastery at Corbey near his home. The founders of the monastery had their roots in the spiritual leadership of Columban, a distinguished Irish missionary monk. Ansgar's first assignment was to establish a new monastery among the Saxons (Germany). He held the office of "preacher" among the brothers, but this was just a prelude to his principal life's calling.

A struggle broke out in the ruling house of Denmark about who was to become king. One of the claimants, Harald, had the favor of Emperor Louis the Pious. He was successful in gaining control over only a part of the country. While this partial victory was not good for the empire's prestige, the Emperor used it as a staging area for Christian missions among the Danes. Just when the effort seemed to have failed, Harald decided to be baptized. For this momentous event, he went in 826 to Mainz (Germany), where he was received with great pomp by the Emperor.

The Emperor decided that a missionary should return with Harald to evangelize the Danish people. It was considered a dangerous job and

109

Ansgar was summoned for the task. Many of his friends tried to talk him out of going because no one had ever succeeded in mission work among the Danes before. Only one fellow monk offered to go with him. The work must have been strenuous, for Ansgar's companion returned fatally ill to Corbey two years later. The mission was not a great success.

Then an unexpected event took place. Representatives from the trading center at Birka, near Stockholm, came to Emperor Louis asking for missionaries. Birka was no unimportant place. (I was impressed by a display of artifacts from Birka, much of it made of solid gold, that I saw at the Museum of Science and Industry in Chicago.) Once again, Ansgar was sent with an assistant while another missionary was dispatched to King Harald in Denmark.

On their way to Sweden, Ansgar and his companion were robbed by pirates and arrived penniless in Birka. This did not deter them, however. The king received them and pledged his support of their effort to convert the Swedes to Christianity (even though he himself was not a Christian). After a few months, they returned to the Emperor, having had good success.

Ansgar's work, however, had hardly begun. In 831, Hamburg became the new center for an archbishop with the responsibility to send missionaries into Scandinavia. Ansgar was chosen to become the archbishop, and a better person could not have been found. After a trip to Rome, he began the project to convert the entire northern world.

What made Ansgar's mission plan different from the missionary expeditions among the Saxons is that it was to be done with purely spiritual resources. The army and the the sword were not to be used. No one else believed that it was possible to do effective missionary work without armed force. As a part of his plan, Ansgar bought Danish and Slavic boys from slavery and trained them to become missionaries. Just when the work was beginning to go well, however, the Vikings burned Hamburg (845), including the church and monastery.

Still Ansgar didn't give up. He was appointed archbishop of both Hamburg and Bremen in 848. His fame won the confidence of Denmark's King Horic and he was permitted to build a church among the Danes. The heathen king had cast lots before an assembly and he was committed to the outcome, which was favorable to Ansgar.

There is an interesting legend about an army of pagan Swedes that was attacking a city. Things looked bad for the city, and the omens which the defenders got upon consulting the pagan gods were unfavorable. Some of the merchants remembered the teaching of Ansgar and suggested that they should cast lots about whether to consult the Christian God. This time the omens were favorable and the city fathers were able to negotiate an advantageous peace treaty. The victorious army was so impressed that it returned home to keep Christian holy days and give alms to the poor.

It was a difficult time, however, and the coastlands where Ansgar was doing his mission work were constantly raided by Vikings. Still he did not give up his task, but worked until his death on Feb. 3, 865. By that time the empire was falling apart and the conversion of these lands was delayed for several generations.

Ansgar's work was not in vain and was not forgotten, though the pagan heart melts slowly even after conversion. The last pagan king of Denmark, Gorm the Old ("Gamle"), tried his best to stamp out Christianity in his realm and destroyed the Christian churches. It was his son, Harald "Blautand" ("Bluetooth"), that made Denmark Christian, according to the runestone in the churchyard at Jelling, not far from the Lego toy factory in Jutland. Harald's conversion may have been influenced by the powerful Christian kings of Germany who kept putting pressure on the Danish borders. A grandson of Harald, Knut the Great, became one of England's most powerful Christian kings during the Viking age.

Today Ansgar is a favorite of the Danes, just as Olaf is a favorite of the Norwegians. Many Danish organizations are named after him. There are about a dozen Lutheran churches in America today named "St. Ansgar," as well as several Roman Catholic parishes. St. Ansgar, IA, is named after this missionary bishop. Eventually, Ansgar's plan to subdue the Norsemen with the Gospel of Peace was successful. It has changed the lives of many of us.

CHAPTER 36

The Reformation In Denmark And Norway

T
HE RELIGIOUS REFORM MOVEMENT that broke out in Western Europe during the 16th century moved in many different geographical and doctrinal directions. While there had been previous attempts to challenge and change the church before this time, none was successful. It was a dangerous endeavor which produced many martyrs. John Wycliffe (1328-84) in England, John Huss (1372-1415) in Bohemia, and Girolamo Savonarola in Italy (1452-98) all experienced the fires of religious intolerance. The age of religious freedom had not yet arrived.

It was in a little back-water city of Saxony in Germany that the unexpected events began that were destined to reshape western society. The movement led by Martin Luther was primarily a religious event, but it touched off a fire that had long been smoldering due to resentment towards the church's vast land holdings and control of wealth, while exempted from taxation. The feudal system also contributed to the repression of the people.

Humanism was another factor that encouraged reform. Renaissance scholarship and freedom of inquiry promoted the study of the Bible in the original Greek and Hebrew texts. Disiderius Erasmus of Rotterdam (1467-1536), a Dutch humanist, scholar and critic, had a powerful influence on the thinking of those times.

Even though Scandinavia was in an area isolated from the mainstream of events, it could not be sheltered from the reform movement of Germany. In Denmark, a Carmelite monk, Poul Helgeson, an admirer of Erasmus, prepared the way for the eventual Lutheran takeover, though that was not his intention. He approved of much of Luther's teaching but did not want separation from Rome. This was the case with many of the reform-minded church leaders.

King Christian II (reigned 1513-23) favored a national church with the king as the head, yet aligned with Rome. It was not uncommon for the king to be in conflict with the nobles and in 1523 Christian was deposed by them in favor of his nephew, Frederick I (reigned 1523-33). Christian went to Wittenberg and listened to the preaching of Luther while staying at the home of Lucas Cranach, the famous artist. Impressed, he commissioned a translation of the Bible into Danish. But since he was a brother-in-law to Emperor Charles V, who thought of himself as the protector of Roman Catholicism, Christian later renounced his Lutheranism in the hope of regaining his throne. He began with an invasion of Norway where he was supported by the archbishop. Defeated, he was arrested and spent the rest of his life in jail.

Frederick remained nominally loyal to Rome but protected the Lutherans and built a theological college at Haderslev which became a center of Danish Lutheranism. For three years (1533-36), Denmark was torn by a civil war. It ended with Frederick's son, Christian III (reigned 1536-59), coming to power. He was a deeply religious man and a practical politician. Recognizing that the bishops controlled most of the nation's wealth, he promptly arrested them and deprived them of their lands and temporal power. A new church constitution (approved by Luther) was adopted, and "superintendents" elected by the pastors replaced the bishops.

In exchange for becoming the head of the church, the king bound himself to worship God and maintain the practice of the Christian faith. This has been done faithfully in Denmark down to the present monarch, Queen Margaret II. The new superintendents (later called bishops again) were ordained by Rev. Jonas Bugenhagen of Wittenberg, a close friend of Luther. Christian III became an absolute monarch and Norway became a mere province of Denmark instead of being a partner in a dual monarchy.

While the Reformation in Denmark involved a lengthy struggle, including a civil war, the religious change in Norway took place by the command of King Christian III. It came at a time when the political, cultural and religious life of the country was at its lowest ebb. The Danish Church Ordinance of 1537 was ratified by the legislative assemblies (diets) in Oslo and Bergen in 1539. The archbishop, Olaf Engelbrektsson, found himself virtually alone in wanting to keep the ties with Rome and fled the country. Most Catholic priests became Lutheran priests (prester), which they are still called. Among the strongest supporters of the Reformation were the priests' sons, for now their parents could be married like other parents and they would become legitimate. It also meant that their mothers would become women of honor instead of privately kept mistresses. (Although celibacy was the rule for the clergy, it had proved to be unenforceable in Scandinavia.)

The first Lutheran bishop appointed to Norway was Geble Pedersson, also ordained by Bugenhagen. While the Reformation was mostly peaceful in Norway, there were places where the people fiercely resisted the king's ordinance. Some of the old church records were burned and religious artifacts identified with the old religion were destroyed. This has been a great loss to genealogical research.

In Denmark, many beautiful wall paintings inside churches were covered with whitewash and are just now being restored. As a result, however, the paintings were also preserved. We saw some of these in a well-preserved church building from the 1200s at Sindal in North Jutland, an ancestral home of some of my wife's family. We also visited some of the old monasteries which still stand but are now used for other purposes. It took about two generations of indoctrination before there was a major change in the piety of the laity. Spiritual reformation did not really come to Norway until the preaching of Hans Nielsen Hauge (1771-1824), a farmer who called the nation to repentance.

As a result of the Reformation becoming a law in Norway, the Danish influence became strong. The Danish Bible, catechism, and other religious books were used. Until 1813, all clergy were educated in Copenhagen. There was not a Norwegian translation of the Bible until after 1814, when Norway came under the rule of the Swedish king. That's why the Bibles and liturgies used by Norwegian immigrants were more Danish than Norwegian.

The Hanse, merchants from Lubeck and other north German cities, were among the earliest to practice Lutheranism in Norway, especially in Bergen. A beautiful church built by the Hanseatic merchants still stands near the harbor in that beautiful city. One of the early effective bishops was Jorgen Eriksson (1571-1604) of Stavanger.

The 16th century was not an easy time in which to live. There were many good people, but intolerance, disease and the social caste system repressed the aspirations and potential of most people while giving opportunity to a privileged few. Still, our ancestors managed to survive. They could never have believed the times in which we live. I'm glad to be living today despite the dangers that surround us.

Martin Luther - reformer.

CHAPTER 37

King Olav V And
The Church Of Norway

HE WAS BORN JULY 2, 1903, in London, and baptized Aug. 11 with the name Alexander Edward Christian Frederick, after his English and Danish forefathers. From the day of his birth, he was destined to live no ordinary life. When he was just two — on Nov. 27, 1905 — his parents, Prince Carl of Denmark and Princess Maud of England, took up residence in Norway's royal palace as King Haakon VII and Queen Maud. Young Alexander, re-named Olav, was instantly loved by Norwegians everywhere.

The affection of the people of Norway for the young Crown Prince (now king) was shared by the Norse immigrant families around the world. His first trip to America, together with Crown Princess Martha (from the royal house of Sweden) in 1939, began a deep friendship that continues to the present day. The people of Minot still talk about his stop in this community. Following a state visit to Canada in 1987, His Majesty planned a trip as a private citizen to Norwegian-Americans in Minnesota and Iowa. On Nov. 27 (82 years to the day after he arrived in Norway), 1,300 people gathered in Minneapolis to honor him. The $37.50 per banquet ticket was no deterrent. My wife and I had invitations, but were not able to attend. It would have been a memorable event.

Much can be said about Norway's popular king. The one thing that has greatly impressed me about Olav V is his concern for the Church of Norway of which he is the head. If all the people of Norway shared the King's devotion to the Gospel, there wouldn't be standing room in the churches on any Sunday morning. He's a regular church-goer, wherever he happens to be. Even when he attends soccer games or is at a ski tournament, the king never misses Sunday worship.

How did this all begin? With the right parents, I suppose. His paternal grandmother, Queen Louise of Denmark, was a devout and highly talented Christian. She read every day to her children from the New Testament. She "had inherited the intelligence and spiritual vitality of the Bernadottes," according to Sigurd Lunde, a contributor to a new book, "A King and His Church," published in Oslo (1987). She also was affiliated with the inner mission circles in Copenhagen. This is typical of the piety found in the Danish royal family to this day. Olav's parents were also faithful worshippers and supporters of mission work. Among the guests in the Danish palace was Lars Skrefsrud, the renowned missionary to the Santals in India.

On our 1983 visit to Norway, my wife and I visited with Trygve S. Woxen, pastor of the Asker parish near the royal farm estate at Bygdøy, just west of Oslo. He often preached to the Royal Family and spoke highly of them to us. When the church was built, a separate entrance was provided for the King to enter. He advised the pastor, however, that when he attended Asker Church it would be through the regular doorway. He worships, sings hymns and takes communion as a regular participant with the congregation.

After the death of Haakon VII, Olav V was consecrated king at the Nidaros Cathedral in Trondheim on June 22, 1958 — exactly 52 years after his father's coronation. Olav chose to have a consecration service with prayers for his reign, rather than to wear the crown. At this service, the crown was placed at the foot of a silver crucifix atop the altar. He knelt before Trondheim's Bishop Arne Fjellbu (born in North Dakota) for the prayer: "Eternal God of power, bless our King; be his Lord and Sovereign always. And bestow every good gift upon his household in this life and in the life to come." Then they sang "A Mighty Fortress is our God." Bishop Johannes Smemo of Oslo preached the sermon, after which they sang "God save our gracious King."

In response to this moving ceremony, the King said "for my part it was no mere external formality. I can say with certainty that it was a sincere act." For over 30 years, Olav V has carried out his role as head of the church faithfully and effectively. Sadly, Olav's wife — Crown Princess Martha — died just a few days after their silver anniversary in 1954. (My good friend and former professor, Dr. Herman A. Preus, told me of attending her funeral.) As a result, Princess Astrid — Mrs. Johan Martin Ferner in private life — has often accompanied her father on state visits.

Besides visiting congregations in Norway, the King has taken a strong interest in Norwegian Seamen's Missions around the world. In 1982 he

117

laid the cornerstone for the new Mission in Houston, and in 1983 he attended the 25th anniversary of the Mission in Kobe, Japan. He has also expressed appreciation and support for the work of the Lutheran Free Church as well as the Pentecostals, Salvation Army and other denominations in Norway. In 1967, on a trip to Rome, King Olav V paid a visit to Pope Paul VI at the Vatican.

One of King Olav's most interesting trips appears to have been his visit to Ethiopia in 1966. Emperor Haile Selassie personally met him at the airport in Addis Ababa and saluted him. A huge banner greeted him as they entered the city: "Welcome King Olav V! The Lord will keep your going out and your coming in!" quoting Psalm 121:8. The main purpose of the trip was to visit Norwegian mission stations in Ethiopia. The King had a special interest in the radio station RVOG ("Radio Voice of the Gospel") in Addis Ababa operated by the Lutheran World Federation, the most powerful station in Africa. When the pro-Soviet Socialist government overthrew Haile Selassie in 1974, it became a propaganda tool of the new military government.

Wherever he travels, whether in Norway or abroad, the King pays special attention to children. While in the Ethiopian capital, he opened the Norwegian School. He has also given strong support to relief work among the poor and hungry. When Princess Astrid visited nursing home residents while attending the Norsk Høstfest in 1983, she was doing what her father the King frequently does. Among the retirement homes the King has visited in America are Ebenezer in Minneapolis and Lyngblomsten in St. Paul. At Lyngblomsten, he met a man who had attended his father's coronation.

For the King's 75th birthday in 1978, the people of Norway raised 13 million kroner as a gift (about $2,500,000 at the time). He gave half of the amount to the Norwegian congregations in Copenhagen and Stockholm and the rest was put into a trust fund of which the interest of 10% goes to the Norwegian Seamen's Missions and a mission hospital in Irgalem, Ethiopia.

Wherever Norway's King goes, people meet him with great expressions of joy and gratitude for his presence. It's a sad commentary on the state of affairs in our country that heavy security is required when he comes to America. This is not the case in Norway and in most countries. When he visited Ethiopia, only two civilians attended him. One day in London, I'm told, a lady met him on the street and said: "You look just like King Olav!" He smiled and thanked her for the compliment.

The people of Norway are justly proud of their King, who so excellently embodies their highest values. We who are the children of immigrants from that land of the Midnight Sun share in this pride.

The consecration of King Olav V.

119

CHAPTER 38

Sigrid Undset —
Norwegian Nobel Laureate

THE FIRST TIME I ENCOUNTERED the writings of Sigrid Undset (1882-1949) was in 1940 as a freshman in the Colfax High School library in southeastern North Dakota. It was a very modest library, to say the least, hardly more than a few bookcases, but it provided some excellent reading.

I checked out Undset's "The Bridal Wreath," part of a the "Kristin Lavransdatter" trilogy set in 14th-century Norway in the mountainous area near Trondheim. Since our school was in a predominantly Norwegian ethnic community, it's not surprising that its library contained this famous trilogy. Another major work of Undset's is "The Master of Hestviken," a series of four related novels set in 13th century Norway.

Sigrid Undset was born in Kallundborg, Denmark, the oldest daughter in a family of three sisters. Her father was a famous Norwegian archaeologist who kindled her interest in Norway's medieval history. Her first novel was set in the Middle Ages, but the publisher rejected it and urged her to switch to modern topics. She tried it for a while and then returned to her favorite theme, explaining, "the human heart does not change in the least through all the ages." The subjects which run through her writings are love, sexuality and our accountability to God and to other people. Her writings involve struggle betweeen the realistic and the ethical. That's not an easy task.

Fame came to Undset in 1911 through her novel "Jenny." Norwegian television has produced this story about the struggle for women's liberation, with Liv Ullmann playing the lead. The story is set primarily in Rome, where Jenny went to become an artist. She had the talent but failed because her emotions got in the way of her work. The book caused a sensation because of Undset's frankness in expressing women's feelings.

A niece of Undset's, Charlotte Blindheim, wrote of the famous author in the "Scandinavian Review" (1982). There was an aura of respect and

120

awe for this celebrated aunt whom she calls "Moster" (mother's sister) Sigrid. It's a term of respect, affection and closeness that my wife's mother has often used of her family in Denmark. In a "moster" relationship, cousins feel almost as close as brothers and sisters.

Sigrid was married in 1912 to Anders Svarstad. They had three children, two sons and a daughter. The daughter was mentally retarded and the oldest son, Anders, was killed during the invasion of Norway in 1940. She never got over the sorrow of her son's death.

Undset's great fame came in 1928 when she was awarded the Nobel prize for literature. When the Nazis invaded Norway, she fled to the United States for the duration of the war. While in America, Undset supported Norway's war effort by writing novels for the Norwegian Information Service. She also wrote an essay about a childhood friend who was shot down over Normandy in 1943. After the war, Undset returned to her own house in Lillehammer, called Bjerkebaek, where she died in 1949.

Bjerkebaek, completed in 1924, was a substantial house — one might even call it a villa. Her niece writes that "every object was stamped with Moster Sigrid's highly personal taste, every room marked by her sure sense of each thing's own beauty." She especially remembered the 12 Christmas Eves that she and her sisters spent at Bjerkebaek.

Undset had a great love for botany and her house was always well furnished with plants and flowers. Her son, Hans, wrote of this love: "Her relationship with flowers came to be legendary even in her own lifetime. She got around plants. She communicated with them. And I don't insult either her or you when I say that as difficult as her association with people could be on occasion — just as undifficult was her association with flowers. It wasn't feigned. They didn't ask stupid questions. In a word, they didn't bother her." That tells us a lot about this great author. During the war years, she travelled to New England from her residence in New York City to study flora.

Bjerkebaek was never the same after the war. The Germans had occupied the house for three years and Undset had lost two of her children. She never wrote another novel. Peter Egge, a long-time friend wrote of her: "She was solitary as a genius always is, despite friends and world renown. She lived a life of inner struggle, accompanied by unspoken, defeating fears and secret glorious victories. The struggle was a precondition of her genius."

Undset liked to read to children, especially from the Sagas and English lyric poetry. She also came to enjoy Shelley, the Bronte sisters, Emily Dickinson and Willa Cather. Reading to children is, in my opinion, a virtue worthy of note.

It was no minor scandal in Norway when, in 1924, Undset decided to become a Roman Catholic. From then on, she wrote from her new point of view. Having been raised in a "lukewarm" Lutheranism, she seems to have been drawn to pre-Reformation Norway through her studies and writings of the Middle Ages. The following year, Undset divorced her husband and never remarried. She also broke with the liberal and feminist company of her youth.

A few years ago, a Benedictine Brother at St. John's Abbey in Collegeville, MN, corresponded with me about Sigrid Undset, stating that he wished to visit her grave to pray there. My wife and I have an author friend in Norway who, like Undset, converted to Roman Catholicism. I told her that this made her a "Protestant" since she was protesting against the State Church. After some thought, she accepted the epithet.

Sigrid Undset was a remarkable person as well as a famous writer. I get the feeling when reading "Kristin Lavransdatter" that she was writing about herself, but transplanted back 600 years in time. Her father died when she was 11 and this put the family into difficulty. For 10 years, 1899-1909, she supported them by working as a clerk by day and writing by night. With the publication of "Jenny" in 1911, she no longer needed the clerking job.

Anyone who wants to know about Norway in the Middle Ages can hardly do better than to read Undset's novels. It takes patience, however, because they are long and require a lot of deep thought. The historical setting may also be unfamiliar, but for those who stick with it, the rewards are great. We who claim the Norse heritage are all in her debt.

CHAPTER 39

Knute Rockne — An Untold Story

OR THE SCHOOL YEAR 1950-51, the faculty of Luther Theological Seminary assigned me for an internship to the Logan Square and Humboldt Park areas of Chicago's northwest side. It was a pretty big change for a North Dakota farm boy who had never planned to live in a city larger than Minneapolis, and then only for going to school.

It turned out to be an exciting year and I'm still glad for the experience. It was an unexpected education. This area had a heavy concentration of Scandinavians at the beginning of the century. There were still quite a few left when I was there 50 years later, but many had moved out to the suburbs. Today, Spanish is the most common language in this community, now populated primarily by Puerto Ricans.

This was the community where Knute Rockne (1888-1931) had grown up, and there were still people living at the time of my internship who remembered him. This immigrant lad from Norway, who made Notre Dame's "Fighting Irish" famous for football, became better known than any president or graduate of the school. When I lived in Glenview, a northern suburb of Chicago from 1967 to 1973, I had a friend who was a Holy Cross priest from Notre Dame. He loved to talk about the famous exploits of Rockne on the gridiron.

Later, as a pastor in New Rockford (1957-61), I ministered to the wife of Theodore J. Lund, who had confirmed Rockne. Lund was pastor at the Hauge Lutheran Church near Logan Square. The Rocknes were members of another "Haugean" church named Immanuel. Immanuel Church had a pastoral vacancy when Knute was in confirmation so Lund helped out. Mrs. Lund shared with me some things which are not well known and which I have not found in any of the written biographical material about him. Lund was in Chicago from 1900-1904. He became pastor of the former Hauge Lutheran Church in northeast Minot in 1912. (The white frame church still stands but is an apartment building today.) Huldas Peterson of Minot remembers Lund well. She went to Sunday school at the Hauge Church when he was the pastor.

The Rockne story goes far back into Norwegian history. When Queen Margaret I forged the Union of Kalmar in 1397, uniting Norway, Denmark and Sweden into one great North Sea power, an ancestor of Knute Rockne named Enidride Erlandson opposed the treaty and moved to Voss in the western mountains of Norway. That's how the Rockne family got identified with Voss. It's an unusually beautiful place, and if you go there today you'll find a monument in Knute's honor.

The Rocknes were an inventive family. Knute's great-grandfather was the first farmer in that part of the country to build and use a farm wagon (with wheels) instead of using a sledge. Knute's grandfather was a blacksmith and hardware merchant and was said to be handy with machines. His father, Lars Knutson Rockne, became a popular builder of two-wheeled vehicles. Germany's Kaiser Wilhelm, who vacationed at nearby Balestrand every year, bought one of them. (See "The Scandinavian Heritage," chapters 80-81.) The English also liked to vacation in Norway's western mountains, and one of them, a nobleman, talked the elder Rockne into going to Chicago to exhibit his buggy at the 1893 World's Fair. He won a prize at the fair — but, more importantly, he liked Chicago so well that 18 months later he and his family decided to make their home in the Windy City.

Knute wasn't cut out to be an artisan. He grew up as a tough street kid who learned how to use his fists, even though he was small. The ethnic rivalry between the Scandinavians and Irish often was resolved on a vacant lot, with an Irish policeman named O'Toole standing watch. If the Norskies got the upper hand, he'd stop the fights. Knute's friends petitioned the city to send them a Swedish cop. At full growth, he stood just 5'8" and weighed only 145 pounds. He grew up in a pious family whose life was centered in the church. The entire family was musical. Knute's instrument was the flute, which he later played in the Notre Dame band.

Rockne did well in all sports but was expelled from high school for cutting too many classes. He went to work at odd jobs about the city, went harvesting in Wisconsin, and spent four years working for the Chicago Post Office. By then he'd saved a thousand dollars to go to college. He picked Notre Dame over the University of Illinois because some friends persuaded him that it would be a good school. He also figured it would be cheaper for him. So on Nov. 28, 1910, at the age of 22, Knute resigned his postal job and enrolled at Notre Dame.

Until that time, the "Irish" hadn't done much in football. It had been Notre Dame's practice to take boys off the farm and boys from poverty areas and help them to get an education. The school for boys began in 1844 in such a state of poverty that it got its Indiana charter only with the help of a Methodist friend. The big day came at the Army-Notre Dame game in 1913, when Knute was a senior. Army was rated as the team to beat that year, and the game was expected to be lopsided. Rockne, as team captain, changed football forever in that game by introducing the forward pass. Later he was to introduce the platoon system. These tactics totally confused the game plan of their opponents and the Irish went on to defeat the Cadets and shock the sports writers.

Knute planned to become a physician, so he took a heavy load of math and sciences. His transcript is impressive and he graduated magna cum laude — not bad for a high school dropout from an immigrant family. Upon graduation he became a chemistry teacher who laid the groundwork for the invention of synthetic rubber. How then did he become a football coach? According to his grandson — Knute Rockne III, who coaches a sophomore team at Bright High School in Midvale, UT — Notre Dame offered him $5 more and he needed the money. His record as head coach (1918-1930) is well known: 105 wins, 12 losses and 5 ties. His teams had five undefeated seasons. He is still the winningest coach the Irish have ever had.

He guided some great players. George Gipp was immortalized by the phrase, "Win one for the Gipper." Jimmy Crowley, Elmer Layden, Don Miller and Harry Stuhldreher became known as the "Four Horsemen." (The other players on the team were called the "Seven Mules.")

For many years Rockne was known as the "lone Norse Protestant" on the Notre Dame Campus. On Nov. 20, 1925, he joined the Roman Catholic Church, perhaps out of deference to his wife and children, according to Mrs. Lund. She told me that he continued to remember her husband, who had confirmed him, with a Christmas present each year until Rockne's death in a tragic air crash in 1931.

THE SCANDINAVIAN SPIRIT

Those who knew Rockne well had high respect for him. He had a great sense of humor and frequently told jokes about himself, but in such a way as to cause others to think about themselves. If you ever visit Voss in the beautiful mountains of western Norway, be sure to visit his memorial near the railway station. It will warm your heart.

The 1988 Norsk Høstfest honored Rockne by posthumously inducting him into the Scandinavian-American Hall of Fame. He was represented at the award ceremony by his daughter, Mary Jean Kokendorfer of Tulsa, OK.

Knute Rockne.

CHAPTER **40**

The Reformation In Sweden

C HANGING THE COURSE of a nation often involves pain—
ful and bloody struggle the outcome of which is rarely pre-
dictable. No one in Sweden would have guessed that the
Reformation of the Church which began in Germany with
Martin Luther (1483-1546) would change the course of the Swedish nation as well.

According to Prof. T. K. Derry of Oslo, the new teaching entered the
Northern countries through three main channels: German preachers
moving north, students who returned home from studies in Germany,
and the Hanse merchants who spread their faith in foreign communities
where they had business establishments. Some kings also played active
roles in establishing a church that would be subject to their control.

Since the coming of Christianity to western and northern Europe,
there had always been a strained relationship between kings and
bishops. Both vied for power and control of the people and their wealth.
Sweden was united with Denmark and Norway in the Union of Kalmar
in 1397, largely as a result of the superior military power of Denmark.
The Swedes were at first unable to throw off the yoke of their Danish
neighbors. Resistance movements, however, kept appearing and were
crushed with force. In these political maneuvers, bishops played strongly
partisan roles.

After an unsuccessful Swedish attempt at revolt led by Sten Sture (see
chapter 23), King Christian II of Denmark invaded Sweden with the
backing of the Pope and Emperor Charles V. Sten Sture was killed and
the local leaders were invited to a peace conference on Nov. 7, 1520.
They were assured that there would be full pardon for their resistance
and that all would be forgiven. Once the King was in control, however,
over 100 of the patriots were executed in what became known as the
"Blood Bath of Stockholm." This was justified by the pretext that since
they were also "heretics" they had no protection under the law. Before
King Christian returned to Denmark, more than 600 people had lost

their lives. The intention was to destroy the leadership of the resistance movement. The result, however, was to doom Denmark's future in Sweden.

A young Swedish nobleman, Gustav Vasa, had been taken hostage to Denmark and imprisoned. Learning that his father was among those who were massacred, Gustav escaped and made his way back to Sweden where he rallied the people and was declared king on June 6, 1523. He first invited the Pope to reform the church. The Pope demanded that Bishop Trolle, who had participated in the "Blood Bath," be restored to office. Gustav couldn't agree to that because the bishop was pro-Danish. This led to the establishment of a Lutheran Swedish State Church over which the king was the head.

From earliest times there has been a close connection between the Scandinavian countries and Germany. When the Reformation broke out over the Indulgence Controversy at Wittenberg University in 1517, students of theology from Sweden were on hand to witness the events. Among these were Olavus Petri (1493-1552) and his brother Laurentius (1499-1573). They were born in Orebo, 150 miles west of Stockholm, sons of a blacksmith, and were educated at the Carmelite monastery near their home.

Olavus went for further study at the new university at Wittenberg in the spring of 1516. Shortly thereafter (1517) Martin Luther became famous as the author of the "95 Theses." Young Petri received a master's degree and returned to Sweden in November, 1518 full of zeal for the Reformer's teachings. Having a degree from a German university was a matter of prestige in those days as it is today. Olavus was soon in great demand and he became a teacher in the Cathedral School in Stockholm. In 1524, King Gustav Vasa appointed him as secretary of the Stockholm City Council. Then the king commanded that a pulpit be erected in the Cathedral and authorized Olavus to preach sermons in Swedish. Sermons had not usually been a part of the worship service in the Middle Ages. (I've seen the pulpit. It's about 14 feet above the nave and is highly ornamented with beautiful wood carvings.) The following year, Olavus renounced his vow of celibacy and was married.

Laurentius Petri also went to study in Wittenberg and returned to Sweden in 1527, after which he was appointed by the king to a professorship at Uppsala University. Four years later, Laurentius was elected archbishop of Uppsala, Sweden's most prestigious diocese, at age 32. He presided over the office until 1573. One hundred seventy priests took part in the election and the new archbishop received 150 votes.

The circumstances of Laurentius's consecration as archbishop had one especially interesting consequence for the Swedish church. The rite of consecration, which occurred on Sept. 22, 1531, was performed by Petrus Magni, Bishop of Vasteraas, who himself had been consecrated a bishop by Pope Clement VII in 1524. As a result, "Apostolic Succession" became a part of the Church of Sweden's tradition, unlike the churches of Denmark and Norway whose first Lutheran bishops were consecrated by a professor of theology. "Apostolic Succession" means that there is a direct physical line of succession from the apostles to the bishops, which "legitimizes" their authority in the church. Although the Church of Sweden continues this tradition today, it places no special emphasis on it.

Olavus and Laurentius published the first Swedish Bible in 1541. Laurentius is especially remembered for his liturgical work. The Swedish church has a reputation for excellent music and liturgy, a tradition which was maintained in the former Augustana Lutheran Synod in the U.S.

It should not be supposed, however, that the Reformation issue was settled so simply in Sweden. After the death of Gustav Vasa in 1560, his successors struggled over the country's religion. Although Erik XIV (reigned 1560-1568) had Calvinistic leanings, he left most of the affairs of the church in the hands of Archbishop Petri. Erik's brother, John III (reigned 1568-1592) displayed sympathies for a "reformed Catholicism" and married a Polish princess.

John's son, Sigismund (reigned 1592-1599), who was reared in the Roman Catholic church, had become king of Poland in 1587. It was his intention to restore Sweden to obedience to Rome. Before he could lead his army over from Poland, however, his uncle, Duke Karl, entered the field with a military force to keep foreign influence out. In 1593, Karl called a convocation of the church which adopted the "Augsburg Confession" as the teaching of the Swedish Church. The "Book of Concord," which contains the historical writings of the Lutheran Church, was not officially adopted until 1663. Sigismund was defeated in 1598 and Karl IX became the ruler of Sweden. Anyone who rejected the Church of Sweden's teaching was in danger of banishment from the kingdom. There was little tolerance for dissenters in those days. The Reformation in Sweden was completed once and for all during the reign of King Gustavus II Adolphus (reigned 1611-1632), known as the "Lion of the North." Gustavus Adolphus College in St. Peter, MN, is named after him.

The Petri brothers are remembered by Swedes today with great respect. Erik Yelverton, an Anglican clergyman, has written: "Of all the Primates (Archbishops) who have occupied the See of Uppsala since its foundation in the 12th century, none is more honoured in Sweden today for his achievements than Laurentius Petri of Neriki."

Today there is full freedom for all churches and religions in Sweden. If you ever visit Stockholm, be sure to see the Cathedral ("Storkyrkan") and the pulpit from which Laurentius Petri preached.

CHAPTER 41

Charles Lindbergh And
The 'Spirit Of St. Louis'

"**T**HE LAST HERO" is the way biographer Walter S. Ross described Charles Augustus Lindbergh. There was no doubt about the hero status of this tall, handsome, boyish-looking Swede from Minnesota. When Lindbergh returned to New York after his triumphant flight to Paris, he was greeted with the city's greatest parade. It's estimated that up to 4,500,000 admirers lined the sidewalks leading to Central Park on June 13, 1927, and more than 3,500,000 pounds of ticker tape was dropped on his entourage. The first air mail stamp was dedicated to him. He was honored by the governments of the United States, France and Germany and received many private honors as well.

The 1920s were a turbulent era and America needed a hero. Historian Page Smith, now retired from UCLA, notes that "the times had been difficult and demoralizing ones" and that "many thoughtful Americans despaired of the future of the Republic." He stated that "leaders were in disrepute, politicians, alive and dead, had come under severely critical scrutiny." The young flier from Little Falls had captured the affection of the world and taken people's minds off their troubles.

In his autobiography, "We," Lindbergh wrote about his family background. Their name in Sweden had been Manson. Grandpa Ola Manson, born in 1810, was a peasant farmer who broke out of his economic servitude and was elected to the Riksdag (parliament) at age 39. He became a friend of the Crown Prince, who became King Charles XV in 1859, and was named his secretary. A man of high principles, Manson's goal in government was to campaign for social reform. He succeeded in outlawing the whipping posts. He fought to make it illegal for employers to beat their hired help and campaigned for voting privileges for people other than the nobility, clergy, farmers and property owners.

The privileged classes were enraged at his efforts and managed to trump up charges of embezzlement against him (for he was also a loan officer in a bank at Malmø). Tiring of the reactionary spirit that

131

prevailed in his homeland, Manson — now Lindbergh — took his family in 1860 to Sauk Centre, MN, where he built a 12 by 16 foot log cabin. This was quite a comedown for the onetime congressman and secretary to the king. Before he left Sweden, members of the parliament gave him a medal made of solid gold. Upon arriving in America, he traded the medal for a plow. Trinkets meant nothing to him, and a plow could come in handy in the new world.

The same sterling qualities were passed on to his children. His son, Charles August Lindbergh, Sr. — named after the king of Sweden — became a lawyer and made his home in Little Falls. Later he was elected to the United States Congress five times. His wife had degrees from both the University of Michigan and Columbia University. She had gone to Little Falls to teach chemistry. Her father was a pioneer in the field of porcelain dental art and had a successful dental practice in Detroit.

Charles, Jr, was born Feb. 4, 1902, in Detroit. Because of his father's political career, he never attended a full year of school in one place until he entered the University of Wisconsin. After a year and a half, young Charles decided that the University was no place for him. His interests were his motorcycle, his gun, open fields and especially the sky. He enrolled in a flying school in Lincoln, NE, against the wishes of his father. His mother approved, however, and went barnstorming with him around the country. Later he enrolled in the Army Air school at Brooks Field, TX, and graduated at the head of his class in 1925.

Six years earlier, a New York financier had offered a prize of $25,000 for the first successful solo air flight from New York to Paris. Charles was determined to win it and managed to secure the backing of some young financiers from St. Louis, MO. He ordered a plane with a 200-horsepower radial air-cooled engine and with navigating instruments to be built in San Diego. The plane was named "The Spirit of St. Louis" in honor of the men who financed the project. Bernt Balchen, a famous Norwegian aviator, helped design the flight plan.

Enroute to New York, Lindbergh landed at Lambert Field in St. Louis. A replica of the plane is now on display at the Lambert Field Terminal in St. Louis and another is at the Charles A. Lindbergh Terminal in Minneapolis. The original plane is in the Aerospace Museum (part of the Smithsonian Institute) in Washington, DC. The plane's top speed was

130 miles per hour; its fuel capacity of 400 gallons gave it a range of about 4,000 miles. Paris lies about 3,500 miles from New York, so the margin for error was not great. The courageous young pilot took off from Roosevelt Airfield on Long Island at 7:54 a.m. on May 20, 1927, and landed at Le Bourget in Paris the following day after a flight of 33 1/2 hours.

That was by any standards a daring feat. It had never been done before and his chief competitors for the prize were planning to fly trimotor planes with extra crew. In his autobiography, Lindbergh wrote that his greatest challenge was sleep. He went to a hotel in New York to get some rest before the flight, but a friend came to visit him. Landing in Paris, however, proved to be even more dangerous. The huge crowds were in such a jubilant mood that they had to be held back by the police or they would have torn him apart. He was rescued and driven to the American Embassy, but someone stole his log book out of the plane. It was never recovered.

Lindbergh became an instant hero, but his moment of glory was followed by some very dark days. I remember being told by our rural grade schoolteacher, Katherine Ista Anderson, that Lindberg had gone to Europe and was invited to inspect the air forces of England, Russia, France and Germany. Unfortunately, he wasn't a very sophisticated diplomat. He didn't say what the western press wanted to hear. Lindbergh praised Germany's Luftwaffe, calling it the best air force in the world. The Nazis were delighted and decorated him for it. Immediately, he was branded pro-Hitler and anti-democratic. I can also remember Dorothy Thompson, a popular newscaster during World War II, saying, "I am absolutely certain that Lindbergh hates the present democratic system."

Nothing could have been further from the truth, and history soon vindicated Lindbergh's judgment. In England, Billy Mitchell worked desperately to build up the Royal Air Force. Some of the American press suspected Scandinavians of being pro-German — especially the Swedes. Norwegians, likewise, were often accused of being pro-German during World War I. Scandinavians have a reputation for independent thinking and even today feel no obligation to agree with their allies on all points. Linbergh campaigned hard to keep the United States out of World War II. His strong anti-Soviet views seem to have been a part of his "America First" rally participation in Madison Square Garden in May, 1941. From our present perspective, we'd have to say that Lindbergh was politically unwise. Still, he certainly was no friend of the Nazis. For his convictions, he was denied a United States Air Force commission during World War II.

Famous people are often targets of tragedy. Charles and his devoted wife, Anne Morrow Lindbergh, had their greatest heartbeak when their 20-month-old son, Charles III was kidnapped on March 1, 1930. The story of the German carpenter from New York, Bruno Richard Hauptmann, in whose home was found $13,000 of the $50,000 ransom money, was front page news for years. People's hearts went out to the Lindberghs so much that even the noted Chicago gangster, Al Capone, offered $10,000 to get the child back. The body was found on May 16, 1932. Hauptmann was arrested in September, 1934 and convicted. I can't remember anyone mourning his death in the electric chair on April 3, 1936. The media, however, had exploited the story to the hilt and the Lindberghs never recovered from the wound.

Though active on corporation boards and a constant world traveller, Charles Lindbergh was a very private person, not wanting anyone even to write his biography. Honor was restored on April 7, 1954, to the famous Swede from Minnesota when he was made a Brigadier General in the Air Force Reserve.

Lindbergh died of lymphatic cancer on the island of Maui on Aug. 25, 1974. The Rev. John Tincher, a United Methodist pastor from Burlingame, CA, held the funeral service the following day, reading these words: "We commit the body of General Charles A. Lindbergh to its final resting place, but his spirit we commend to Almighty God, knowing that death is but a new adventure in existence and remembering how Jesus said upon the cross, 'Father, into Thy hands I commend my spirit.'"

CHAPTER 42

The Conversion Of Iceland

THE STORY OF ICELAND reflects its geological history. It is believed that the island was created by a series of volcanic eruptions that occurred some 20 million years ago. The nearby Westmann Islands, however, are said to be only 7,000 years old. Other smaller islands have also been formed and then disappeared into the sea. In between these violent eruptions all has appeared peaceful except for the hot springs which continue to flow.

The first known inhabitants of the island were Irish monks fleeing from Vikings who had invaded and plundered their homelands during the seventh century A.D. The search for serenity led them to this place called "Thule," or "Ultimate Outpost." Their solitude, however, was not to last forever. Norwegian refugees, unwilling to endure the oppression of King Harald Haarfagre (872-930), loaded up their livestock and horses and sailed to that distant and dimly known island to the west. Upon the arrival of the Norsemen, the monks fled, leaving all their possessions behind.

Norse migration to Iceland actually began in about the year 860. By 930, some 20,000 had arrived. Their names are preserved in the "Landnamabok," which lists the genealogy of settlers. They came not only from Norway; about 13 percent of these immigrants were second and third generation Vikings from England, Ireland, Scotland and nearby islands. One of these was Aud, the widow of Olaf the White, the Norwegian king of Dublin. A considerable number of Irish and Scottish settlers also came, some as slaves, some as wives and children of mixed blood.

Included among those from the British Isles were a number of Christians who bravely maintained their faith in the face of the pagan majority. Estimates vary, but it is conservatively surmised that at least 10% of the Icelandic people have Celtic, or Irish, origins.

The center of Icelandic paganism was at Thingvellir where the "Althing" (Parliament) was established in 930. It was a place of human

135

sacrifice, and yet a model for democracy in its time. Blood feuds often settled private disputes. This is how Erik the Red, father of Leif Erikson, came to be banished from Iceland and spent three years of exile in Greenland. He had been too ready to use the sword.

The decisive momentum to make Iceland Christian came from Norway's King Olaf Tryggvason (reigned 995-1000). Olaf was a fanatical Christian evangelist who didn't hesitate to use both bribery and force to effect conversions. The first missionary efforts in Iceland had begun in 981, but had met with little success. When Olaf became a Christian, he promised never again to wage war on England and vowed to bring all Norway into the "true religion." One of his missionaries, Stefnir Thorgilsson, wrecked pagan temples and burned idols in Iceland. As a result, a persecution of Christians was approved by the Althing in 996.

Because of Olaf's missionaries and other pressures, the Althing met on June 23, 1000, to decide whether Iceland should remain loyal to the Norse gods (Odin, Thor, Frey and others) or become Christian. By this time, Christians had become quite numerous in Iceland. It was agreed to submit the matter to Thorgeir, a pagan priest who was the Lawman and presided over the Althing at Thingvellir. King Olaf Tryggvason held hostages in Trondheim and this was no small influence on the outcome. Civil war was also hanging in the balance.

Thorgeir went into his tent and covered his head with a robe for 24 hours. On the evening of June 24, he emerged and announced: "Let us avoid extremes, and take a middle course; let us all have one law and one faith." He ruled that Iceland should officially become Christian and that the people were to be baptized as soon as possible. He also declared that the private worship of heathen gods was not forbidden, so long as people were not caught doing it. The exposure of infants and eating horse meat, both pagan customs, were not officially prohibited.

The king generously rewarded those who helped bring about the conversion of Iceland and thus the new faith was established. Soon thereafter, Olaf was ambushed at sea and killed. He had insulted the pagan queen of Sweden while proposing marriage; she vowed revenge and was successful. Had the Althing met after Olaf's death, the issue may not have been decided in favor of Christianity.

Churches were built all over the island as private chapels on the farms, for each farmer got a tax exemption for the land on which the chapel stood. It took over 100 years to consolidate the church's organization. Despite the strife in the church, a tradition of strong scholarship emerged. Some of the priests went to Europe for their training. Tithing was introduced in 1096, based on Charlemagne's system of levying a 1 per cent tax on all property.

Norway continued to interfere in Iceland's affairs, treating it as though it were a colony. In 1262, King Haakon Haakonsson took advantage of Iceland's internal weakness and claimed a monopoly on trade with the island nation. The Althing agreed to recognize his monopoly and to pay him taxes. Surprisingly, the result of this action turned out to be good for Iceland, for peace was established and blood feuds were stopped. Two ecclesiastical centers were maintained during those years, Skalholt in the south and Holar in the north. Norwegian bishops were appointed to replace native Iceland prelates.

The "Black Death" struck Norway in 1349, and in 1402 a ship arrived in Iceland carrying passengers infected with the deadly disease. Everyone in Skalholt died except the bishop and two laymen. The early years of the 15th century saw some unusually hard winters, disease, fires, and storms at sea, all of which weakened Iceland. The leadership of the Icelandic church in the Middle Ages included both pious saints and notorious sinners. Ancient Norse superstitions and witchcraft lingered on, though officially discredited. In 1397, both Norway and Iceland came under the rule of Denmark's king.

When the Danish King Christian III proclaimed Lutheranism in 1536 to be the official religion of Denmark and Norway, he also enforced it in Iceland. The transition from Catholicism to Lutheranism was far from peaceful, however. One of the benefits of the Reformation was the printing of the Bible. The churches and the liturgy, however, changed very little until the Pietistic movement of the 18th century.

Although the Evangelical Lutheran Church in Iceland is a state church and the pastors are state officials, all churches and religions have full freedom. Other denominations include Adventist, Pentecostal and Roman Catholic.

THE SCANDINAVIAN SPIRIT

Iceland has a remarkable history and has a long history of democracy. It's a place and a people worth getting to know.

Iceland — an island called "Thule."

CHAPTER 43

Nathan Søderblom —
Swedish Ecumenical Pioneer

WHEN WE MOVED TO Webster Groves, MO, a suburb of St. Louis, in November, 1961, I was expecting to begin doctoral studies at Concordia Seminary while serving as pastor of Bethany Lutheran Church, a small congregation of Danish background. It was also the intention to give our children the experience of living in a large metropolitan community. As much as we loved the wide open prairies of North Dakota, we thought it would be to their advantage to learn how to live in a large urban area.

This was about the time when Pope John XXIII announced the Second Vatican Council to be held in Rome from 1962 to 1965. Being interested in such events and open to people of other traditions, I decided to learn about it. The Council's agenda was "aggiornamento," a renewal of the Roman Catholic Church which included "ecumenicity." The word "ecumenical" refers to the worldwide promotion of Christian unity and cooperation. It's based on the belief that "oneness" is an essential quality of the Christian faith. Ecumenism was not invented by Vatican II, but it gave it a tremendous boost. The mutual intolerance and standoffish politeness of previous times were no longer to be the pattern of relationships in the Christian world.

Our move to St. Louis couldn't have occurred at a more fortunate time. Not only did the the ministerial associations promote the ecumenical theme, but the St. Louis Archdiocese extended courtesies to the public never before accorded. His Eminence, Joseph Cardinal Ritter, was particularly gracious. I became a good friend of Msgr. Joseph Baker, Ritter's "peritus" (specialist) in canon law who accompanied him to Rome. As a result, I was frequently invited to speak to Roman Catholic congregations to share with them my understanding of the faith as experienced by a Lutheran Protestant. I was always cordially received.

The ecumenical impetus had been hastened when Protestant and Roman Catholic clergy were imprisoned together in Nazi concentration camps for opposing Hitler. One of the earliest ecumenical leaders in modern times, however, was a Swedish Archbishop named Nathan Søderblom (1866-1931). He was born in the province of Halsingland into a pious Lutheran parsonage, an environment that gave him a passion for the ministry. His home and the times were influenced by an evangelical revival. There was also a great love of music in his home, and he learned to play the piano, the organ and the French horn. Two strong influences on his life were the writings of Martin Luther and those of Albrecht Ritschl (1822-1889), a German theologian and historian. He also greatly admired the music of Johan Sebastian Bach.

While attending the University of Uppsala, Søderblom joined a student missionary group. This gave new direction to his life because it led him to understand the international spirit of missions and to become a serious student of science. In 1890 he attended a Christian Student Conference at the home of Dwight L. Moody in Massachusetts. There he met John R. Mott, a great 19th-century mission leader.

Unlike the ancient Vikings, this modern Swede was committed to world peace. Three principles guided his thinking in this quest. First, he took seriously the words that Jesus was the "Prince of Peace" and that peace is God's will for the world. Second, he believed that peace in the hearts of men had consequences with respect to how they ought to behave. This meant that personal renewal and the promotion of peace belonged together. Third, the church's witness for peace required unity within itself. He believed that the goals of peace and ecumenism are one. The Nobel Peace Prize was given to him in 1930.

Søderblom was ordained in 1893 and became a chaplain in an Uppsala mental hospital. The next year he married Anna Forsell and moved to Paris to study at the Sorbonne. He became fluent in French and completed a doctorate in 1901. While there, he ministered to Swedes in France.

His graduate studies completed, Søderblom returned to Uppsala to teach theology at the University. There he formed friendships with Einar Billing, Gustaf Aulen and Anders Nygren, all of whom became famous theologians and churchmen. During these years he also worked to establish close ties with the Church of England, with the result that "intercommunion" was established in 1922. From 1912 to 1914 he held professorships in both Uppsala and Leipsig. In 1914, Søderblom became the Archbishop of Uppsala and Primate (head bishop) of Sweden. As Archbishop, he added contemporary music to the Swedish hymnal.

The early years of the 20th century witnessed several notable international church meetings. Among these were the Lambeth Conferences in England, which had begun in 1867. There was also a World Student Christian Federation meeting in Constantinople in 1911. These gatherings had a strong impact on Søderblom. In 1925 he hosted a conference in Stockholm that brought Anglican, Orthodox and Protestant church leaders together to search for ways to bring about Christian unity.

Another project to which Søderblom gave attention was building a chapel in memory of St. Ansgar on the island of Birka in 1930, celebrating 1,100 years since the first Christian mission began in Sweden (see chapter 35).

Søderblom was elected to the Swedish Academy of Sciences in 1921, a highly prestigious honor. In 1931 he gave the famous Gifford lectures in Edinburgh, Scotland. His strenuous work schedule, including writing 700 books and articles, eventually took its toll: he died later that year. He was buried in the Uppsala Cathedral, Sweden's most famous church.

Great leaders don't just happen. They travel many roads and learn how to survive testings by fire. This was the case with Søderblom. He was controversial without being arrogant. He was given many honors but did not seek them. He was often criticized by famous contemporaries, but none of them did more to promote the spirit of ecumenism than did this humble scholar and churchman on whose tombstone were inscribed the words of Luke 17:10, "So you also, when you have done all that is commanded, say 'we are unworthy servants, we have only done what was our duty."

Søderblom thought of himself as an "evangelical catholic." The term has become popular in our time but was a rarity in those days. He cited the Swedish translation of the Apostles' Creed which reads, "Den allmaneliga Kristna tron," which means "the universal Christian faith." "Allmaneliga," which means "all mankind" or "universal," is the Swedish equivalent for the Greek word "catholic."

Though the official Vatican response to Søderblom's ecumenical efforts was not positive, Max Pribilla, a Jesuit from Munich, Germany, praised him, saying, "May God resurrect the catholic Søderblom." John XXIII and Vatican II were the answers to his prayer. Nathan Søderblom, the tireless Swedish Archbishop, is a name to remember during the week of Christian Unity, Jan. 18-25.

Nathan Søderblom — ecumenical leader.

CHAPTER 44

The Early Norsemen

SCANDINAVIA HAS BEEN inhabited ever since the glaciers receded some 10,000 years ago. We don't know, however, who those first inhabitants were except that they were hunters and wandering tribesmen. They went north to follow the seasonal migration of the reindeer and other wild game.

About B.C. 2500-2000, agricultural techniques were introduced as migrations of new people of Germanic origins pushed into Denmark, Sweden and Norway. Finland was inhabited by a migration that passed through Hungary and Estonia, except for the Sami (Lapps) who appear to have come from Mongol stock.

Ignored in their isolation of the early days, the Norsemen came to the attention of their neighbors to the south in A.D. 793 when a band of them suddenly appeared in longships at the holy island of Lindisfarne. There they brutally plundered the monastery and returned home to tell about the easy loot available in England. From then on, Christian historians painted a villainous picture of them as heathen terrorists, which in fact many of them were.

But there was another side to these people. Many of them were quite civilized and took no part in piracy on the seas. They were good farmers, skilled artisans in working with cloth, wood, metal and bone carving. They also had a democratic form of government that was ahead of anyone else in their part of the world. For 250 years, these "Vikings" were a dominant force in the North Sea lands, along the coastlands of western Europe and up the rivers of Russia.

What more can we know about these people? Were they a single pure race or did they come from mixed origins? What we know has to be pieced together from many sources: runestones, archaeology, legends and sagas, language study, numismatics (the study of coins) and educated guesses. Some of our best written records come from the early Icelanders.

THE SCANDINAVIAN SPIRIT

Anthropologists identify two types of Norsemen. There were the long-headed (dolichocephalic) people who are tall, blond and blue-eyed. These are characterized as being adventurous and easy-going; and the broad-headed (brachycephalic) people described as conservative, distrustful, dark-haired, quick to become enthusiastic, emotional in politics, religion and personal relationships. While the tall, long-headed, blond and blue-eyed type are found in large numbers in these lands, Sweden has the highest percentage of this type and Denmark the fewest. Norway is a more equal mixture of both. One should not, however, be too rigid in drawing conclusions from these claims.

Not all Norsemen were Vikings. Properly speaking, "Vikings" refers to those who made a profession of trade, piracy and land-taking. These had been northern activities long before the "Viking Age."

The earliest reference to these lands comes from the voyage of Pytheas of Massalia, a Greek geographer, in B.C. 330-300. He described the north coast of Denmark quite accurately. Despite their great power, the Roman legions were never able to conquer the Norsemen. They did, however, employ many "Germanic" people as mercenaries and even invited them to settle in the Empire as a buffer against further attacks. The Romans explored the coastlines of this region in A.D. 5, but never attempted to occupy it, so far as we know.

Between A.D. 400 and 550, over-population led many Norsemen to migrate to England. Originally they were invited to settle there after the Roman legions departed, but once there they came in greater numbers and drove the Celts into what is now Wales. The Angles and Jutes from Denmark and the Saxons from northern Germany took over the land but it returned to heathenism, having been Christian under Roman rule. The Prince Valiant and King Arthur stories provide an interesting picture of the struggle between the newcomers from northern Europe and the earlier settlers.

Impressive grave sites from the Merovingian Period (A.D. 550-800) have been found near Oslo and Uppsala. Cremation was the usual way of disposing of bodies before the coming of Christianity: the bodies and goods were burned on a pyre and then covered with mounds.

Those early Norsemen were known to their neighbors by a variety of names. The "Eruli" or "Heruli" seem to have had their original home in southern Jutland. Driven out by the "Dani" ("Danes") about A.D. 200, they invaded Gaul (France) in A.D. 289. Later they plundered the coast of Spain. They were also famous as mercenaries, but they are best remembered for their skill at writing with runic characters.

The Roman historian Tacitus paid tribute to the Swedes of about the year A.D. 100 as the most powerful and best organized of the northern nations. In the early days, Scandinavian kings were petty rulers who had small areas under their control. Many battles were fought before any of these lands came under the rule of a single monarch.

One of the most interesting of these ancient kings was Harald Blautand ("Bluetooth") of Denmark. His father was the hard-headed Gorm the "Gamle" (the "Old"). Gorm was the first to rule over all Denmark and was a devotee of the pagan gods to the end. His wife Thyri was Christian, however. It is surmised that she was descended from an English royal house. According to Prof. Gwyn Jones from Cardiff, Wales, in his book "A History of the Vikings," Thyri was remembered for her beauty, chastity, wisdom and saintliness. (My wife and I visited the burial mounds of Gorm and Thyri at Jelling, Denmark, in 1985. They're each 50 steps high.)

Harald Bluetooth was the first king of Denmark to embrace the Christian faith. It's difficult to know, however, how much instruction and conviction lay behind his claim to have "made the Danes Christian." His Christianity, such as it was, may have been the result of influence from his Christian mother, military pressure from the neighboring German king, Otto I, who was Christian, or pressure from the Danes in England who had been converted to the new religion. By being baptized, he protected his southern boundary with Germany and thus was able to wage war in Sweden and make claims in Norway. Very few people in positions of power appear to have acted with pure motivations.

In his old age, Harald fled Denmark to escape attack from his son Svein "Forkbeard." After gaining control of Denmark, Svein conquered England and returned to the paganism of Gorm. But Svein's son, Knut the "Great," became a Christian king of England who is remembered for his saintliness. He became the most powerful ruler in the North Sea lands after defeating Olaf the "Saint" in the Battle of Sticklestad north of Trondheim in 1030 (see "The Scandinavian Heritage," chapter 31).

145

THE SCANDINAVIAN SPIRIT

It's unfortunate that historians have concerned themselves so much with kings, battles and intrigue. I'd like to know much more about the everyday life of common people. There's a trend in our times to tell of the past as "people's history," rather than exclusively as a political and military chronicle. The ancient world was a dangerous place for children. Unless the head of the house approved of a newborn child, it was put out to die. Too many mouths could spell disaster when there was a food shortage. It was not much safer for women and for people low on the economic scale. If we think that morals in our time are in jeopardy, we should not be deluded into supposing that the ancient world was a paradise.

Life has mostly been a struggle for survival. Marriage had little to do with romantic love. It is only in our time that luxuries and plenty have been assumed by the masses to be their right. Our ancestors would have thought they'd reached heaven (or, Valhalla) if they could have seen our age.

CHAPTER 45

The Mystery Of 'Sutton Hoo'

D
URING THE SUMMER OF 1939 the attention of the world was fixed on the German Wehrmacht, Hitler's war machine. As a result, the greatest archaeological discovery in England's history was overshadowed by the opening shots of World War II. When the war ended almost six years later, Europe was too preoccupied with rebuilding itself to be concerned about the ancient treasure at Sutton Hoo in Suffolk County of eastern England. The treasure is now in the British Museum.

The impression of a wooden ship had been discovered in the sandy soil of an earthen mound. An excavation in July, 1939, revealed that there had indeed been a ship buried there, but all the wood had decomposed; only the iron nails were in place. The probability is that it was a burial ship dating to about A.D. 625. The jewels and armor found at the site made it the richest treasure ever uncovered in Europe. But whose treasure had it been? Was someone buried in the ship and if so, who? Scholars are still searching for the answers.

People who are interested in Scandinavian heritage sooner or later have to deal with the "English connection." The whole North Sea was the world of the travel-minded Norsemen, and England was one of their favorite stopping places. Even today, many Danes and Norwegians go to London for their shopping. The north Germans and the English were rivals to obtain the rights to Bergen as a trade center for their merchandise in the late Middle Ages.

I'm especially interested in the Scandinavian connections with Suffolk County because people from Surnadal, southwest of Trondheim, migrated to Suffolk, possibly before the Norman conquest in 1066. This may have been a reward for siding with Knut the Great (d. 1035) in his battle with St. Olaf at Sticklestad. Among those settlers were some of the Fiske (Fisk) families, whose descendants settled in New England during the 17th century. One famous member of this family is Carlton Fisk, the catcher for the Chicago White Sox.

THE SCANDINAVIAN SPIRIT

Suffolk County had been attractive to Scandinavians long before the Viking Age (793-1066). During the migrations of the 5th and 6th centuries from southern Denmark and northwest Germany, the Angles, Jutes and Saxons came in such large numbers that they eventually dominated the culture of Britain and gave it a new name "Angle-land" (England). A similar "mass migration" occurred during the large 19th-century movement of Scandinavians to America. When the letters from America came back to the homeland, thousands more got "America Fever" and sailed westward. The lure of "land for the asking" was irresistible.

The ship discovered at Sutton Hoo is considered to be a forerunner of the later Viking longships that were used so successfully during the period of their power. The armor found in the ship appears to have come from Sweden. Burial in such ships was common in Sweden for royalty and aristocrats during the Anglo-Saxon period.

But who might have been buried at Sutton Hoo? One theory is that it was Raedwald (ruled 599-624), a king who was descended from the Wuffingas ("Wolf-people"). The Wuffingas had come from Sweden and took their name from Wuffa, who ruled from 571 to 578 and was the founder of the dynasty. His father, Wehha, was the first of the East Angles to rule in England. This royal family continued to supply rulers in England until the death of King Edmund in 930. The claim is also made that the Wuffingas had been royalty in Sweden and may have come from the royal house of Uppsala. There were always more royalty than there were kingdoms so that may have motivated them to try their luck in England.

There are some problems, however, in resolving the mystery. The main one is that no body was found. Scientific tests of the soil in the middle of the ship near the armor revealed no trace of human remains in the soil, though there was a high phosphate content near the sword. The phosphate may have come from the remains of an ivory chess set, however. Acid in the sand which covered the ship may have dissolved all traces of bones and teeth.

Another suggestion is that the "Sutton Hoo man" was not buried there at all. He may have been entombed at some other place and the ship could have been simply a memorial to him. Michael Wood, in his book

"In Search of the Dark Ages," believes that a body had been buried there but somehow it disappeared. If the body belonged to Raedwald, what happened to it? Raedwald had been converted to the Christian faith and was baptized, but he recanted when his wife urged him to abandon the new faith. They then compromised and had both a Christian and a pagan altar in their private chapel. The relevance of all of this to the mystery at hand is that some people think his body may have been moved from the pagan mound and given a secret Christian burial.

One of the interesting artifacts found in the ship was a highly ornamented whetstone which could have been used to sharpen the owner's sword. It measures almost three feet long. Since the whetstone had never been used, it may have been a part of the ceremonial equipment to accompany him on the journey to Valhalla. These sceptres were frequently found in Swedish burials. The circumstantial evidence indicates that it was probably a king who had been buried and Raedwald seems to fit the picture.

In addition to jewelry, many coins were also found at the site. They were not dated like ours are today, but it has been determined that they were minted between 620 and 640.

It is said that King Henry VIII had his agents dig for treasure in the Sutton Hoo area. Queen Elizabeth's magician, John Dee, had opened one of the many mounds in the area. Later archaeological digs discovered one of their tools as well as their snacks left behind. It is further said that a gold crown weighing 60 ounces was discovered in the area, but it was sold and melted down.

The archaeologists finished their work on Aug. 23, just nine days before Hitler plunged the world into war. They had found a treasure that had previously only been hinted at in myths, sagas and in the epic "Beowulf" (see chapter 1). It was not known that this kind of splendor had existed at such an early time in England. The extent of the find was enormous: a helmet, a sword inlaid with gold and jewels, the whetstone, spears, a battle-axe, a decorated shield, silver drinking horns, silver bowls, silver spoons, a large bowl bearing the stamp of the Empress Anastasius in Constantinople, a gold buckle, coins and more things of value.

There was also an iron stand, 66 inches tall, which some scholars think could have been a royal standard to carry the king's banners. Such banners were carried in procession to announce the arrival of the king to a community.

Perhaps we'll learn more. Seventeen mounds have been identified in the area and some have still not been excavated. The mystery of Sutton Hoo may be with us for quite a while, but it does add to our knowledge of the English connection for early Scandinavians. Some day I'd like to explore it for myself.

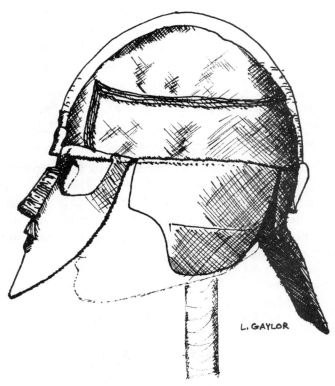

Helmet found at Sutton Hoo.

CHAPTER 46

Alfred The Great And The Vikings

NO OTHER ENGLISHMAN has equalled the fame of Alfred the Great, King of the Saxons. It's difficult, however, to get at the real truth about people who become famous. In addition to the historical facts, many legends become attached to their stories. Sometimes the legends are more interesting than the real history. The problem is to determine which is which.

In King Alfred's case, there was a narrow margin between known greatness and not being known at all. Here's how it came about. The Danish Vikings were raiding England. Hundreds of longships and thousands of battle-trained soldiers arrived in raid upon raid. They conquered Mercia, Northumbria and East Anglia. By 878, only Wessex remained in Saxon hands. In 867 they conquered York and burned it. Terror was their trademark. The Northumbrian king, Aelle, suffered the "blood eagle," a Viking ritual in which the victim was sacrificed to Odin. His ribs and lungs were cut from his body and spread like eagle's wings. After conquering a territory, the Vikings set up a puppet government to rule for them so they could carry on with their plundering.

Alfred was born in 849. His father, Aethelwulf, was king of the West Saxons. His name indicates that he had descended from King Wuffa who had come from Sweden in the sixth century (see chapter 45). Alfred had four older brothers, so it seemed unlikely that he'd ever become king. It also looked like the end of Anglo-Saxon civilization was near at hand. The Danes were victorious everywhere. Ordinarily, they arrived in early summer and returned in autumn. But when Alfred was only two years old, the Danes began wintering in England. The Anglo-Saxons, who had come from Scandinavia and northwest Germany centuries earlier, had converted to Christianity. Their latter-day kinsmen were still heathen.

As a young prince, Alfred was taught to ride, hunt, use hawks and lead soldiers. Had it been a time of peace, he probably would have been sent to a monastery to become a priest. When only four, he was sent to Rome for an audience with Pope Leo IV (St. Leo). From his father, Alfred inherited a religious and thoughtful nature. He was also a poet and had a strong spirit.

Though Alfred had a gentle side to his nature, he did not shrink from the danger of battle and was determined to defeat the Danes. His test came in the winter of 870 when he was 21, the year his father died and he became king. Fresh from victories in the north and east, the Danes pushed on against Wessex, the heart of England. At a place called "Ashdown," where a white horse had been cut into the rocks centuries before, Alfred stood his ground and the Danes lost a king and five leaders. That didn't end the war, however, for the Danes soon returned with a vengeance.

At Wilton, the Danes forced Alfred to retreat. To buy time, he gave the enemy gold ("Danegeld"). After plundering in other areas, the Danes returned and overran Mercia in 874. Once more Alfred bargained with them to effect their retreat. The Vikings knew the Christian calendar of festivals and liked to attack during a holiday. They struck on the 12th day of Christmas in 878 and took the food stores laid up for winter. It appeared to be just a matter of time before Alfred would suffer the "blood eagle."

Many kings would have fled to the Continent and surrendered the land to the invaders, but Alfred kept up a campaign of guerilla warfare while retreating and waiting for a chance to counterattack. A Viking force of 1,200 men had wintered in south Wales and joined another Danish army in battle against the Anglo-Saxons. They won the battle but lost 800 men plus their leader. Alfred called a meeting on May 11, 878 (Pentecost Sunday), at a place known as Egbert's Stone. After preparing themselves for battle by fasting, praying, and taking an oath on the reserved host of the sacrament (to prevent desertion to the enemy), they returned to the White Horse at a place called Edington.

Alfred attacked ferociously, according to his biographer, Bishop Asser, who recorded the event. A great slaughter followed. After two weeks of battle, the Vikings requested terms of peace. Alfred knew he could not drive them all out of England, so he offered to divide England into Anglo-Saxon and Danish England ("Danelaw"). He also required that Guthrum, the Danish General, and his bodyguard of 30 men be baptized. Had they not accepted conversion, there is no doubt that Alfred would have ordered them all killed. He was no "milktoast" Christian! The historian Michael Wood wrote, "No one respected a weak king in the Dark Ages."

Once baptized, the Danes kept their bargain and left Alfred's territory, never to return. They settled down in the eastern and northern parts of England where they created a social revolution by building cities and developing trade. Lincoln, Stamford, Derby, Nottingham and Leicester became a Scandinavian land. There is still evidence of Danish words and phrases surviving in these areas.

The Danes met their match in Alfred the Great. He couldn't drive them out, but neither could they defeat him. He went on to re-establish Anglo-Saxon and Christian culture in central and western England and gained control of London. The walls of the city were repaired and the town was repopulated.

Alfred's most important contribution to England after protecting it from the foreigners was his interest in education. He understood, like many other great rulers, that a decline in education is the downfall of a nation. Previously the monasteries had been the centers of learning, but the Viking raids had reduced them to rubble. He had a few books that he thought "most needful for men to know" translated from Latin into Anglo-Saxon. They are books still worth reading. Among these were Bede's "Ecclesiastical History of the English People," Pope Gregory the Great's "Pastoral Care," and St. Augustine's "Soliloquies." Fragments of two original copies of these translations survive in the British Library. Bishop Asser's biography and a collection of writings by Alfred are available in The Penguin Classics.

What was Alfred like as a person? Bishop Asser described him in his youth as oversensitive, high-strung, strongminded and inventive. He was also something of a hypochondriac, constantly suffering a nervous illness. He was not the sort of person that you'd expect to become the leader of an army. It was with great effort that he became a literary person, largely due to the influence of the church.

While a strong believer in the "peace of the Lord," Alfred was also a practical politician who didn't allow bishops to run his kingdom. What made him a great ruler was the fact that he had a vision for England.

153

He was not just concerned with the next battle. In his last years he wrote a preface to Boethius's "Consolation of Philosophy" and the Danes settled down in England to live within the territory awarded them by Alfred. There were more struggles with later invasions of Danes, but Alfred had brought peace to his people and the English still honor him by calling him "the Great."

CHAPTER 47

The Adventures Of Erik 'Bloodaxe'

THE JUDGMENTS OF HISTORY are still coming in on the Vikings. Historian David L. Edwards, formerly chaplain in the British House of Commons, has written in his book "Christian England" that the Vikings were "thugs" who took advantage of a military vacuum in their times. Emperor Charlemagne had destroyed the once mighty Frisian (Dutch) fleet, but his successors weren't able to maintain control of the seas.

According to Edwards, the Viking terror from the North had as great an impact as the Moslem armies in the south in frustrating the hope that dawned on Europe when the Christian Charlemagne was crowned Emperor in Rome on Christmas Day in the year 800. Edwards wondered that Christian civilization either survived or expanded in those days. Winston Churchill also wrote about those perils in his "History of the English Speaking People." While Charlemagne lived, he was the protector of Roman Christianity and his enemies kept a safe distance from his armies.

Erik "Bloodaxe" was one of King Harald "Finehair's" nine sons and richly deserved the name "Bloodaxe." Harald was the first of the Norwegian regional kings to gain control over the whole country and Erik was Harald's choice to succeed him. His qualifications included physical strength, a decisive mind, and kinship with King Erik of Jutland in Denmark. He was married to Gunnhild, the daughter of Gorm, the first king to rule over all Denmark. Gunnhild had a reputation for beauty, brains and her father's vengeful spirit.

When Harald died, the struggle for succession pitted Erik against his 15-year-old brother Haakon, who was being brought up in the court of the powerful King Athelstan of England. Erik killed two of his brothers and seemed on the way to seizing control of Norway. A powerful group of farmers opposed him, however, and arranged to have Haakon brought back from England. Unable to stop Haakon's power move, Erik sailed west with his family, ships, wealth, and a small army. After a stop in the Orkney Islands (settled by Norwegians), he went plundering in Scotland and Germany.

In 947, Erik arrived in Northumbria, where a revolution was brewing and the leaders invited him to be their king. They believed that Erik could defend them against the powerful Anglo-Saxon rulers in southern England. A part of the bargain was that Erik and his family had to to be baptized by Wulfstan, the Archbishop of York. Erik agreed, but it didn't change his Viking ways.

The Northumbrians had a stormy history and were hemmed in on all sides by hostile neighbors. They were experienced at playing their neighbors off against each other. Their highways were unsafe for travel, for law and order were not maintained in the countrysides. Travel was risky without armed escort and even then it was considered unsafe to venture more than six miles from home. Foreign merchants brought their wares in by sea.

York, the capital, was an old Roman center, second only to London as a major trading city in the land. More than 30,000 Danes lived in York at the height of its population. Many of the Danes were fourth generation. Second generation Norwegians were there too, as well as other ethnic groups. York, called "Jorvik" by the Norsemen, was also a city of churches with new ones constantly being built.

(Today York is a major English tourist center. The Viking-age Jorvik features the restored "Coppergate" section, once the home of carpenters ("koppari"). It's open for tourists throughout the year. If you want information on it, write: Jorvik Viking Centre, Coppergate, York YO1, England. You'll be amazed to discover how authentically the old Viking scenes have been restored.)

Erik's first reign in Northumbria lasted less than a year. Before 948 had ended, the Anglo-Saxon King Eadred was back in power. He used terror by sword and fire to break Erik's popular support. He burned Ripon, one of the great cities of Northumbria, including its church. Then he stole the bones of St. Wilfrid, the local saint, to deprive the rebels of heaven's assistance. In the meantime, Erik went "viking" for the next four years. The sagas tell how he ravished the coastlands of Scotland, the Hebrides, Wales and Ireland. His major pirate activity seems to have been in slave trade with the Spanish Moslems. He probably cooperated with the Norwegians in Ireland who made a major business of slave traffic at Dublin.

Slavery was the most profitable business in peacetime for the Vikings. They raided the major church festivals crowded with pilgrims. Ireland, being the most Christian of the North Sea lands, was particularly victimized. The Viking slave traders also covered the markets of Italy, Germany, France and eastern Europe, however. Many captives were delivered to Spain, from where some were sent to the Middle East, others to the Far East. The men were forced into military service or work brigades and the women either became domestic servants or were put in harems. Few of the kidnapped people ever saw their homelands again. It was such a good business that the Spanish Moslems sent representives to Scandinavia to contract for a continual supply of slaves. One shipment saw 9,000 Italians being sent off to Egypt. "Blue men," as the Africans were called, were also sold in the northern lands as slaves.

Erik returned to Northumbria in 952 and was again invited to be king. He defeated a combined English and Scottish army, though at heavy cost. Then he appeared as a pious Christian monarch paying homage to the shrine of St. Cuthbert. His strongest supporter was Archbishop Wulfstan who opposed Anglo-Saxon rule. The Archbishop was captured by the Anglo-Saxons, however, and imprisoned. Erik never succeeded in consolidating his power and was not able to control the seaways. As a result, his second reign lasted for only two years.

A dreadful battle took place between Erik and his enemies in 954 and he and all his men lost their lives. Treachery played a role in his defeat: he was betrayed by the son of a Norwegian-Irish king named Olaf. After his death, Archbishop Wulfstan was set free and restored to power. Despite his ecclesiastical title, he governed much more in the style of a secular ruler than as a servant of God.

Erik's spirit did not end with his death, for Gunnhild and her sons carried on his pirating activities. This also provided an excuse for Gunnhild's brother, Denmark's King Harald "Bluetooth," to renew his military operations in southern Norway on behalf of his nephews.

For all his crudeness, Erik must have had some popular appeal. When he died, Northumbrian writers were kind to his record. A later poet wrote a special story about how Erik entered Valhalla, the hall of the gods, as one of their greatest heroes: "Hail to you Erik, be welcome here and come into the hall, gallant king!" Eulogies still make interesting reading. It just depends on who writes them.

CHAPTER 48

From Vladimir To Glasnost —
1,000 Years Of Christianity In Russia

TO PEOPLE GROWING UP TODAY, it may seem strange to think of Russia as a religious nation - since its leaders are required to be atheists. Despite the government's claim to be "godless," the church in Russia celebrated a millenium — 1,000 years of history — in 1988.

The Russian Orthodox Church traces its historical origin to Prince Vladimir (Valdemar) of Novgorod. He was a great-grandson of Rurik, founder of the Scandinavian dynasty which ruled in Kiev of the Ukraine. Rurik, a Danish prince, and two of his brothers were invited to organize the first government in Russia. Their task was to defend the people against enemies. In those days the name "Rus" (Russians) referred primarily to the Swedes. The name was given by the Finns: it means people who came "rowing" their boats (see "The Scandinavian Heritage," chapter 15).

When he was 16, Vladimir's father Sviatoslav died. A power struggle followed and Vladimir was forced to flee to Scandinavia. At 26, he returned with an army, defeated his brother who had claimed power, and consolidated his rule from Poland to the Volga. Then he moved his capital to Kiev and decided that the country should be Christian. In 988 Vladimir proposed marriage to Anna, the sister of the Emperor Basil in Constantinople. It was agreed on condition that Vladimir would become Christian, and he was baptized that same year. The Emperor reneged on the agreement, however, and Vladimir attacked the Crimea to claim his bride. The wedding was held according to the rites of the Greek Orthodox Church.

Vladimir became a zealous Christian. He got rid of his former wives and mistresses, destroyed idols, became a crusader for education, built churches and monasteries, supported missionaries and became a champion of the poor. Like many Christian rulers of his time, he relied on physical force to win converts. Why did he establish Christianity as the official religion of the land? His grandmother, Olga, who had accepted

159

the new faith in 955, may have had something to do with it. We know of a church built in Kiev as early as 945.

Drastic changes took place in Russia as a result of Vladimir's influence. He was especially concerned about the poor. Whenever there was a royal feast, the leftovers were distributed to the poor. Timothy Ware writes in his book "The Orthodox Church," "nowhere else in medieval Europe were there such highly organized 'social services' as in 10th-century Kiev." Vladimir was also motivated by a sense of Christian mercy. He took steps to improve the judicial system and abolished the death penalty. Torture and mutilation were also abolished and corporal punishment was seldom used. Even criminals were treated with mercy. Two of his sons, Boris and Gleb, supported their father's policies. After Vladimir's death (July 15, 1015), however, they were murdered by orders of an older brother. They chose death for themselves rather than to see others killed when they were attacked.

The church in Russia developed under the guidance of Greek leadership until 1237, when the Mongol Tartars ruled the land. Kiev and all of its beautiful buildings were destroyed. When the Tartar rule was overthrown in 1448, the new Russian leadership came from Moscow. The Russia that now emerged was vastly different from the socially concerned government of Vladimir.

When the Turkish army captured Constantinople in 1453, the church in Russia declared itself independent. Moscow rose in importance and was soon called "the third Rome." The first Rome had been conquered by foreigners and Constantinople, the second Rome, was charged with heresy. One of the most gifted leaders of the Russian Church was the Patriarch Nikon (1605-1681), who tried to restore Greek ways to the Russian church. Unfortunately, he was not a diplomat and caused a split between his ways and the "Old Believers" who wanted to maintain the Russian customs. The politically ambitious Nikon tried to bring the state under the control of the church. Although his religious reforms were adopted, he was deposed in 1667.

Peter the Great ruled Russia with an iron hand and suppressed the Patriarch's power. He replaced the office of Patriarch with a Holy Synod to rule the church. The constitution for the Synod was copied from the Protestants of Germany. Officers were appointed by the Czar and thus were beholden to him. This remained the pattern of governance in the Russian Orthodox Church until the Revolution of 1917.

When Czar Nicholas II abdicated on March 15, 1917, the church leaders voted to restore the office of Patriarch. They elected Tikhon, Metropolitan (bishop) of Moscow, as their leader. Peace for the church was short-lived, however. Lenin and the Bolsheviks came to power on Nov. 7, 1917. In August 1918, a month after the Czar and his family were executed, the Metropolitan of Kiev was also brutally murdered by the Bolsheviks.

Despite many years of atheistic propaganda and government pressure, the church in Russia is far from extinct. It is estimated that more than 10% of the people attend worship regularly, which is higher than in many of the countries of western Europe. During World War II, Stalin temporarily lifted the repression of the church in order to rally support for the war effort. The church people, who have always had a strong loyalty to "Mother Russia," responded with vigor. Some American writers were impressed and believed that Russia had "turned the corner" on religious freedom. Emil Ludwig, for example, made that mistaken claim in his biography of Stalin.

Paul F. Scotchmer of Seattle, a consultant to the National Association of Evangelicals, published an article entitled "Glasnost, God and Gorbachev" in the Jan. 21, 1988, Chicago Tribune. He raised an important issue about "glasnost," the supposed new policy of "openness" and "publicity" in the Soviet Union. Much has been made about this policy since Gorbachev's rise to power. Scotchmer is not convinced that glasnost is being applied to the church. He notes that clergy pay five times as much income tax as other people. The policy of registering all baptisms and weddings with the government, he claims, is used to repress people. He also notes that the number of Orthodox churches was reduced to fewer than 8,000 from 54,100 in 1914. Scotchmer called on the Soviet leaders to allow its people freedom of conscience.

The great contribution of the Russian church to the world has been its deep spirituality and capacity for suffering. One of my favorite writers is Anthony Bloom, a Russian Orthodox Archbishop. His book "Beginning to Pray," published by the Paulist Press, is an inspirational classic. Bloom notes that when Yuri Gagarin, the Soviet Cosmonaut,

161

returned to earth and declared that he had "never seen God in heaven," one of the Moscow priests remarked: "If you have never seen him on earth, you will never see him in heaven."

When you read about the millenium of Russian Christianity, remember Vladimir (Valdemar), the great-grandson of a Danish prince, who made the decision that was to change the course of a whole nation for a thousand years and more. We haven't seen the end of it yet.

CHAPTER 49

M. Falk Gjertsen —
A Pastor Under Fire

THINGS ARE NOT ALWAYS what they seem, and frequently not as claimed. But it's often difficult to know the difference.

The story of Melchior Falk Gjertsen (Yairt-sen) is a case in point. He was born at Kaupanger, near Bergen, Norway, on Feb. 19, 1847. His father, Johan, who was educated in theology, was a teacher. The family moved to Chicago in 1864. The next year, Johan became a pastor in Racine, WI, and young Falk went to Augustana Seminary in Paxton, IL. After graduating in 1868, he spent the next 13 years as a pastor in Illinois and Wisconsin. (I'm indebted to Nina Draxten's book "The Testing of M. Falk Gjertsen," published by the Norwegian-American Historical Association, for much of my information about this interesting figure in Scandinavian immigrant history.)

Then came the big move that was to change his life forever. In 1881, Gjertsen went to Minneapolis to become pastor of Trinity, the oldest Norwegian Lutheran Church in the city, founded in 1866. Soon he became a leading citizen in the rapidly growing city. He was active in organizing a Temperance Society, the Associated Charities of Minneapolis, the United Norwegian Lutheran Church (1890), and the Lutheran Free Church (1897). He was best known for his role on the School Board, however. Elected in 1887, he introduced many reforms and improvements: free text books, manual training (woodworking), elimination of basement classrooms, and establishing four high schools so that all pupils would be within walking distance of one of them. He served as both secretary and president of the board.

All was going well when Gjertsen, at age 53, made a trip to Norway in the spring of 1900. He arrived in time to speak for the 17th of May (Syttende Mai) Constitution Day celebration at a "prayer house" (bedehus) in Bergen. Gjertsen was recognized as one of the outstanding preachers among Norwegians in America. People were profuse in their praise. Moreover, he was a local hero who had returned from America as a success.

Little did he realize, however, that this day would lead to troubles that would cloud his life as long as he lived. Attending the service was a licensed lay preacher and his young wife, Michael and Esther Biernakowsky Paulsen. Mrs. Paulsen had been deeply "touched" by the message, according to her husband and wished to discuss the needs of her soul more fully with the visitor from America.

Gjertsen was unaware that Mrs. Paulsen was a woman with a hidden past. She seemed to be totally sincere. She even persuaded her husband to request that Gjertsen take her back to America with him, but the request was declined. This didn't stop her from making further attempts to get Gjertsen's attention, however. Wherever he went on his speaking tour and visits, there was Mrs. Paulsen — at the railway stations, stopping by the homes where he was a guest and even seeking entrance to his hotel room. He treated her politely and expressed kindness as towards a daughter.

Gjertsen returned to America in September and resumed his work at Trinity Church. All was going well when just before Christmas a letter arrived from two pastors in Norway denouncing Gjertsen as unfit for the ministry and charging him with "impropriety" towards Mrs. Paulsen. They reported that Mrs. Paulsen had shown them a sensuous letter believed to have come from Gjertsen. The letter was unsigned and undated, but Mrs. Paulsen claimed that Gjertsen had definitely written it and that he had caused great harm to her marriage.

Needless to say, Gjertsen was shocked and immediately wrote to Mrs. Paulsen expressing sorrow that she would make such unfounded charges. Although insisting that the charges were entirely false, Gjertsen — in view of his position of high trust and prominence in the city — decided that he could not simply ignore such serious charges. A similar letter outlining the charges had been sent to Prof. Georg Sverdrup, President of nearby Augsburg Seminary and a leading member of Trinity church. Gjertsen decided that he had to go back to Norway to clear his name. Trinity granted him a leave of absence for this purpose and funds were raised for his legal costs.

Once back in Norway, Gjertsen learned that Mrs. Paulsen had quite a reputation. A Bergen bank employee claimed that his family life had also been ruined by her. He offered to sign a deposition acknowledging his illicit encounters with Mrs. Paulsen. Unfortunately for Gjertsen, the bank pressured him to withdraw the statement because the publicity would have been harmful to them.

The civil authorities were also uncooperative, probably because, they didn't want to embarrass the state church. After several frustrating and unsuccessful attempts to clear his name, Gjertsen returned to Minneapolis, a troubled man.

The issue centered on the anonymous letter. It seems that Gjertsen's correspondence with Mrs. Paulsen was misinterpreted. His religious language was capable of being understood in different ways (something like the opening paragraphs of Paul Wellman's novel, "The Walls of Jericho"). Since Gjertsen had destroyed the letters sent to him by Mrs. Paulsen, there was no way to prove if there was a case for reading between the lines. Mrs. Paulsen produced other letters also, but these were thought to be forgeries. It turned out that she had an accomplice who had copied Gjertsen's penmanship. It was later revealed that this woman also had a shady reputation and went by two different names. The forged letters made Gjertsen out to be a philanderer and a cad. She did not charge him with adultery but with being "amorous."

Despite yet another trip to Norway to try to resolve the matter, Gjertsen never did succeed in clearing his name. The Paulsens dropped from public view after 1901 and were not heard from again. Gjertsen returned to resume his duties at Trinity Church. Things didn't go well, however, as the Minneapolis Tribune and some of the Scandinavian newspapers carried headlines on the scandal every week. In 1902, under pressure from one element in the congregation, he resigned from Trinity and founded nearby Bethany Church. In 1908, leading citizens of the city persuaded him to again become a candidate for the School Board and he was easily elected. He was instrumental in getting Norwegian and Swedish language study introduced as electives in the high schools.

Gjertsen also became active in the Sons of Norway. When the noted Norwegian writer, Bjørnstjerne Bjørnson, died in April, 1910, Gjertsen delivered the funeral eulogy to an overflow crowd at the City

Auditorium. This is noteworthy, for Bjørnson was known for his anti-clericalism. Gjertsen also became an advocate of peace and of the working classes which is where most of the Scandiavians found themselves.

After retirement in 1911, the Gjertsens moved to San Diego for a short time but then returned to Minneapolis. In the summer of 1912, he addressed a crowd of 2,000 people at Hillsboro, ND, for a mid-summer festival. He also took part in laying the cornerstone of the Lyngblomsten Home for the Elderly in Minneapolis. In the spring of 1913 he became suddenly ill and died of a pleurisy attack on April 22. His funeral was the largest ever held in south Minneapolis up to that time. The Tribune lavished praise on Gjertsen as a most worthy citizen. Mrs. Gjertsen lived in Minneapolis until her death in 1939. The anonymous letter was never discussed in family.

Men of the cloth, like other people in the public's eye, have often been targets of slander. While people must bear responsibility for their own actions, those like Gjertsen rise again, even though they have been deeply wounded. Whatever went on between Gjertsen and Mrs. Paulson (if anything), he believed enough in himself to live again, instead of dwelling in self-pity. He survived under fire.

There's a lesson in this story. If you want to rebuke someone, say it to his or her face. If you want to praise someone, put it in writing. It's a lot safer that way — and fairer, too.

CHAPTER 50

Marcus Thrane —
Radical Norwegian Social Reformer

NORWEGIANS AROUND THE WORLD celebrate "Syttende Mai" as the greatest day in the modern history of Norway. May 17, 1814, was indeed an important day, but the constitution adopted on that date didn't automatically bring freedom and equality to the Norwegian people. Nearly another century was to pass before Norway truly became free and independent.

One of the people who became impatient with the constitution was Marcus Thrane (Thrah-neh), born in Oslo on Oct. 14, 1817, just three years after the great document was signed. Prof. Terje Leiren, University of Washington, has written an excellent biography on him entitled "Marcus Thrane: A Norwegian Radical in America" (Norwegian American Historical Association, 1987).

The constitution was technically illegal as Norway had been signed over to the king of Sweden at the treaty of Kiel the preceding January. The men who drew up the document at Eidsvold did a good job of expressing the ideals of the Norwegian people at the time, but they had no power to enforce it. In fact, the signers ran the danger of being treated as revolutionaries. The fact that they had borrowed many ideas from the American and French revolutionary constitutions did not endear them to a Europe whose monarchies were becoming nervous about holding on to their power.

There were 37 farmers on the committee that wrote the constitution, but after the delegates went home it was the aristocratic members who took charge. The first step was to get the Swedish king to honor the constitution, which he did with a few changes. That wasn't enough, however, for Marcus Thrane. He had been born into a family of wealth but his father lost it all when Marcus was just three years old. The elder Thrane, a member of the Board of Directors of the Bank of Norway, had "borrowed" some funds to cover a risky investment that didn't work out. He repaid his debt but was broken both financially and socially.

THE SCANDINAVIAN SPIRIT

Marcus grew up on a slim budget but was a determined young man. He travelled on the Continent and learned French in Paris. Then he returned to Norway and entered the University at Oslo to study theology. He developed an intense antagonism against the upper classes and started to crusade for more power to the workers, including a labor voice in running the government.

Thrane's first position of influence was as editor of a newspaper in Drammen. He wrote openly about the need for government support of industry to guarantee wages and he opposed the policy that allowed the sons of the wealthy to buy their way out of military service. He also advocated loans to working people to buy inexpensive housing. He took the social teachings of Christianity seriously and wanted Norway to be reformed according to them. As a result, he was fired in 1848 because the privileged classes were alarmed at his radical ideas.

This didn't deter Thrane. He became a champion of the labor movement and established his own newspaper in 1849. He claimed that Christ was a revolutionary and a "true socialist." He gathered over 12,000 signatures and sent a list of grievances to the king in Stockholm. He asked for help for the cotters (share-crop farmers) to enable them to own their own land, no exemptions from universal military training, reforms in the judicial system and better schools. The king rejected all the requests, but the movement grew.

The government offered Thrane a position in the bureaucracy, hoping thereby to silence him, but he rejected it. On the morning of July 7, 1851, he was arrested and imprisoned for seven years. His wife's health was broken by the ordeal. Frustrated in his attempts at social reform, Thrane went to Germany to study photography and returned to become one of Norway's first professionals in the business.

After the death of his wife, Thrane and his four daughters left for America. The date was Feb. 2, 1864. His son, Arthur, remained in Norway to complete his studies at the University. The Civil War was raging, but this did not deter him. He went to Chicago, where he proceeded to establish a Norwegian-language newspaper. His goal was to elevate Norwegian immigrants to a level where they would not be looked down on by other ethnic groups.

168

Thrane attacked slavery, supported the public schools and championed the rights of workers. He severely criticized the Norwegian clergy in America, calling them a "stumbling block to civilizaton" for the immigrants who ought to be becoming "Americans." He saw the immigrants being indoctrinated with the oppressive social ideas of the Old World. There was one exception. He liked Paul Anderson who founded the first Norwegian Lutheran Church in Chicago — the one that today is known as "Lakeview." (When my son Mark was going to college in Chicago, he attended this church.) M. Falk Gjertsen, a prominent Minneapolis clergyman, opposed Thrane, but he was praised by Kristofer Janson, a pastor who had converted to Unitarianism.

Social reform on behalf of Norwegian immigrants was Thrane's passion. Among other things, he advocated an eight-hour work day. A skilled writer, he also wrote and produced several plays on social themes. Some were fairly successful, though none earned much in the way of income for their fiery creator.

Thrane's most ambitious publishing venture was a philosophical-religious journal named "Daglyset" (The Daylight). Influenced by French philosophers, he advocated elimination of prejudice, superstition, ignorance and stupidity and called for "free thinking." Though he called himself a socialist (pre-marxist), Thrane continued to support private ownership of property. He often quoted Thomas Paine who said, "The world is my country and my religion is to do good." Thrane was an idealist who believed in the perfectability of human society.

Until 1872, when a worker's rally was crushed in Paris, Thrane had not been a revolutionary. Soon thereafter, however, he helped organize a rally in Chicago where the red flag was displayed and the slogan "Workers of the World Unite" was displayed on a banner.

Thrane lost confidence in constitutions and came to believe that the American office of president was an aristocracy that kept the working people in bondage. His view of America was undoubtedly influenced by his disappointing experiences in Norway. In the great Chicago fire of Oct. 8, 1871, half of the city burned. It destoyed all of the Scandinavian printing presses, so the journal ceased and Thrane was suddenly deprived of his livelihood. He moved temporarily to St. Louis. He also visited Norway but discovered that he had been forgotten.

THE SCANDINAVIAN SPIRIT

Thrane's son Arthur was a physician in Eau Claire, WI. Thrane went to live with him, having concluded that reform was impossible. When he died on April 30, 1890, he left instructions that his funeral was to be conducted without clergyman, sermon or other religious ceremonies. A memorial service for him in Chicago was attended by some 500 people. A band played the "Marseillaise," music of the French Revolution (and now the French national anthem) and everyone sang Norway's national anthem, "Ja, Vi Elsker Dette Landet."

Though I'm sure I would have disagreed with Thrane on many issues, I find much to admire in him. In his concern for the poor and politically oppressed he was far ahead of his time. Much of what he advocated we now take for granted. Norway rejected Thrane during his lifetime, but has now adopted many of his reforms. His body has been returned to Norway, with honors! While theologically a "heretic," Thrane understood the social issues of the day better than those who condemned him.

"Prophets" are a strange breed of people. Their calling is to be "gadflies." First we reject them and then we praise them. It's a risky business.

CHAPTER 51

The Mystique Of The Normans

HISTORY AND MYTH are an interesting blend. Writers of such tales are something like weavers who blend cotton and polyester. The "blended" stories are more interesting than history and more believable than myth. But once blended, it's very difficult to disentangle them.

The story of the Normans is such a mixture of myth and history. Much has been written about the descendants of the Vikings who established themselves as a major power in France, conquered England in a single battle and then established brilliant kingdoms in Italy and Sicily. A helpful book is "The Normans and their Myth," by R. H. C. Davis, Professor of Mediaeval History at the University of Birmingham in England.

As long as Charlemagne (d.814) was emperor, the Vikings avoided direct conflict with his lands. The death of his son, Louis the Pious (840), was their signal to move in. They attacked Nantes in France on St. John's Day, June 24, 842, when the city was filled with visitors. The slaughter was merciless. A Danish fleet of 600 ships attacked Hamburg, headquarters of the Archbishop Ansgar in 845, looting and burning it to the ground (see chapter 35). Ansgar barely escaped wih his life. The same year, another Danish fleet of 120 ships attacked Paris on Easter Sunday. King Charles the Bald paid them 7,000 pounds of silver to leave. The Seine River in northwest France was the highway to Paris for the Norsemen. More heavy raids were carried out in 856-861 and 885-891.

Not until 911 did the French find a way to defend themselves against Norsemen. The French King Charles made a treaty with their leader, Ganger Rolf (Rollo). He gave the Norsemen the land they already occupied provided they swore allegiance to him, kept other Vikings from entering France on the Seine, and became Christians. They accepted the offer and became ardently Christian and French. However, a few years later they added to their territory at the expense of the French king. They occupied and ruled over Normandy ("Duchy of the Northmen") for almost 300 years, until 1204 when the France reconquered it.

But in the meantime, the Normans became great architects, statesmen, patrons of scholarship, lawyers, churchmen, skilled knights, and wealthy. They were so skilled at horsemanship that their services were sought all over Europe as mercenaries. Many of them went to Italy and Sicily. Professor Davis calls this "one of the most romantic episodes in medieval history." Northern Italy was a part of the German Holy Roman Empire at that time. The southern part was under the rule of the Emperor in Constantinople and Sicily was a Moslem state.

The Normans entered Italy about 1030 as mercenaries and played one leader off against another until they controlled the southern part. They conquered Sicily. They were frequently in a military alliance with the Papacy to defend the Pope against the German emperors. They'd also raise the price for their services, depending on how badly they were needed and would switch sides if they thought their deal wasn't good enough. The last Norman king of Italy and Sicily was William II. In 1186, three years before his death, he arranged the wedding of his only daughter to Henry, the son of the German Emperor, Frederick Barbarossa, because he had no male heir. When William died, a civil war broke out. The Normans were divided and the Emperor took possession of their kingdom in 1194. That was the end of the Norman kingdom in Italy and Sicily.

But in those years of conquest, the Normans played a major role in Mediterranean politics. They had even planned a conquest of Constantinople. Many of them became members of the famed Varangian Guard which protected the Emperor. They also became the guardians of the church and assumed the role of piety, though not without the sword. The Normans in Italy and Sicily adapted themselves to the culture of the people over whom they ruled. It was only later, as their "myth" began to grow, that they reclaimed their Scandinavian heritage. Nostalgia influenced their effort to establish a history that had the flavor of romance.

Back in France, the Scandinavian blood line became thin among the ruling classes. Many of the original settlers came as warriors and did not bring wives as they had to England and Ireland. So they intermarried with the French and became a vigorous hybrid race. After settling

172

down, most of them forgot their language and customs, like many of the Scandinavians who came to America in the 19th century. The Scandinavian heritage has been retained in America chiefly in those places where there's been a high density of Scandinavian population and where local leadership has kept it alive. There never was any sizeable Scandinavian population in Italy or Sicily, though considerably more in Normandy. The Danes made up the largest part of the Scandinavians in Normandy. There were also a considerable number of Norwegians from Ireland, including those who had moved from Ireland to northwest England.

The Normans are best remembered for conquering England in a one-day battle at Hastings on Oct. 14, 1066. Duke William put together an army which included soldiers of fortune from many nations besides Normandy. His battle with Harald Godwinson of Viking and Anglo-Saxon stock was won by good strategy. Harald didn't lack bravery or ability. He'd fought a fierce battle in the north of England against an army led by the mighty King Harald Hardrada of Norway three weeks earlier. William had landed without opposition and was well entrenched by the time Harald met him in battle. One Norman arrow ended the war and the history of England took new directions.

The Normans weren't content just with the occupation of England. They remade it into their own image. French became the official language and the great Anglo-Saxon cathedrals and other public buildings were torn down to be rebuilt in Norman style. For two centuries, English was almost an "underground" language in its own country. The Normans were ruthless in suppressing rebellions. A large tapestry preserved in the Old Archbishop's Palace at Bayeux in Normandy is a famous piece of propaganda telling of the conquest.

Normandy was frequently visited by Norsemen. Olaf Haraldsson, known as "St. Olaf," visited Normandy on one of his pirate expeditions and was baptized at Rouen about 1013. History shows that he took his conversion seriously and became a great king. His respect for law and religion may have come from his stay in Normandy.

The Norman rule in England was relatively short, lasting only until 1154 when Henry II from the Plantagenet family became king. Only one of his great-grandparents had been Norman. The Scandinavian blood line had thinned out even more. Yet no event in all England's history has affected it so much as the Norman era. Despite the distance separating the Normans from their Scandinavian past, it is to Scandinavia that their historians have turned to establish their beginnings. After 1154, they became Anglo-French, but their influence on the English language seems destined to last forever.

The interest in "roots" has taken hold of Scandinavians in the United States and Canada. This comes as a surprise to many people in their ancient homelands. People need an identification with their past. It's difficult to know who you are if you don't know who you've been. The myths which become a part of our history make a more interesting story to tell our children.

CHAPTER 52

The Hongs Of Northfield

A FEW MILES TO THE SOUTHEAST of Wolford, ND, a grain elevator bearing the name "Hong" used to mark the horizon's landscape. I knew almost everyone in that community from 1952-1957 while pastor of the Wolford Lutheran Church. I was surprised to learn that the grain elevator was named after the father of a famous Norwegian-American professor at St. Olaf College in Northfield, MN, Dr. Howard Hong. (The elevator burned down in the mid 1960s).

Howard Hong was born in Wolford on Oct. 19, 1912, but moved to Minnesota with his parents as an infant. I became acquainted with his uncle, Rev. George Nerison, who used to spend summers in Wolford during his retirement years. In his teens, Howard worked for Gamble-Robinson in Willmar, MN, sorting vegetables and fruit. Earning a degree from St. Olaf College in the depth of the Great Depression (1934), Howard went on to study at Washington State, the British Museum and earned a PhD at the University of Minnesota in 1938. His list of achievements is too large for full comment in this story.

Edna Hong grew up in a Norwegian-American home at Thorpe, WI, and received a St. Olaf degree in 1938. She has had a distinguished career as a homemaker, translator, writer and lecturer. As a child, one of her jobs was to keep the woodbox filled. Out of those beginnings have come keen insights into life that she continues to impart.

The Hongs were featured in a book entitled "Growing Up in Minnesota," in which ten writers reminisced about their childhoods, edited by Chester G. Anderson (University of Minnesota Press, 1976). In it the Hongs tell about their eight children (two of whom were adopted from Latvia). Howard was also a tree farmer. I remember friends who had attended St. Olaf telling me how the Hong's Northfield house was built around a tree.

They have not only been endowed with great talents, but the Hongs have been humanitarians. Howard was Field Secretary for War

Prisoners Aid of the United States, Scandinavia and Germany from 1943-1946. After the war, he was Senior Representative in Service to Refugees for the Lutheran World Federation in Germany and Austria (1947-1949), and served in a similar capacity for the World Council of Churches in Germany at the same time. In addition to his teaching at St. Olaf and travels, he also found time to lecture at Holden Village on Lake Chelan, WA, during the summers of 1963-1970.

It was as a translator and interpreter of Soren Kierkegaard that the Hongs achieved special fame in the academic world. The Kierkegaard Library at St. Olaf College is named after Howard and Edna. It's a center for study and scholarly reflection. The space for the center is on the sixth floor of Holland Hall, an attic of a building patterned after the fortress monastery of Mont St. Michel on the coast of Normandy. Built in 1925, it became the architectural model for most buildings on the campus.

More than 7,500 books and other materials fill the library shelves, including their own personal collections of works by and about the famous Danish philosopher. One hundred sixty microfilm reels of Kierkegaard's manuscripts and papers from the Royal Library in Copenhagen are available to researchers. One file contains more than 3,000 articles, clippings, reviews, notes, and leaflets written about Kirkegaard, both during his lifetime and after. The Hongs presented the Library as a gift to St. Olaf College and it's open to all people of inquiring minds. Dr. C. Stephen Evans, Associate Professor of Philosophy at St. Olaf, is curator of the Library.

Howard started seriously studying Kierkegaard when a student of Prof. David F. Swenson at the University of Minnesota back in the 1930s. Swenson had a profound influence on future scholars through his teaching of Kierkegaard. When he died, his wife learned Danish so she could continue his work. Howard is now the general editor of the definitive 26-volume Princeton University Press edition of "Kierkegaard's Works."

In 1983, the Hongs became the first recipients of the Minnesota Humanities Commission's annual Public Lecture Award. The award was to recognize Minnesotans who have "made significant contributons to the understanding of humanities." The citation reads: "The work of Edna H. and Howard V. Hong is exemplary in showing that the private lives of scholars and the public lives of stewards can be woven into whole lives of service on behalf of the humanities."

The first book I read by Edna Hong was "Muskego Boy," published in 1944. I still regard it as one of the best children's books written. Another book by Edna, "Wild Blue Berries" (1987) is a mystery novel about a young pastor, Paul Amundson, which takes place on the north shore of Lake Superior. He discovered that his great-grandfather, Poul Amundson (1885-1912), and his great-grandmother, Margaret (1891-1912), had just begun their married life and church ministry in northern Minnesota when they both suddenly and mysteriously died. They had mistaken poison berries for blueberries. The strange part was that they knew the difference between the berries and yet met their fatal ends from the "Clintoni borealis," a blue-bead lily.

Four generations later, the young pastor discovered that their deaths were murders of revenge because his great-grandfather had not married one of the young women of his parish. To complicate it more, young Paul had arrived at the parish of his great-grandfather as a bachelor and fell in love with the great-granddaughter of the offending party. It's an exciting story how the tale unravels and the "curse" of the past deed had covered the descendants of this intrigue of jealousy. The book is especially interesting to those who want to learn some of the old Norwegian words that have been forgotten by most people today. It also has a good understanding of human nature and soul care.

The Hongs are also sensitive to the life situation for Native Americans. Edna's book "The Way of the Sacred Tree" (1982) gives a knowledgeable picture of American Indians, their wisdom, traditions and suffering. Howard discovered early in his life that much of the history written about the earliest Americans was neither honest nor respectful of their humanity.

Many honors have deservedly been given to the Hongs. Howard received the J. A. O. Preus Award for Humanitarian Service in 1953 and was named "Midwest Father of the Year" in 1954. Both Howard and Edna received Denmark's "Knight of the Order of Dannebrog" in 1978. In 1987, they received the Doctor of Humane Letters from Carleton College, the across town neighbor to St. Olaf, in addition to many other honorary degrees.

The best testimony to the Hongs, however, is what former St. Olaf students tell about them. Their home welcomed students for visiting and learned discussions. Their children grew up in an atmosphere of openness and charity. I admit to being impressed by my many seminary classmates who were St. Olaf grads. They received a quality liberal arts education at the feet of this learned, but unassuming, professor. Those are the best credentials any teacher could have.

Grain elevator.

CHAPTER 53

The Wisconsin 'Birkebeiners'

WHILE THE 1988 OLYMPICS were going on in Calgary, the largest cross-country ski race in America was taking place at Cable, in northern Wisconsin, near the Telemark Lodge. More than 6,000 skiers hit the trail on Saturday, Feb. 20 for the 16th Annual Curel American Birkebeiner. There are two trails. One is 55 kilometers (about 34 miles) and the other is 29 kilometers (about 18 miles).

Even though the dates conflicted with the Olympics, the organizers did not feel that the competition was harmful. Konrad Hallenbarter of Switzerland, winner of the 1987 Birkebeiner, was in Canada competing for a gold medal. He returned in 1989 and took second, losing to the 1988 and 1989 winner, Orjan Blomquist of Sweden, by four-tenths of a second. The publicity of the Olympics increased the attendance from the previous year. In 1987 the lack of snow was a problem and the race had to be cut down to about seven miles. However, in the year of the Olympics, northern Wisconsin had more than 18 inches of snow.

Skiers from all over the skiing world are attracted to the Wisconsin event, even though there is no money for winning. Orjan Blomquist came hoping to win as his brother, Anders, won in 1986. Blomquist said, "Compared to other races here in America, I think this is one of the very best." Recognition is given for both the best men and women skiers. The 1989 winner in the women's division was Elizabeth Youngman of Newbury, OH, who races bicycles in the summer. She is also No. 1 in the Greater American Ski Chase (GASC).

The "Birkebeiner" ski meet, founded in 1973, was named after Norway's Birkebeiner Rennet, a race which celebrates the flight of Prince Haakon, an heir to the Norwegian throne in the early 13th century. He was carried by his father's warriors on a secret journey to safety in the dead of winter. As a child, he was in constant danger of being killed or kidnapped. His arch-enemy was his half-brother, Jarl Skule Baardson, not of royal blood. Together with his mother, Haakon was brought to Trondheim in a journey full of hazards and hardships to be under the protection of King Ingi. There he was reared to become king.

At age 13, he became King Haakon IV and ruled Norway from 1217 to 1263, though his coronation did not take place until 1247. His grandfather, King Sverre (reigned 1184-1202), had been a powerful ruler. He had come to power through a peasant uprising of people called "Birchlegs." They were so poor that they wrapped their legs in birch bark. This is the derivation of the name "Birkebeiner." These peasants forced the election of Haakon at a Thing, even though he was illegitimately born. His father was King Haakon III who ruled for only two years (reigned 1202-1204). Ingi Baardson ruled Norway from 1204 to 1217.

From 1198 until Haakon IV took command, Norway was under an Interdict by Pope Innocent III, one of the most powerful papal rulers of the Middle Ages. It was an attempt to discipline King Sverre's Birchlegs. There had been a struggle between the church and the king which resulted in the bloodiest and most bitter war in Norway's history. The Archbishop of Lund read the "bull of excommunication" against the Birchlegs. Sverre did not blame the Pope but the bishops for "misinforming" the papacy about affairs in Norway. The king held the upper hand, but his followers were a ravishing rabble, burning the homes of their enemies and showing no mercy. He tried to control their cruelty and forbade them when he was able to wreak pillage and revenge. With the accession of Haakon IV to the throne of Norway, the Interdict was lifted and Norway returned to the fold of the Faithful in the church.

Haakon IV's rule was not always peaceable. There were uprisings among the lower classes of people against the tyranny of the sheriffs and other royal servants. The wealthier classes also rebelled. In 1228, the farmers hanged the last of the rebel leaders and peace came at last. The struggle was not between the king and the nobles, but rather with those who wanted to be kings. The alignment with the nobles, however, separated the king from the people who had supported him. Legal issues were settled in the Thing assemblies and the old folk laws prevailed.

It was during Haakon's time that many stave churches were built. Once there were over a thousand of these beautiful structures. Today there are 33. These are the most famous of all Norwegian monuments. They were put together without nails or spikes out of pine trees. The interiors were built according to the plan of the Romanesque basilicas with choir (place for singers), three aisles, and rounded arches. They had elaborate wood carvings, especially at the entrance. The ceiling, pillars and walls were decorated with brilliant primary colors. The frequent use of dragon carvings is a dominant motif on the outside of the churches.

Those who wield power frequently abuse it. Haakon IV was no exception. He tried to bring all of the overseas colonies of Norwegians under his control. The Orkneys, the Hebrides, and the Isle of Man were considered the proper spheres of influence for the kings of Norway.

His two major political achievements were to bring Iceland and Greenland under Norwegian rule, with the help of the bishop of Trondheim who claimed spiritual authority over the church in those distant islands. Snorri Sturluson, Iceland's great saga writer and speaker, had been a confidant of the king in Trondheim. But when Snorri opposed the royal policies and resisted the king's attempt to seize the island, Haakon had him murdered in 1241 on his own farm. This signal for Norway's taking over the land was accomplished between 1262 and 1264, after Iceland's resistance was exhausted. The Icelanders agreed to pay taxes and turn over their fines to King Haakon for every murder committed in the land. They were allowed to keep their ancient law codes.

The acquisition of Greenland was another of Haakon's accomplishments. A bishop had been sent from Norway who was instructed to act as the king's agent. The walrus tusk business was highly profitable for Haakon. In exchange he sent iron and timber to the Greenlanders.

The king of Scotland, Alexander III, repeatedly tried to buy the Hebrides islands from Haakon. He refused each offer. When word came that the Scots were going to attack the Hebrides, Haakon, now an old man, called for a levy of soldiers and gathered the largest fleet any king of Norway had assembled. Neither king wanted battle, so Alexander waited until the winter storms set in. This forced the Norwegian fleet to return. Haakon, exhausted and ill, died just before Christmas 1263 and was buried in Kirkwall in the Orkney Islands. His son, Magnus VI (reigned 1263-1280), sold the Hebrides and the Island of Man to Scotland by the Treaty of Perth in 1266.

THE SCANDINAVIAN SPIRIT

The Norwegian empire of Haakon was solid because it was built by colonization instead of conquest. This was the time when Norway was, according to historian Karen Larson, "mistress of the most far-flung colonial empire and the greatest sea power of the North."

It all started with the "Birchlegs" risking their lives to carry a small child through perilous winter travel in forests and mountains. What if they had failed? The history of Norway in the Middle Ages would have been a different story.

Every year, skiers from many parts of the world gather at Cable, WI, to celebrate the rescue of a prince with a ski race. They ski up to 33 miles for a prize without money. That's the spirit of the "Birkebeiners."

Cross-country skier.

CHAPTER 54

The Swedes Of Lindsborg, Kansas

I FIRST HEARD ABOUT Lindsborg, KS, from Bud and Beulah Mattson, who were friends of our family when we lived in St. Louis. Both of them graduated from Bethany College in Lindsborg and were proud of it.

My awareness of Lindsborg was revived by a letter from Irwin Fisk of Pasadena. He'd gotten a copy of my Scandinavian Heritage article "Tracing a Family Name" and asked me to share more information on the Fisk(e)s. Irwin edits an annual newsletter with a fairly large circulation which traces its history to Symond Fiske who lived in Suffolk County England back in the 1400s. A native Kansan, Irwin and his wife had purchased a house in Lindsborg and were excited about the Swedish history and customs of the community.

The Swedes of Lindsborg are lovers of culture. Each year, between Palm Sunday and Easter, they put on the "Messiah Festival of Music and Art." The first festival was held March 28, 1882, in Bethany Lutheran Church. The eight-day festival is busy all week long with an excellent program. I saw a live telecast of Lindsborg's "Messiah" concert on Public Television in 1986.

Many people return to Lindsborg each year like it's a religious pilgrimage. They meet in the Presser Auditorium on the Bethany College campus which seats 1,900 people. The choir is limited to 400 singers. The orchestra has about 60 members. Soloists come from New York as well as Kansas. Handel's "Messiah" is performed on Palm Sunday and Easter, and Bach's "St. Matthew's Passion" is presented on Good Friday. Organ workshops and concerts are also held.

The 1988 celebration was a special event. It honored Dr. Elmer Copley, Conductor of the Bethany Oratorio Society since 1960 and who retired that year. For 29 seasons Dr. Copley has poured his talent and energy into dedicated service to the community. He was Distinguished Professor of Music (Voice) on the Bethany faculty. His choirs have received excellent reviews both in Scandinavia and America. He has continued his work in music after retirement from the Bethany faculty.

The Midwest Art Exhibition is a part of the festival. It's the largest in Kansas and has been held since 1900. This is held in the Birger Sandzel Memorial Gallery on the campus of Bethany College.

How did Swedes ever get to Kansas? From the start, Lindsborg was destined to be a center of high quality culture. Olof Olsson was educated in Sweden to be both a pastor and a church organist. In 1869, at age 28, he led 250 of his parishioners from Sweden to make their home in America. Over 100 of them settled in the Smokey River Valley of Kansas. After only six weeks, Olsson organized Bethany Lutheran congregation and became the recognized leader of the community. Just two weeks after arrival he began the naturalization process to become an American citizen. A year later he became the superintendent of schools of McPherson County and organized eight grade schools. He was also elected to the state legislature where he sponsored bills to protect immigrants from exploitation on the labor market and to protect farmers from having their land overrun by the great cattle drives from Texas to Abilene.

The Swedish school which later became Bethany College opened its doors in October 1881. Ten students, both boys and girls, were enrolled, but before the year ended there were 27 students. The second year they had three classrooms with a faculty of five and 92 students. The organizer was Carl Swensson, a young seminary graduate only 22 years old. Chosen by Olsson, he proved to be an excellent choice. J. A. Udden, who later became an eminent geologist, taught all the classes except religion in the first year. Swedish congregations of Kansas gave support to the school and in its third year (1883), they had a new steam-heated brick and stone building with classrooms, dormitories and a dining room. They offered teacher education, classics and scientific courses, emphasizing both Swedish and English.

The 1880s began as "boom" years in Kansas. Farm land was easily available through the railroads and the Homestead Act. Credit was easy to get and heavy mortgages were common. The rainfall was generous and the crops were abundant on the rich prairie soil.

But as you could guess, the prosperity didn't continue forever. The lean years came. Rainfall failed in 1887 and for several years afterwards.

Crop failures brought bank failures. The eastern banks withdrew their loan money. One newspaper cartoon said, "In God we trusted; in Kansas we busted!"

Bethany College felt the pinch. The financial support which had been available at the beginning dried up with the drought. As creditors clamored for their mortgage payments, faculty salaries were paid in promissory notes. It got so bad that King Oscar II heard of their plight and asked the churches of Sweden for an offering to help the beleaguered college. Only $809.78 was collected. Swensson never gave up hope. His motto was "morgon blir det battre" ("tomorrow will be better").

Meanwhile, the Augustana Synod of Swedish Lutherans began to worry that they had too many schools to support. Their "flagship" was Augustana at Rock Island, IL. President Hasselquist may have feared that Bethany would rival the Illinois school for funds during those hard times. Swensson, however, held firm in his insistence that Bethany was a good investment for the Swedes. In 1889, the Bethany Academy became Bethany College and Swensson became its president. Even though they were deeply in debt, he talked the college board into building a dormitory for girls and a 4,000-seat auditorium for the annual "Messiah" presentation. By 1891, there were 334 students in all of its departments, including 33 in college studies. We need to remember, however, that even to get a high school diploma in those days was a prestigious achievement. Bethany graduates were no academic slouches. Twenty-one graduates between 1898 and 1902 continued their graduate studies at Yale.

Lindsborg, KS, is still full of Swedes and they are proud of their heritage. It's too bad that King Carl XVI Gustaf and Queen Silvia didn't have time to visit this community while they were here for the "New Sweden '88" days. They'd have received a royal welcome. However, if you should drive through Kansas, stop in a Lindsborg and visit with these fine people. They'll treat you like royalty. They're a hardy people to have survived on the prairies while remembering the best of their heritages, both Swedish and American.

If you'd like more information on the Lindsborg Swedes, write to the American-Scandinavian Association of the Great Plains, P.O. Box 265, Lindsborg, KS 67456. They publish a periodic newsletter.

CHAPTER 55

Vikings In Oklahoma?

L EE COTHRAN, WHO SPENT four years at the Minot Air Force Base, wrote a letter of appreciation to me for the "Scandinavian Heritage" column. By the time Lee went back home to Arkansas, he had become quite interested in Scandinavians from being in the Northland.

In an article entitled "Norse Runestones in America" (see "The Scandinavian World," chapter 76), I had mentioned runestones found in Oklahoma. That's a long ways from the Viking home base. Lee was particularly interested in the "Heavener Runestone" on Poteau Mountain in the Oklahoma State Park at Heavener, OK, having previously seen it. He visited it again and sent me a brochure printed by the Oklahoma Tourism and Recreation Department. He also included a close-up photo of the writing on the stone.

I found the booklet highly interesting. People, including many noted scholars, are often skeptical that the Vikings ever got past New England. But like the people of Alexandria, MN, who have made a great deal out of the "Kensington Stone," the people of Oklahoma take their runestone seriously.

According to the oral history of some Choctaw Indians in the 1830s, they discovered this stone while on a hunting trip. It was on reservation land to which they were relocated after they were forced to leave their homes in Mississippi. They were pretty astonished to see the eight strange looking symbols carved in the rock.

In the 1870s, white men began to come into those parts. Some bear hunters claimed to have found the runestone. In 1898, the stone was seen by Luther Capps. Logging was a major industry of the area in those days. A five-year-old girl, Laura Callahan, remembered having been shown the runestone in 1904 by her father. When Carl F. Kemmerer discovered it in 1913, people called it "Indian Rock." A decade later, Kemmerer sent copies of the lettering to the Smithsonian Institute in

Washington, DC, for identification. It turned out to be runic characters, the written, though not spoken, language of the Norsemen 1,000 years ago.

The first person to try to find out the meaning of the stone was Gloria Stewart. She spent over 30 years researching those strange letters. The area was overgrown with tangle-brush and moss covered the carvings. It was then renamed the "Heavener Runestone."

The oldtimers in the community told that once there had been many such stones. All but two were destroyed in the 1930s and 40s by souvenir hunters. Unfortunately, no copies of the inscriptions were made before they were destroyed.

The heavener stone stands in a vertical position in a deep ravine, protected from the wind. It's 12 feet high, 10 feet wide and is 16 inches thick. The characters are six to nine inches high. A variety of scholars who were specialists in ancient history, runology, geology, philology, archaeology, and anthropology, have shown interest in the carvings. A meeting attended in 1959 by a Viking scholar, a geologist and members of the Oklahoma State Historical Society concluded that neither Indians, French nor Spaniards could have done the rune carving. The only other answer seems to be that Vikings had travelled up the Mississippi River and followed tributaries into the Heavener area.

Land was donated in 1965 to create a park and to protect the stone. A steel cage was built around it to protect it from vandals. The park was dedicated in 1970.

The translation of the writing has been a major obstacle. Six of the rune inscriptions were from Old Norse of about 300 A.D. and two came from about 800 A.D. A runic scholar from Norway transliterated the letters as GNOMEDAL, but there is no such word in Old Norse or any other known language. Several scholars who had not actually seen the rock or studied the carvings decided that it was a modern fake. They did not realize, however, that the fine-grained Savanna sandstone is a very hard rock which would take a skilled carver. Neither had they seen the weathering on the rock.

Alf Monge, a former U.S. Army cryptographer, has offered an explanation which seems a possibility to me. Monge, born in Norway, claims that the runic writing spells GAOMEDAT, but that it isn't meant to be a word. He identified it as an ancient practice of Norse clergymen who wrote crypto-puzzles, almost like riddles with hidden messages. He translates it as a date - Nov. 11, 1012. This is St. Martin's Day on the old Norse calendar, the "primstav." The date commemorates a venerable Christian bishop of Tours in France, after whom Martin Luther was named on his baptismal day in 1483. Monge explained that the two different alphabets were intentional to give the month, day and year.

But how did this come to be written way out in Oklahoma? Just 12 years earlier the first Norse ships arrived in eastern Canada. The colony didn't last more than a few years. The theory is that one of the ships went exploring in the Gulf of Mexico instead of returning to Greenland and that members of its crew found their way up the Arkansas and Poteau Rivers to Heavener in 1012. The Christian influence of King Olaf Tryggvason would explain the reference to St. Martin's Day.

In 1967, some 13-year-old boys found another inscription, dated Nov. 11, 1017, about ten miles away dated Nov. 24, 1024, was found with five runic characters. A fascinating similarity in writing style is found in the Shawnee Indian inscriptions. Could it be that the Shawnees might have copied or learned some things from those Vikings, or was this just accidental?

Nobody knows who the mysterious writers were. My guess is that Vikings may very well have found their way into central United States. That was a time of expansion for them. They travelled far into Russia, into the Mediterranean lands and into the islands of the north Atlantic. There was no place that they were afraid to go. They didn't all have success, however. Many drowned at sea and few of those who strayed too far away returned home again.

The runestones carry mysteries that will be with us for a long while, but there is a lot of interest in them. I had a letter from John V. Bodin of Cokato, MN, who'd read the story on the Kensington Stone in my book, "The Scandinavian Heritage." Of Swedish descent, he's been a long-time student of these runic mysteries and has made a trip to the site where the stone was found three miles northeast of Kensington, MN.

I suspect that a few more stones with runic writing may lie buried in the earth along the rivers of America. Let's hope that those who discover them will not just dump them into a trash heap. There's a lot more we'd all like to know about early visitors to America.

If you drive through eastern Oklahoma, look up Heavener and its famous runestone. Heavener is about 50 miles south and a little bit west of Ft. Smith, AR. Then decide for yourself if the Vikings wrote it and what they might have been doing in those hills.

CHAPTER 56

The Swedes In North Dakota

1 988 WAS THE "YEAR OF THE SWEDES" and they celebrated it with gusto and pride. The Swedes had been in America for 350 years! In 1975 when the Norwegians celebrated 150 years since their immigration began under the leadership of Cleng Peerson, there were special celebrations in 12 cities across the United States.

The Swedes had celebrations in 88 cities. From Boston to San Francisco, from Houston to Minneapolis, and from Seattle to Tampa, people were hyped up to remember that little settlement of about 500 people who built log cabins on the banks of the Delaware River in 1638. It was a glorious time in Swedish history. Swedish armies were respected and feared. Their greatest king, Gustavus II Adolphus (reigned 1594-1632), called the "Lion of the North," had rescued northern Germany from the armies of the Holy Roman Empire. It's the only known army in modern history that didn't have "camp followers" to spread venereal disease among the troops. Instead, chaplains led the soldiers in prayer twice a day and a sermon once a week. They sang hymns in battle. (See "The Scandinavian Heritage," chapter 53.)

One of the early Swedish settlers, Peter Minuit, bought Manhattan Island from the Indians for $24 and founded the first Swedish settlement there in 1638. It took another 233 years for the first Swedes to become established in North Dakota at Harwood near Fargo. Between 1880 and 1914, many Swedes resettled from Illinois, Iowa and Minnesota to North Dakota. They also settled in Christine (a town named after Queen Christina, daughter of King Gustavus II Adolphus), Sheyenne, Oakes, Kulm, Kintyre, Wilton, Washburn, Battleview, Lignite and Perth. The largest concentration is in the Wilton-Washburn area. Twenty North Dakota towns have Swedish place names besides Christine. Among these are Kloten, Wasa, Calmar and Svea.

Though there was a lot of dissatisfaction among Swedes about the state church in their homeland, they built many churches in America.

190

One of the picturesque buildings they constructed was Zion Lutheran Church near Souris in 1903. The community was settled in 1896. Today there is no congregation but the building is carefully preserved. The first Swedish Lutheran Church in the state was the Maple-Sheyenne congregation at Harwood. Though mainly Lutheran in their homeland and in America, Swedes also became active members of other denominations.

About 25,000 Swedes settled in North Dakota by 1910. That's only about one fifth the number of Norwegians, so they are often overlooked. Since many of them moved to communities already settled by Norwegians, they often joined existing congregations. Scandinavians generally tended to intermarry, so that Swedes soon became mingled with the Danes, Finns and Icelanders as well as Norwegians. They were attracted to America by free land. The railroads advertised for settlers so they could claim the land offered by the government in exchange for building the rail lines.

Swedes, like Norwegians, have been political activists in the New World. The Youngdahls and Andersons of Minnesota have made a strong impact on the state. John Anderson, a congressmen from Rockford, IL, ran for President of the United States in 1980. They are still trying. John Norquist, an underdog candidate for mayor of Milwaukee in 1988 defeated a better known candidate who had been lieutenant governor and acting governor of Wisconsin. Just 38 years old and without the backing of a political establishment, Norquist, a former machinist, campaigned in typical Swedish style of promising to work for greater harmony in the community. The Swedes are "peacemakers." They haven't been in a war for over 175 years.

The spirit of Swedish pride was featured at the North Dakota Heritage Center in Bismarck, called the "North Dakota Swedish Heritage" display. The panels with the pictures and information on Swedish settlers were beautifully done. They were also displayed at the Norsk Høstfest in Minot. The same informational panels were exhibited in communities around the state. Each participating community also displayed its own local Swedish artifacts.

Prof. James Kaplan of Moorhead State University was the chairperson for the Swedish celebration in North Dakota. He held a statewide convocation to commemorate the Swedish immigration to America at Jamestown College. Count Peder Bonde, Chairman of the Swedish National New Sweden '88, was the speaker. They also had films and displays, and a concert by Per Sorman and Kjell-Ake Nilsson, popular Swedish folk singers.

Kaplan is not Swedish, but he's as excited about Sweden and Swedish culture as any person you'll ever find. He grew up in Worcestor, MA, a city with many Swedes. Most of his friends were Swedish. When he was a Fulbright exchange teacher in France (he teaches French at Moorhead State), he took a job with the Swedish YMCA. He learned Swedish easily and soon travelled all over the country. When dressed up, he wears two pins. One says "Dare to be Swedish," and the other is the Swedish flag.

There were Swedish celebrations in Bismarck, Devils Lake, Fargo, Grand Forks, Jamestown and Minot in North Dakota. Fargo had a modern Swedish film festival and the Fargo-Moorhead Symphony Orchestra gave a concert of Swedish music at Concordia College. Devils Lake had a presentation of "You Can't get to Heaven though the U.S.A.," a play featuring a Swedish Lutheran pastor and an Italian Catholic priest. Swedish musical groups also toured in the state.

The Swedish immigrants to America were mostly farmers. Many of them, especially in North Dakota, are still farmers. However, most have moved to cities and brought skills needed by the building trades and industry. When I lived in New Rockford, I became well acquainted with the Swedish congregations in Sheyenne and Oberon. My next door neighbor was Ole Mattson who had been sheriff of Eddy County. So far as I know, he was the only member of First Lutheran Church who fasted before communion. It's a mark of Swedish piety.

To illustrate how far the Swedes carried on with their celebrating in 1988, the Chicago Bears and the Minnesota Vikings played a pre-season exhibition football game in Gothenburg, Sweden,. That's where they build Saab automobiles. If you can't get to Sweden, I suggest that you watch the newspapers for some Swedish events. You might be surprised how many people will turn up that you didn't know were Swedes. They're a proud people.

CHAPTER 57

The Spring Grove Norwegians

"VELKOMMEN TIL SPRING GROVE" (Welcome to Spring Grove) is the headline on the brochure describing a famous Norwegian-American community in southeast Minnesota. Spring Grove claims to be the first Norwegian settlement in Minnesota. They hold a three-day celebration in May to coincide with the "Syttende Mai" (17th of May) festival, which commemorates the Norwegian constitution of 1814. They've been celebrating this event annually since 1971.

Norwegians began moving into Fillmore and Houston counties in 1852. Lars Tollefsen of Hallingdal, Norway, brought his family to Riceford, just inside the Houston County line, that year. When the railroad by-passed Riceford in October 1879, Lars moved some of the buildings into Fillmore County to the railroad where the town of Mabel was established just seven miles from Spring Grove. Riceford then became a ghost town. The Tollefsens had previously lived a short time in Wisconsin.

The following year, Norse settlers started coming in caravans. A few years later, many of them moved to the Dakotas and Montana. There were quite a few Fillmore county people in the Wolford, ND, community. One of the churches of those early settlements was named "Bloomfield." (There's also a Bloomfield Church at Upham, ND, and one north of Glendive, MT, near Lindsey. My earliest roots in America come from near Blooming Prairie, a short distance to the west of Spring Grove. After a dozen years, my great-grandparents moved to Walcott, ND. It was the typical pattern of early immigrants.)

The Spring Grove folks plan an interesting weekend for visitors in their Syttende Mai festival. They have a quilt show, a parade, some "Big Stakes Bingo," arts and crafts, a Fiddler's Bee, some historic bus tours, evening entertainment, and a Norwegian church service on Sunday with a dinner served by the local Sons of Norway. Hikers may like to go on the "Folkemarsj," a 10 or 20 kilometer walking trail through some of their most scenic countryside.

A local genealogist, Georgia Rosendahl, is on hand to help people discover their Scandinavian origins. She has traced the roots of the earliest settlers to the present descendants. Georgia's father-in-law, Peter Julius Rosendahl (1878-1942), who farmed near Spring Grove, produced the "Ola og (and) Per" cartoons from 1918-1935. They were printed in the "Decorah-Posten." I'm indebted to Georgia for some of the information in this story.

Since Decorah, IA, is only 22 miles away, they offer a trip to Vesterheim, the most prestigious Norwegian-American museum in North America. Just another 50 miles away is Norskedalen, near Coon Valley and Westby in Wisconsin. Norskedalen is a 350-acre site nestled in the palisades of the Mississippi River which looks a lot like parts of Norway. Tours were arranged to visit the Steam Engine Museum in Mabel. The steam engines draw about 35,000 people on Labor Day weekend for an old time thresher's show. It began in 1953 on the Gerhard Clauson farm near Hesper, IA.

The Spring Grove folks also offer a tour of the Amish community near Harmony. Over 100 Amish families live there. Besides farming with horses, they make quilts, baskets, furniture and other crafts to sell. One of the host farms has a barn built by Mr. Allis of the Allis-Chalmers company. The famous racing horses, Dan Patch and Tommy Briton, were raised here. Nearby is the largest limestone quarry in southern Minnesota.

Syttende Mai isn't the only celebration these Scandinavian enthusiasts of southeast Minnesota hold. In July they put on Rodgers and Hammerstein's "South Pacific." The production takes place in Ye Olde Opera House, a community theatre. In addition to reserved seating, people bring blankets and sat under the stars while listening to "Some Enchanted Evening." A "Fall Foliage Festival" is held in October. Anyone who has taken a drive along the Mississippi in early October knows what a feast of color it is to the eyes. They call this the "Bluff Country." But by whatever name it's called, this is a delightful place of American beauty.

Spring Grove is near Burr Oak, IA, the home for the "Little House on the Prairie." Laura Ingalls Wilder's books have their setting in this area. There's a historic site named after the famed author in Spring Grove.

There are caves to visit in the area. Mystery Cave is near Spring Valley and Niagara Cave is near Harmony. For people who want to know more about the early settlers to the area, the Fillmore County Historical Centre in Fountain is open Monday through Friday.

Trinity Lutheran Church in Spring Grove was organized in 1855 by the Norwegian Synod with 700 souls. That was a pretty big membership for a beginning congregation. They had grown to 1,200 by 1914. Among those 1,200 were four Swedes, a German and an American. Trinity is a congregation with vision. Not only did they have a ten-acre cemetery, but they had an additional 60 acres of farm land. In 1893, they built a brick church that cost $20,000. Their first parsonage cost $5,000 in 1858. The Spring Grove Norwegians took a lot of pride in their church. Today they have over 1,600 members in a town of less than 1,300. Besides Trinity, there are many more congregations of Norwegian origin in the Spring Grove area which are active to this day.

How did it happen that so many Norwegians found their way to southeast Minnesota? After Cleng Peerson's famed voyage in his sloop named the "Restauration" in 1825, whose passengers settled in upstate New York, later Norwegian immigrants went to the Fox River Valley west of Chicago. They kept on moving, however, and soon were in Racine County, WI, and in the Madison and LaCrosse areas. They came in such large numbers that there wasn't land enough for them in the earlier settlements. They'd stay with other Norwegians, often people from their home communities in Norway. A barn was not considered a bad place to sleep as they moved on to their eventual destinations. Always they heard the stories of more land for less money out west.

They were fortunate for the most part. The land purchased near Indian Hill, southeast of Milwaukee, was no paradise. But if you drive through that area today you will find beautiful farmland with well kept buildings. They did better in their land purchases in western Wisconsin and in Minnesota. My father told me that some were too eager for land as they came to the Dakotas. Many came in the winter when snow covered the ground and were victims of sharp land agents. The sales pitch often turned out to be much better than the soil. Once purchased, it was too late. They were deep in debt. Still, many of them stuck it out and did well, despite drought, rocks, grasshoppers, hailstorms and disappointing grain prices.

So if your Norse roots should have a Spring Grove connection, you'd enjoy visiting with these good friends at one of their festival times. For more information, write Karen B. Gray, 222 Highway 44E, Spring Grove, MN 55974. The people of Spring Grove have not forgotten their heritage. May their kind continue.

CHAPTER 58

Swedish-Soviet Relations

S WEDEN AND RUSSIA HAVE KNOWN each other for a long time. The Swedish Vikings ventured mainly to the east and onto the rivers of Russia in their quest for trade. They organized the first Russian kingdom at Kiev and gave their own name, "Rus," to the land. Norwegian kings also visited Russia. Both Olaf Tryggvason and Olaf Haraldsson (St. Olaf) were in exile among their fellow countrymen in Russia when life was too dangerous back home.

The boundary between Sweden and Russia was often contested. Many battles were fought, the Swedes won a few, but lost more. In 1808, the Russians moved into Finland, then Swedish territory, and occupied it until 1917. With the aid of Kaiser Wilhelm's army, the Finns drove out the Soviets after the Bolshevik revolution.

Sweden remained neutral during both World Wars, but has kept a wary eye on its boundaries to the east. In the last few years, however, the Soviets have been trespassing Swedish territorial rights. This is in spite of the good public relations image that Mikhail Gorbachev has going for him in the West.

Ernest Conine of the "Los Angeles Times" wrote an article entitled "Why are Soviet subs in Swedish waters?" He stated that Soviet "minisubs have actually landed frogmen on Swedish territory." Soviet defectors, he noted, have said that "in event of a war in Europe, the Soviets would land saboteurs and assassins assigned to eliminate political leaders and key military personnel in enemy countries."

The Swedes take this threat seriously but don't protest loudly about it. They have, however, moved some military personnel into new secret quarters. While the Swedes have assured the Soviets that they will not be a part of any aggressive actions against them, they've also made it clear that they'll fight to defend their territory.

In the late 1970s, the Soviet subs started moving into Swedish territory. A Soviet sub ran aground near the Karlskrona naval base in

October, 1981. When questioned, the Soviet captain said his radio equipment was broken down and that his gyrocompass and depth gauge were malfunctioning. But six more Soviet subs were discovered in the fjord near Stockholm just a year later. Were they all lost?

What ideas could the Soviet military leaders have on Swedish territory? Western military experts see Sweden as a convenient route for an attack on Norway in case of war. Norway is a member of NATO while Sweden is officially neutral. Soviet commandos would move in first to destroy Swedish defenses.

The Swedish policy of neutrality has kept them from making an international issue of the Soviet incursions on their territory, even though they have frequently been vocal about the foreign policies of other countries. But one has to understand that it is common for small countries to sometimes criticize their friends and be silent towards their potential enemies. The danger is that such silence will invite more violations. It's a Scandinavian trait to give subtle signals when they mean to be protesting loudly. A veteran Swedish diplomat, Sverker Astrom, surprised people when he suggested at UCLA that the United States should take the lead in getting the Soviets to stop violating Swedish territory.

To make things look better, Soviet Prime Minister Nikolai Ryzhkov visited Norway and Sweden on a good will tour in January 1988 and settled some old disputes about fishing rights in the Baltic Sea and agreed to supply natural gas to Sweden.

Swedish Prime Minister Ingvar Carlsson has issued a warning that "blood will flow" unless these violations stop. Officially the Soviets deny that any infringements are taking place and that "right wing" elements in Sweden are causing all the trouble. In contrast to Carlsson, the late Prime Minister Olof Palme drew criticism for his neutralism. An article by Henrik Bering-Jensen in the Feb. 8, 1988, issue of "Insight," stated that "Soviet Foreign Minister Andrei Gromyko in Stockholm in January 1984 . . . promised to respect our neutrality policy."

Swedish naval officers complain that they are not allowed to sink the Soviet subs. They've been ordered to try to force the subs to surface instead by dropping the depth charges at a safe distance in order to avoid a diplomatic crisis. Still Soviet submarines keep coming into Swedish waters. Thirty violations were noted in the last half of 1987, some as close as a dozen miles from the business district of Stockholm.

Any visitor to Sweden soon learns that the Swedish people are pro-American even when their government doesn't talk that way. It has been suggested that the Soviets are testing Swedish neutrality to see just how pro-Western they are. When Ryzhkov was in Stockholm, he told the Swedes, "Bomb us, by all means." It appears he was taunting them to break their position of neutrality, knowing that the Swedish government will do all in its power to maintain their peace which has lasted for over 175 years.

The Nordic countries are in a difficult position. Denmark and Norway are under the protection of NATO. But their borders are close to the heavily armed Warsaw Pact nations, whereas the Scandinavians appear to pursue peace like there is no evil to fear.

Finland is the most sensitive of all the Scandinavian countries about its relations to the Soviet Union. They are careful not to disturb Soviet paranoia. Yet in my visit to Finland and talking to people, they made no hesitations to express their pro-American feelings. I got the impression that they are expecting the United States to be their umbrella against the Soviets even without a formal alliance. The only reason that Finland has any degree of freedom today is because Roosevelt and Churchill denied Stalin's request to include the Finns in the Eastern Block at the Teheran Conference in December, 1943. Stalin did admit, according to Charles E. Bohlen's "Witness to History: 1929-1969," that "any country which fought with such courage for its independence (as Finland) deserved consideration."

All countries operate security and counter-espionage programs against foreign spying activities. The Soviets are experts at espionage and have had a strong secret police since the days of the Czars. Peter Wright's book, "Spy Catcher," claims that the Soviets have penetrated the security systems of most western nations. Wright believes that the head of the British Military Intelligence (MI5) for domestic surveillance was headed for many years by a Soviet agent who was a British citizen. The British government tried to block the publication of this book both in England and Australia.

THE SCANDINAVIAN SPIRIT

This information is troubling to us who have family connections in Scandinavia. These are a peace loving people who have often turned "the other cheek." Yet we remember the heroic resistance of Finland and Norway in World War II, and how the Danes frustrated Hitler's attempt to turn them into a "caged canary." During those years, the Swedes assisted their Scandinavian neighbors at considerable cost and risk while maintaining their neutrality. Peace requires courage, but it also helps to have some powerful friends.

CHAPTER 59

The Adventures Of Svein 'Forkbeard'

IF THERE EVER WAS a Viking buccaneer that pleased the hearts of the warlike Norsemen, it was Svein Haraldsson, better known as "Forkbeard" (Tjugskegg). Today we'd pronounce his name "Sven." He was the son of Harald "Bluetooth" (Blautand), son of Gorm the Old (Gamle). Those were mighty men. Gorm was the first king to unite Denmark under one rule. Harald supported the Christian faith. Svein gained his fame by conquering England.

Svein was born to be a warrior. He even drove his father out of Denmark. At the sea battle off the island of Svold, he ambushed and defeated his brother-in-law, Olaf Tryggvason, who jumped overboard in full armor and drowned rather than surrender to Svein. Alliances have a way of changing. Olaf had come to England as Svein's ally, though they were destined to be enemies. After Tryggvason's death, Svein also claimed rule over the southern part of Norway.

It was not by accident that Denmark was a military power in those days. The tiny North Sea land had become a heavily armed encampment with four major marshalling points. These staging areas had elaborate castles for protection. It was a "brilliantly organized military machine," according to Danish historian Palle Lauring. The Danish soldiers were no longer peasant farmers and adventurers who left home for a summer to get rich quickly. They had become full fledged professionals. I visited the ruins of the largest fortress named Aggersborg on the Limfjord just north of Aalborg (see "The Scandinavian World," chapter 34). To this day it looks like the place where the ghosts of those old Vikings might still be lurking and ready to jump out at you.

For almost 200 years before Svein was king (reigned 985-1014), Danes had raided and settled in England, but had made no determined effort to conquer it. Most of the Danes lived in an area called "Danelaw" in eastern and southeastern England. As you can imagine, the Christian Anglo-Saxon English, though they were distantly related to the

Danes, fought fiercely against these intrusions into their land by these heathen foreigners.

Ethelred, the English king, earned himself the nickname "Unready." Even though he knew that the Danes would return each year for new plunder, he was never ready for battle to defend the people. Instead he followed the rule of appeasement and paid the Danes to leave with immense amounts of gold and silver collected from the people. Then the Danes went home and returned the following year for more easy money. Each year the ransom was higher. In 994, 16,000 pounds were demanded. It went up to 24,000 in 1002, 36,000 in 1007, 48,000 in 1012 and 83,000 pounds in 1018.

The invasions operated like a business. The money was used to buy more weapons and finance new invasions. It had to be repeated every year and the ante was raised to maintain the armies. Mercenary soldiers don't work for free. Many of the coins and jewelry (brooches, arm-rings, ingots, etc.) turned over to the Vikings have been found in large hordes mainly in Denmark and Sweden, and a few in Norway. I saw some of them which had been unearthed in the island of Birka (Sweden) on display in Chicago.

Ethelred made a foolish move on the night of St. Brice, Nov. 13, 1002. He ordered the slaughter of all the Danes living outside the Danelaw. Among those murdered was Lady Gunnhild, the sister of King Svein. A great cry for revenge rose up from the Danes in England and Svein rallied the people for a powerful invasion of the island. Almost every Danish noble family had lost relatives in the bloodbath.

England's fate was sealed by this blood-revenge. During the next two years Svein moved across England destroying and burning at will. Ethelred's attempt to build a navy came to nothing but confusion, destruction and desertion. Then Svein went back to Denmark to consolidate his power. He sent two great warriors in his place, Torkil the Tall and Olaf the Fat (later known as "St. Olaf").

Now it was the Viking's turn to commit a disastrous blunder. While the English were gathering up the silver and gold to pay them to leave, the Danes captured Canterbury in revenge for the St. Brice massacre. They seized Archbishop Aelfeah, who refused to pay a ransom or allow anyone else to pay for him. Angered, a Danish soldier crushed his head with an axe. With that, Torkil and Olaf switched to the English side. They may have been soldiers of fortune, but they had respect for law and would have no part in such violence.

This brought Svein back to England where he took control again. After more fierce fighting, he captured London and made himself "Caesar of the North." King Ethelred fled to Normandy without even putting up a fight. Five weeks later, Svein fell off his horse and died at age 55 on Feb. 3, 1014. Some people believe he was murdered.

Historians rate Svein a genius as a ruler and military strategist, despite his penchant for cruelty. He was a cool-headed manipulator of men and events with a keen sense of timing. He knew how to move the masses of people and knew when they'd rather switch than fight. He left nothing to chance. He recaptured Hedeby, the large Danish market city, from the Germans and brought the surrounding Vikings under his control. He invaded England at one of its weakest times. The pride and power of Alfred the Great and his descendants had come to an end. While Svein favored Christianity, he was tolerant of the pagans. He brought huge amounts of wealth back to enrich Denmark. The wealth was spent on military operations and was not used to improve living conditions for the people.

The English recalled Ethelred from Normandy to be their king again. So Knut (or Canute, as the English write it), Svein's 18-year-old son, set sail with a fleet of 200 ships to claim his father's kingdom. His commander of the army was Jarl (Earl) Erik, a Norwegian, who was to play an important part in Knut's invasion of Norway.

Ethelred died suddenly and his son, Edmund Ironside, took the throne. After a hard battle, the English asked for peace and Knut and Edmund divided the land. Then strangely, Edmund died and Knut became king over the whole land. There is a suspicion that he'd been poisoned.

The English were fond of Knut and have named him the "Great." It is said that he actually became an "Englishman." After making a grand entrance into St. Peter's Cathedral in Rome with the German Emperor Conrad on Easter Sunday, 1027, he went on to dispossess Olav as king of the Norwegians. Then on Nov. 11, 1035, he died at only 35 years of age. With his death, the Danish kingdom in England came to an end. They all do eventually.

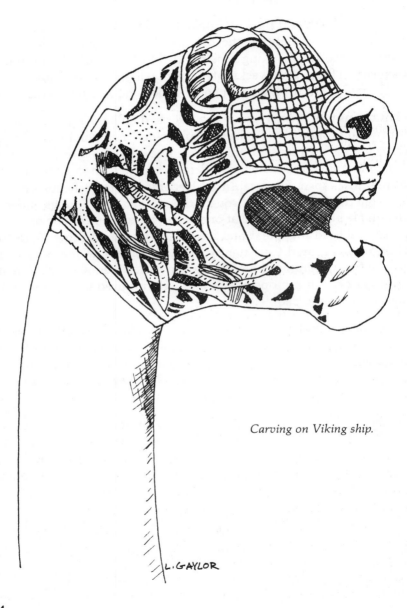

Carving on Viking ship.

L. GAYLOR

CHAPTER 60

The End Of The Viking Age

THE "VIKING AGE" began in 793, when Norwegian fortune hunters ravished the Christian holy island of Lindisfarne off the northeast coast of England. It ended at the battle of Stamford Bridge in October, 1066 when King Harald Hardrada, half-brother to St. Olaf, died in his attempt to claim England for his kingdom. The age both began and ended with violence.

That doesn't mean that there weren't adventurous Norsemen before Lindisfarne or after Stamford Bridge. The rise and fall of kingdoms is a fascinating theme of history. Some are like meteors racing across the sky. Others seem eternal. Many do not outlast their founders. Such were the kingdoms of Attila the Hun, Hitler and Mussolini. By contrast, the Roman Empire seemed destined to last forever, whether in Rome or Constantinople.

Once the Viking outbreak took place from Denmark, Norway and Sweden, it achieved a reputation of terror as it moved with the element of surprise against unsuspecting neighbors. It wasn't long before these Norsemen had gained a foothold in England, Ireland, France, the North Sea Islands and along the rivers of Russia. After their swift rise in the 9th and 10th centuries, it seemed that they might become the permanent power of the North Sea. The 11th century saw them rise to their highest heights and then fade away.

After living for 200 years as conquerors and settlers in Ireland, an invasion by the grandest Viking army ever assembled was crushed at the battle of Clontarf, near Dublin, on Good Friday 1014. A combined army of Irish and Norwegian-Irish fought against the foreigners who were joined by other Irish. The Irish high-king, Brian Boru, inspired his forces to victory only to die on that same day together with his heirs. Four thousand defenders and 7,000 invaders fell in one day. One of the Vikings stopped to tie his shoes during the retreat. The defenders asked him why he was not fleeing. He answered that he wouldn't be able to make it back to his home in Iceland by nightfall anyway. They let him live. And Ireland remained Irish.

Danish and Norwegian kings and other pretenders to power continually fought to rule over Norway. The descendants of King Harald "Finehair," the first Norwegian king to rule over the whole land, kept reappearing even though defeated by the Danes. Olaf Tryggvason was defeated in 1000 at sea by his brother-in-law, Svein "Forkbeard." Olaf Haraldsson died at Sticklestad against Knut the Great, the Danish king of England in 1030. Their sons, Magnus Olafson and Hordaknut Knutson divided the lands and agreed that if one should die the other would inherit all. Magnus was the survivor.

Magnus' uncle, Harald Hardrada (half brother of St. Olaf), returned from his adventures in Russia and Constantinople and secured half the kingdom from Magnus. Shortly afterwards Magnus died. Harald and Svein, Knut's nephew, agreed to divide Norway and Denmark between them. Then Harald Hardrada sailed off to England to conquer the land when the English king, Harald Godwinson, the grandson of a Viking, claimed the throne in 1066. Harald Hardrada, the greatest warrior of his time, fell at the battle of Stamford Bridge when his troops were caught napping in the sun. A couple of weeks later, new conquerors arrived in the south of England from Normandy under the leadership of Duke William, a descendant of Vikings. That was the end of Viking pretensions to England.

When Jaroslav died in Russia in 1054, the Viking character of the rulers in Kiev came to an end. For over 200 years their ships had plied the waters of the Russian rivers to deal in furs and slaves. No longer would they dream of a Viking kingdom among the Slavs.

The Normans would be dominant for a while in southern Italy, Sicily and especially England. But they had become French in their language and ways. While they have had a permanent influence on England, the island country returned to its Anglo-Saxon heritage after a few generations.

The Viking settlers in Iceland maintained their heritage. They settled down to be farmers for the most part. Some of them had gone on to Greenland and a few had explored the northeast coasts of North America. But they never had political influence in other Norse lands.

What caused the downfall of the Viking kingdoms? Prof. Gwyn Jones, from Cardiff University in Wales, has given four reasons in his book "A History of the Vikings." First, "the constant struggle for territory and dominance in and between the three homeland kingdoms" (Denmark, Norway and Sweden); second, "their general inability to propagate elsewhere their political, social, and religious systems;" third, "the fact that they must encounter nations and people, the Franks and English, the Empire, Byzantium, the Muslim Caliphates, and in the long run the Slavs, richer or stronger, and altogether more absorbent and self-renewing than themselves;" and fourth, "most important of all, their lack of manpower."

Prof. Jones' analysis of the Viking's demise is on target. The Norsemen were never properly organized for long term conquest and they overextended themselves. They were typical of the Germanic tribes that gathered about a leader who for all practical purposes "owned" the country. When the leader died, they had to start all over again to build new loyalties. One reason that the Roman empire lasted so long is that it had a mystique about being a nation with a destiny. Emperors were crowned and often assassinated, but the nation lived on with its code of law.

In America, the constitution is the staying power of government. Even presidents may resign, but the nation remains intact. While the Vikings had a strong sense of democracy in their homelands based on their "Thing" laws, the only place that they effectively transplanted it to was Iceland, a land practically uninhabited when they arrived. They never made their style of democracy work in any other land. On the contrary, they were assimilated into the local population and changed language, religion and social customs. Nowhere did they rise to greater leadership achievements than in Normandy.

So what happened to these Vikings? They became "Christian" Danes, Norwegians and Swedes in their homelands. I've asked people in Scandinavia today about their Viking past and they prefer not to talk about it. They regard the Viking age as one of heathen barbarism which they reject today. It appears to me that it's chiefly in America that the pagan Viking past is glamorized. Of course, some of the old names of the pagan gods are still around. You'll find Sons of Norway lodges with names like Odin and Thor. And since Thor was particularly popular

207

among the Norwegians, names like Thor, Thordis, Thorson or Thoreson, Thorvald, Torgerson, etc. still persist. My maternal grandfather was born Thoreson near Lyngdal in Numedal, Norway, but changed his name to Thompson in America. So did a lot of others.

Nations rise and fall, sometimes swiftly. President Lincoln referred to our constitutional freedoms in his Gettysburg Address when he said "Now we are engaged in a great civil war, testing whether that nation, or any nation so conceived and dedicated, can long endure."

The Viking power lasted about 250 years. That's a lot longer than their Christian neighbors wished. Today they've become the world's foremost advocates of peace. Miracles can still happen.

CHAPTER 61

The Sons Of Norway 'USA Soccer Cup'

A S BASEBALL IS TO AMERICA, soccer is to most of the world. Soccer is, however, also coming into its own in the United States. I'd paid little attention to the game, which Europeans refer to as "football," until we moved to St. Louis in 1961. The "Gateway City" to the West is one of the strongest soccer centers in the country. It's a major sport in the schools. St. Louis University has had strong teams. My sons were taught the fundamentals of the game so well that they became varsity players in the Maine Township High Schools in the Chicago suburbs when we moved there in 1967.

Every Scandinavian city has soccer fields. A few years ago, a team from Lorenskog, near Oslo, came to North Dakota to play some exhibition games. The locals played well, but the Norwegians returned home undefeated, while making many friends in America.

More than 7,000 young athletes representing 320 soccer teams from 11 countries participated in the fifth annual USA CUP in July, 1989 at the Sports Complex in Blaine, MN, suburb of Minneapolis. More than 820 games were played. Six hundred coaches and hundreds of referees and volunteers participated. That's more than are in the U.S. Olympic Festival. The goal is to have 500 teams "to promote friendly competition, growth of character and international understanding by bringing together athletes from around the world for a week of social activity and soccer." The USA CUP, modeled after the Norway Cup, has become the largest youth soccer tournament in the United States. The Norway Cup held in Oslo, the largest event of its kind in the world, is limited to 1,000 teams. The tournament is held in late July and early August. It began in 1973. The first USA CUP was held in 1985 with 68 teams and 1,200 players participating.

The opening ceremony for the USA CUP takes place in the Hubert H. Humphrey Metrodome in Minneapolis on a Sunday evening. The teams march in a colorful parade of flags, uniforms and banners. More than 10,000 people came out to watch the ceremony, which is conducted in Olympic-style pageantry.

The Minot Soccer Association sent two teams to the USA CUP in 1989. The Thor Lodge 67 Sons of Norway in Minot annually supports the local players in getting to the Twin Cities. Jeff Jensen, one of the Minot players, was enthusiastic about making this annual trek to the USA CUP. He said that it was fun to meet players from foreign countries as well as from all parts of the United States. He especially mentioned players from Mexico. Jeff said that competing with teams which play an excellent brand of soccer helps the Minot players to improve their game.

There are four age levels for both the boy's and the girl's divisions: Under 12, under 14, under 16 and under 19. There are also three classes of teams: A, B and C. Visiting teams stay in local homes. The "home-stay" is considered by Sons of Norway an essential part of the event. For example, a team from Trandby, Norway, was hosted by a team from Anoka, MN. The first game of a visiting team is against its host team. One of the chief benefits of the games is the friendships that develop between young people.

The USA CUP now attracts players from eastern Europe. In 1989, two teams from the Soviet Union participated for the first time. Other countries which have sent teams include Brazil, Canada, Columbia, Denmark, Haiti, Holland, Hungary, Italy, Japan, Mexico, Nigeria, Norway, the Philippines, Sweden, Taiwan and West Germany. The Norwegians were surprised to discover that many people in America can speak their language.

The Blaine Sports Complex has 17 soccer fields and is the future home of a national training center for soccer. The players are instructed to be polite both on the field and off. Gaelyn Beal, writing in the September, 1987 "Viking" magazine, stated "these Japanese were from the under 14 boys soccer team from Ibaraki, and after politely trouncing their opponents from Des Moines, they ran over to their opponents' side, lined up, and politely bowed. Then there was a flurry of souvenir exchange as the teams traded patches, pins and pennants."

There's a lot of fun off the soccer field too. The host teams take their visitors to see some of Minnesota's special attractions around the Twin

Cities, including the lakes and a Minnesota Twins baseball game. The Minnesota Strikers, a short-lived professional soccer team, had shown interest in the USA CUP. Striker players have played exhibition games for the youth and offer soccer clincs. Visiting players bring along some extra money, not just for shopping in the malls, but to buy soccer equipment that may not be available in their home towns.

Awards are given both to the winning teams in each bracket and to individual players. Referee and sportsmanship awards are also given. Many families plan their vacations to be with their children at these games. For people who've become "bitten" by the soccer bug, it's hard to stay away. I remember going to a lot of soccer games when our sons played in the suburban Chicago high school leagues. I can understand a little better that fans in the Latin American countries become highly emotional in the support of their teams.

Response to the USA CUP has been appreciative. It's a sign that soccer is coming of age in America. One Minnesota coach expressed high praise for the event: "This tournament has done more for soccer in the U.S. than anything I've seen in four years. The sportsmanship among the teams and players is top rate." A coach from Dallas stated "it has got to be the best run and most fun-filled tournament in the country."

There will be injuries, of course, but more than 60 medical volunteers are recruited who offer first aid in case of twisted ankles, bruised knees, heat exhaustion or other accidents.

Minnesota Governor Rudy Perpich proclaimed that the "USA CUP is the fastest growing international sporting event in North America." The governor stated that "Youth Soccer has a tremendously positive impact on young people, families and on communities." And it's only just begun!

If you happen to be in the Minneapolis area in early July, you are welcome to join in the festivity. There is no admission charge to watch the games. But be careful, you might want to stay for the whole tournament. For more information, write: Sons of Norway USA Cup, 1455 West Lake Street, Minneapolis, MN 55408 or call 612-827-3611.

211

CHAPTER 62

A Tribute To 'Besta'

"**B**ESTA" IS SHORT FOR "BESTA MOR," meaning "Grandma."
It means the "best mamma" in Norwegian. Norwegians and
Danes also use the terms "Mor-mor" (mother's mother) and
"Far-mor" (father's mother). "Besta" could also refer to a
grandfather, "Besta Far," but in this story it's about a grandmother.

Elsie Heiberg Hjellen (pronounced "Yellen") wrote a story about her
grandmother, Johanna Marie Slettebak (1830-1924). I'm indebted to
Leona Olson Pfund of Ada, Minnesota, for my information about this
noble lady of pioneer days.

Family names were often changed in Old Norway. Besta's grandfather,
born Rodseth, took the name Slettebak from the farm of his wife's family, located near Lake Brusdalsvatne in the area of Aalesund. The land
was given to them by Besta's parents. That's also how Vice President
Mondale's great grandfather became Mundal, though born Vangsness.

Norway was highly class conscious in those days. Elsie Hjellen wrote
in her book that the "fornemme" (the elite people) of the city used to
visit the farm during the summer. They brought along delicacies such
as "kaffe brod" (coffee bread), "sukker kavring" (sweet rusks), kringle
and white bread for the visit. This insured their welcome.

Grandpa Slettebak was remembered as a strict man with his one surviving son and seven daughters, as well as having a red beard. The
children all learned to milk cows, tend sheep and cattle, and work in
the fields. In the winter they brought wood across the lake to heat their
house. As a result, the daughters who married farmers were well prepared for life.

Their youngest child met with tragedy while still a toddler. They were
by a sand pit getting sand for scrubbing and polishing an unpainted
floor. The little child came too near the pit and was accidentally buried
alive when a cave-in took place. Even though Besta dug in the sand until

her fingers bled, it was too late. In her grief, she wore only black and white clothes for the rest of her life.

Shortly after this tragedy, in 1882, the Slettebaks immigrated to a farm near Twin Valley, MN. Besta's husband died in March, 1887. By 1893 she had disposed of all her property. Together with her youngest daughter, Ludvikka, she came to make her home for a number of years at the Jorgen Heibergs. That's why Elsie came to have such vivid memories of her grandmother. Probably because of her generosity, she didn't realize much money from the sale of her property. One of her prized possessions was her bridal outfit, including a silver crown, which was lost in the trunk coming over from Norway.

Once in retirement, Besta busied herself with kitchen work, including doing the dishes and making lefse. Elsie wrote that she was a "whiz" at that. She added both white and dark flour to the mashed potatoes and rolled them out with a grooved rolling pin. She had her "spa," a spatula made of wood, to flip the lefse as soon as it started to bubble. (I remember helping my father make lefse over our wood burning cook stove on the farm exactly the same way.)

People of today would be surprised to see how dressed up the women of a hundred years ago were for special occasions. They wouldn't have been caught dead in blue jeans. This included going to church, and especially to funerals. It was a common sight to see Besta dressed up with gloves, hymnal and purse. She often walked the two miles along the railroad track and always arrived early, never after the bell rang.

Like lots of people who were serious about their piety, the church was important to Besta. She belonged to the "Hauge Synod," named after Hans Nielsen Hauge (1771-1824), a farmer who led a religious revival in Norway. The Haugeans had a deep faith and placed a lot of stress on the outward behavior of Christians. One of her hopes was that a grandson would become a pastor.

Prayers at mealtime and at bedtime were a regular part of life for immigrant families. Many Norwegian-Americans still use the mealtime prayer in the language of their homelands: "I Jesu navn gaar vi til bord, at spise or drikke paa dit ord. Dig Gud til aere, os til gavn, saa faa vi mat i Jesu navn. Amen." (In Jesus' name we go to the table, to eat and drink upon your word; to thee, O God, be glory and to us be the gift, so we receive our food in Jesus' name). There was also an after-meal prayer that I also learned as a child, but I don't hear it among the Americanized Norwegians of today.

It was a custom in Besta's home to eat fruit before going to bed. Apples, pears, oranges, bananas and grapes were shipped in regularly to her home. The one thing that Besta refused to eat was bologna. She had heard a story that a sausage maker had disposed of his wife by grinding her up for sausage. That completely spoiled it for her.

Children would usually eat what their parents ate, but Mrs. Hjellen told that they would not eat "gammelost" and didn't care for sour milk. Some of the original old timers thrived on such fare. I concur with her that the smell of gammelost is enough to make you want to leave the room. They all liked fish. Living by a river, they had a diet of pickerel, bass, pike, perch, red horse and suckers. They also ate lutefisk, of course, and soaked the dried cod to prepare it. (This was an every winter event on the farm where I was reared. My father would order 100 pounds of frozen Lake Superior herring from Fradet's Fish Company. I looked forward to every meal it. Occasionally, we'd order some of the more expensive fish too.)

Besta went visiting her children in the summer. One of her daughters, Emelie Trandum, lived on a farm near Bottineau, ND. There was also an Uncle Ramus who lived in Bottineau. When she visited another daughter near Oslo, MN (then called Granville), she used to take the steamboat from Grand Forks. The common way to travel over land in those days was by wagon, sitting on a spring seat. This is how milk and cream were transported to market. (I remember riding along when I was a small child.)

The Heiberg home was a regular stopping off point for newcomers from Norway. Among those who came was a nephew, Leif Sverdrup, who later became a famous architect in St. Louis and a Major General as an engineer in World War II. I knew him and wrote of him in the "Scandinavian Heritage" book (see chapter 2). He became one of the best known citizens of Missouri.

Besta had clear views on marriage. Her slogan was: "When the right one comes along, you'll know" ("naar den rette kommer saa vil du vite det"). Maybe that's why there were so few divorces in those days. If it was the "right one," it would work out despite difficult times.

Almost every Scandinavian mother spent a lot of time knitting, especially stockings, mittens and scarves. Babies in those days were almost always breast fed. This gave mothers time to think and resolve their problems. It was also a time for reading to the other children. The modern mother who has to go back to work a few weeks after giving birth is denied this luxury.

Christmas was a special time in Besta's time. No child was allowed to see the decorated tree until Christmas Eve, after supper was eaten. Those were great days. It hadn't changed in my childhood either. Today most people are tired of Christmas before it comes, because we start celebrating so far in advance.

Besta lived to be 94 years old, passing away on July 1, 1924. Her grandson, Martinus Stenseth, a World War I ace and later a brigadier general, circled over her grave and dropped a wreath on it at the time of her burial. She was a small lady, according to her biography, but left a powerful legacy of courage and determination to her family. The world needs more of her kind.

CHAPTER 63

The Erickstad Legacy

WHEN TOLLEF ERICKSTAD, his wife Brita Olson Aardal and their six children emigrated from Jolster, Norway, in 1883, they could not have realized what was in store for them in the New World. Neither could they have foreseen that a grandson, Ralph, would some day become the Chief Justice of the North Dakota Supreme Court. It's a long ways from the mountains of Norway's "Vestlands" (west country) to the state capitol in Bismarck. Not many people are marked for such distinction.

Travelling with Tollef and his family were his brother Elias and family, his 16-year-old sister Andrea, Sam Overbo and his young bride, Anton Myklebust and Lars Knutson Klakegg. Boarding a steamer at the Bergen harbor, they landed at New York and travelled by train to Grafton, ND, where Tollef had a brother, Gunder. Brita also had two brothers, Ole and Samuel Olson in Grafton.

The land at Grafton was already claimed. So Tollef and several other men drove a team of oxen pulling a wagon in search of land available for homestead. The sight of a cow following the wagon amazed the Indians in the Turtle Mountain area. They travelled as far east as the Mouse River near Minot. The soil met their approval, but they decided it would be better to settle nearer the railroad which had come only as far as Devils Lake. They found their future home near Starkweather, 25 miles northwest of Devils Lake and about 75 miles from their families in Grafton.

They must have wondered why they left Norway when they came to that treeless prairie of tall grass and sloughs in DeGroat Township. And just like back in Jolster, there were rocks in North Dakota too, though not as many. One of the agreements made with the government in getting land was that they had to plant trees. After breaking the tough prairie sod with the walking plow and building a house from available timber, they put up hay and returned to Grafton for work in the harvest fields.

216

In November they returned to their claim. The cow became so stiff from walking that she had to be loaded into the wagon. Before they reached their shelter, a severe snowstorm struck. The snowfall was so heavy that the oxen had to be led. A surprise awaited their arrival at the prairie shack — a skunk had taken up residence in their absence. The door and windows were still in the wagon among their winter supplies. The fuel for heating the shelter in the first winter was twisted prairie grass and buffalo chips. They roasted some of their seed wheat to use in place of coffee. (I remember how my father roasted cereal grains when I was a child when the coffee ran out and there was little or no money to buy any, even at 15 cents a pound.)

Before long, more people from Jolster arrived. It wasn't long before a schoolhouse was built which also served as a church. A congregation was organized in 1886 by Rev. Ole Aaberg, an enterprising missionary pastor to the Dakota Territory who lived in Devils Lake. In 1900 the first church was built and named after Aaberg's place of birth — Bergen in Norway.

This was a hardy breed of people. Tollef (1848-1927) and Brita (1845-1923) could have stayed in Norway since he was heir to the family farm. But he sold it when deciding to go to America. Their first home in the Starkweather community was a sod house.

Their son, John T. (1880-1958), was only three when the family came to America. After attending Aaberg's Academy in Devils Lake (founded by Pastor Aaberg) and a short course at the Agriculture College in Fargo, he married Anna Myklebust in Iola, WI, and returned to farm in the Starkweather community. He was also active as a County Commissioner and served as president of the Starkweather Telephone Company.

Their son, Ralph J., born in 1922, came from hardy stock. Those who knew him weren't surprised that his diligent habits for work and study would lead him to a successful professional career. He was one of six children, one whom died in infancy and another at age six. The prairie life took its toll and there were a lot of tears shed by these pioneer parents, as they lived with the uncertainties of life.

Ralph's career which led to the highest law position in the state came after a distinguished career of military service, study and law practice. During World War II, he was a radio operator and gunner on a Liberator

Bomber in the Eighth Air Force. After attending the University of North Dakota and graduating from the University of Minnesota Law School, Ralph began his work as an attorney in Devils Lake in 1949. He also served as the city Police Magistrate, the State's Attorney and was a State Senator when elected to the Supreme Court in 1962. While in the State Senate, he was often in leadership roles.

When I was the pastor of the Mylo Lutheran Parish, 65 miles northwest of Devils Lake from 1952-57, I became aware of this energetic young attorney in Devils Lake. When I moved to New Rockford in 1957, I got my first close-up glimpse of him. He spoke to our Kiwanis Club and impressed us all by his sincere and articulate presentation. I was not surprised when he became the Chief Justice in 1973 and was re-elected in 1978, 1983 and 1987.

Besides his judicial duties, Chief Justice Erickstad has served on many committees. He was president of the Executive Council of the National Conference of Chief Justices and of the National Center for State Courts. President Reagan appointed him to the Board of Directors of the State Justice Institute in 1987. Governor Sinner also presented him with the North Dakota National Leadership Award of Excellence in 1987.

Legal work is not the only thing that has occupied this busy Chief Justice's time. He has been active in the Boy Scouts of America and the YMCA. Both these organizations have recognized his leadership. The Boy Scouts awarded him the Silver Beaver Award and named the 1983 "Chief Justice Ralph J. Erickstad, Eagle Class" in his honor. The Missouri Valley Family YMCA presented him with the First Distinguished Service Award. The University of North Dakota honored him with the Sioux Award in 1973.

In June, 1988, Erickstad was given the Distinguished Service Award from the North Dakota State Bar Association. In May, 1989, he was awarded the National Center for State Courts "Distinguished Service Award" and was cited as "truly one of this nation's outstanding jurists."

There is another significant person in the Ralph Erickstad legacy. He was joined by Lois Jacobson of Minneapolis, a University of Minnesota graduate in business administration, at their marriage in 1949. They have two sons, John and Mark, both medical doctors in Bismarck. Lois has achieved considerable fame for herself. Besides being an attentive mother and a supportive wife, she earned a Masters Degree in Public Administration at the University of North Dakota. She became the President of the Western North Dakota Synod of the Evangelical Lutheran Church in America, in 1988, the first woman to hold this position. In the former denominations, this position was held by pastors. Mrs. Erickstad was one of 70 people who drew up the organizational plan for the ELCA. She has also been Chairperson of the Bismarck Park Board.

Chief Justice Erickstad addressed the Syttende Mai (17th of May) banquet for Minot's Sons of Norway Thor Lodge in 1988, in recognition of Norway's constitution of 1814. He spoke with his usual clarity of thoughts on the United States Constitution. He paid tribute to his Scandinavian heritage, but it was obvious that his first love and loyalty is to "the United States of America and to the constitution for which it stands." We have a better state because of the dedicated and wise judicial leadership of this grandson of the immigrants from Jolster whose first home in the New World was a sod house.

CHAPTER 64

Norman Borlaug And
The 'Green Revolution'

OR ABOUT TEN YEARS I flipped pancakes for the Annual Kiwanis Pancake Day in Minot. In addition to the usual fluffy white cakes served, some were made with a courser flour milled from "triticale." This is a cross between wheat and rye which was perfected by Dr. Norman Borlaug. It's the first man-made plant and has a higher protein content than plain wheat flour and can be grown on soils with marginal plant nutrition.

Borlaug is a hard-working scientist who was one of the pioneers of the "Green Revolution" and has been the Director of the Centro Internacional de Mejoramiento de Maiz y Trigo - CIMMYT (International Maize and Wheat Improvement Centre) in Mexico City.

On Oct. 20, 1970, Borlaug became a household name throughout the world. A reporter from Oslo called Mrs. Borlaug breaking the news that her husband was to receive the Nobel Peace Prize. Borlaug was out in the experimental fields training workers to continue the Green Revolution that the hungry of the world might have food. From that moment, he has belonged to the world.

Norman Borlaug was born March 25, 1914, on a farm near Saude in northeast Iowa, a few miles from the Minnesota border. His grandparents had been born in the Sognefjord area of western Norway. Grandpa Henry was particularly close to young Norman in his growing up years and told him, "Common sense, Norm, that's what the world needs. Education and common sense." These words have stuck in his memory all these years. His father, Nels, reinforced this counsel, "Education, Norm, puts vital power into a man. Fill your head now if you want to fill your belly later on."

His education began in a one-room grade school. We sometimes think that people who become famous must be unusually gifted with brilliant minds and hardly have to study. Borlaug has a brilliant mind but it wasn't all giftedness (sometimes that doesn't turn out to be a blessing).

With tenacious determination, Borlaug went to the University of Minnesota until he completed a PhD. While at the University, he met Margaret Gibson, a student whose family had originally come from Scotland. They were married in 1937.

When Borlaug graduated from eighth grade, the family held a conference to decide if he should go to high school. His second cousin, Sina, who had been his teacher, said, "No question! He's no great shakes as a scholar; his arithmetic is awful - but he sticks. He's got grit! High school will make him."

Borlaug didn't only crack the books. He was also active in sports. At Cresco high school, he was a star athlete in wrestling, football and baseball. At the University, besides waiting on tables and having a job through the National Youth Organization, Norman was a successful varsity wrestler. His determined spirit caught the attention of some of his teachers.

That tenacity stuck with him after earning a doctorate in forestry. He also studied agronomy. He first job was as a microbiologist with the Du Pont Company in Wilmington, DE. His life, however, was not destined to remain in the United States. The Rockefeller Foundation was requested by the White House to help the Mexican government develop its agricultural program and rescue its failing economy. Even though Borlaug had a position which was classifed as vital to the war effort, in 1944 he answered the call to work in Mexico.

It wouldn't be easy. It wasn't just that the Mexican soil had been eroding for generations, the problem was how to develop a short-stemmed, rust-resistant, wheat plant with high yield that would grow in both the tropical regions and the highlands of Mexico. It took years of hard scientific work to complete the job, plus convincing the farmers that this new way of growing wheat was a good thing. Many thought the new cereal grains would poison them. The agricultural scientists and politicians were often his greatest obstacles. To admit that Borlaug was right was to bring shame on themselves for having failed.

Many things have gone into successful agriculture. In an article co-authored with Christopher R. Dowswell entitled "World Revolution in Agriculture" in the 1988 Britannica Book of the Year, Borlaug lists the driving forces behind the spectacular production gains in agriculture.

He cites newly developed high-yielding crop varieties, increased reliance on irrigation and improved techniques for conserving moisture, chemical fertilizers, effective control of weeds, diseases and insects, and better farm machinery.

In January, 1976, Borlaug addressed a convocation at Wartburg College in Waverly, IA, on the topic: "Producing Food for Four Billion." Today, it's five billion. Borlaug sees the challenge both to produce more food and to educate people for population control.

Dr. Borlaug gave the first of the York Distinguished Lecturer Series at the University of Florida in 1985. It was a major address entitled "World Hunger: What to Do." In it he pointed out that it took 17 years (1943-1960) to enable Mexico to achieve self-sufficiency in food production. The statistics cited in the address are impressive. Wheat production in India increased from 11 million metric tons in 1966 to over 45 in 1984. Rice increased from 36 million metric tons in 1970 to 57 in 1983. Pakistan's wheat harvest increased from four million metric tons in 1966 to over 12 in 1983. China, he noted, had overtaken both the United States and the Soviet Union in wheat production, increasing from 22 million metric tons in 1965 to over 80 in 1983.

Borlaug is critical of government regulated economies which control food production, such as in the Soviet Union and most of the Communist countries. (It remains to be seen if Mikhail Gorbachev can change those policies.) Borlaug believes there needs to be private incentive with the government being friendly to the farmer so that prices can support production and that there is adequate storage in the event of crop failure.

As successful as the Green Revolution has been, the battle is not over. In his convocation address to the Punjab Agricultural University in 1987, Borlaug cited the urgent need for more people with scientific training to continue the research because plant diseases keep breaking through the defenses that scientists have built. To continue the work, Borlaug has trained more than 150 scientists from 23 countries.

Borlaug strongly disagrees with those who would restrict the use of chemical fertilizers and pesticides, and would do only organic farming. He calls this "confused science." He also defends the application of DDT when used properly. Borlaug was working at the Du Pont laboratories

222

when DDT was first being tested. He has stated that only 25% of the earth's surface is land, and only 11% of that is suitable for agriculture. Since land is limited, the only way to produce more food, Borlaug insists, is to "increase the ability of existing crop lands to do the job."

As a result of India's increased production, my good friend Leo Holman (d. 1987), was in India and Punjab in 1969-1970 instructing the agricultural leaders how to store their bumper crops. Leo, then retired fom the United States Department of Agriculture and making his home in Minot, ND, made similar trips to Chile, Brazil and Taiwan. While still in the USDA service, he was one of eight specialists who travelled to the Soviet Union to improve their grain storage facilities. Unfortunately, the Soviet grain elevators were in such a sorry state that the officials wouldn't let the Americans make the inspections.

The Norsk Høstfest inducted Borlaug into the Scandinavian-American Hall of Fame in October, 1986. He addressed us with the hopeful message that we can conquer hunger if we want to badly enough. The scientific and technical skills are available, he claimed. He made a strong appeal for the attack on world hunger as a way to peace.

When I met Borlaug, his gentlemanly appearance didn't look like someone who had sloshed through mud in rice paddies, or worked tirelessly in the baking sun while trying to perfect a better grain, or who has argued down the heads of govenment to win his battle against hunger. Besides his work as a Consultant for CIMMYT, he is Distinguished Professor of International Agriculture at Texas A & M University. He has also been a Senior Scientist at the Rockefeller Foundation and was elected to the National Academy of Sciences. When the people of Mexico wanted to thank him with a gift of $5,000, he refused it saying, "I can't take this money. It's impossible for me to do that and still work here in this place."

A helpful biography is "Facing Starvation: Norman Borlaug and the Fight Against Hunger" by Lennard Bickel (1974). Bickel is one of the best known scientific writers in Australia. Dr. E. W. Mueller, former Director of CENCOAD (Center for Area Development) at Augustana College in Sioux Falls, SD, commented after reading the book, "It represents real progress."

THE SCANDINAVIAN SPIRIT

"Norman Borlaug is one of the few enduring heroes of our wild, erupting age," wrote Vance Bourjaily, author of "Country Matters." I agree. Borlaug is a no-nonsense scientist committed to humanitarian goals. When the greatest heroes and events of the 20th century have been evaluated, Norman Borlaug and the Green Revolution are among the select few that deserve to be remembered. He manifests the best in the "Scandinavian spirit" of our times.

CHAPTER 65

The Genius Of The Sagas

HOME ENTERTAINMENT IS BIG business today. You're not with it if you don't have a VCR so you can show movies on your own TV screen. Besides the visual entertainments at home, people go jogging or riding a bike with their headphones attached, listening to stereo music. For those who don't like to watch movies or listen to music, there is an endless supply of reading material available. Books, magazines, newspapers and advertising mailers fill our homes.

None of those things were possible in the Old Norse world of Iceland a thousand years ago. They spent their non-work hours listening to stories which combined history and legend. It's told that a visitor named Thorgils Skardi came to a farmhouse one evening in 1258. The host asked him if he prefered saga-reading or ballad-dancing for the evening's entertainment. Like a true Icelander, he chose to listen to sagas. "Saga" is an Old Norse word for "what is told" or "sayings." Even the English word "to say" is related to the Old Norse through their connection with the Anglo-Saxon language. The emphasis in saga-reading is that they be read aloud in public, rather than silently in private. That's the way the Bible was originally read too.

A saga could be any kind of story in Iceland, oral or written. The Icelandic writers excelled in story-telling from about 1180 to sometime in the 14th century. There were three kinds of Icelandic sagas: Stories about kings (especially Norwegian kings), legends, and stories about Icelanders. The best known of the sagas were royal stories written by Snorri Sturluson written to glorify St. Olaf. The most famous of the Icelandic stories is Njal's saga (Njal is Icelandic for the Celtic "Neil"). Some people think it's the greatest of all the sagas.

Sagas have a different way of telling a story than the modern novel. Novels today spend a great deal of time analyzing the inner feelings and motives of the characters. The sagas give detailed genealogical data about the people and the reader is expected to understand a person's inner character. If a person's father was noble, you'd expect the son to also be noble. The same is true if the father had character defects such as being a thief or a liar. The information is given briefly and did not need to be repeated. The reader was expected to understand. For example, in Njal's saga a reference is made to Hallgerd's daughter as having "thief's eyes." Nothing more needs to describe her. The listener (or reader) knew what to expect in her behavior.

One Icelandic writer stated: "Sagas about worthy men are useful to know, because they show us noble deeds and brave feats, whereas ill deeds are manifestations of indolence; thus, such sagas point out the distinction between good and evil for those who wish to understand it."

Sagas were something like "yarns," stories told for entertainment. During the long dark nights in Iceland, story-telling was the most popular form of entertainment and the Icelanders excelled in it. One writer said: "With sagas one man can gladden many an hour, whereas most entertainments are difficult to arrange; some are very costly, some cannot be enjoyed without large numbers of people, some only entertain a very few people for a brief time, and some entail physical danger. But saga entertainment or poetry costs nothing and holds no dangers, and one man can entertain as many or as few as wish to listen; it's equally practicable night or day, by light or in darkness."

The sagas were the closest thing in medieval Iceland to what we call the historical novel. You get the story, but should not insist on historicity. Styrmir the Learned (d. 1245), an Icelandic scholar, wrote, "You can accept from this composed saga whatever you think most likely, for in old sagas many things are confused. This is only to be expected where oral tradition alone supplies the material . . . I expect that holy King Olaf would not be offended by any inaccuracies in the saga, for it has been written in order to entertain others rather than to criticize the king or out of any malice." In the stories about St. Olaf, he can hardly do anything wrong, even though many of the things which he did offend our 20th century sensitivities. We find them gross and rude. It does not appear that people of those times were offended by the behavior of their heroes.

Women were strong and dominant in the sagas, especially in the story of Njal. They are not seen as romantic characters so much as people who take charge and in some cases are capable of being utterly unscrupulous, like Gunnhild the queen-mother of King Harald Grey-Cloak who ruled Norway fom 961-970. They are clearly individuals and come off as very real. Helga, in the "Hagar The Horrible" cartoon, may be an exaggeration, but she is not far from what the saga women were like. They do not impress me as the kind of persons on which Harlequin romances are based today.

The courts of kings employed professional scribes to write royal histories which were favorable in their estimates. These court poets and writers were called skalds. It paid handsomely for those who could write in prophetic style and offered good omens for the king's future. Sturluson's "Heimskringla" ("Sagas of the Norse kings") are replete with selections of such court poetry in praise of the ruler's wisdom, bravery, oratory and physical skills.

Generations before the stories were written down, the art of storytelling was a highly developed art form among the Icelanders. Since the pre-Christian Norsemen in Iceland didn't have a highly developed alphabet, it remained for the Christian priests and scholars to record them. We'd know very little about the history of Norway's kings if those saga writers had not waded through the immense amount of stories, edited them and added their own interpretation.

It was the Chrisian missionaries who taught Icelanders the Latin alphabet. This advanced the cause of literature. In this way the sagas were preserved for the future. The introduction of Latin also brought the outside world into Iceland through literature from the continent. Since the early bishops were foreigners, they introduced Bible stories and new customs. The residence of the bishops also became the centers of learning.

"Justice" is a prominent theme in the Icelandic sagas. They placed the welfare of the community above the individual, unlike modern writing. The Icelandic saga characters are fully integrated into society, especially farmers and chieftains. In Hrafnkel's saga, the chieftain who murders his shepherd, suffers the consequences of torture and humiliation. Some of the sagas have the themes of love triangles, feuds and violence.

A vulnerable point in the pride of Icelanders was their sense of honor. Blood revenge often followed when someone's sense of honor was violated. They seem to have had very "short fuses." Sometimes they even created a second crisis just to provoke the opportunity to vindicate their honor, even though it meant death. To the old Vikings, death was to be preferred to having your honor discredited.

The setting for the Icelandic sagas was in the days of paganism, before 1000. But even with their new Christian understanding of life, they continued to refer to the old days and ways, though they wrote 200 or more years afterwards.

Saga writing was highly developed at Skalholt in southern Iceland, where a bishop was headquartered. Many of those who became famous in Iceland as writers travelled to Norway to ingratiate themselves with the king. Greed, love of money, and hunger for fame provided the motivation. According to Magnus Magnuson, it is "the Christian virtues of self-sacrifice and humility that eventually stemmed the tide of evil, not the pagan virtues of heroism and pride."

The sagas aren't just stories of long ago, they are full of insight into human character and behavior. Human nature and people haven't really changed much in the past thousand or more years. It's the genius of the sagas that they entertain us while giving us understanding of own inner selves. And they did this long before the advent of modern psychology.

CHAPTER 66

Paavo Ruotsalainen —
Finland's Greatest Religious Leader

EVERY NATION HAS ITS HEROES and anti-heroes. Some of them are not known to us because they left no written legacy or no one wrote about them. It's also true that the genius of some of those people was not discovered until after they had died. Paavo Ruotsalainen (1777-1852), pronounced Root-sah-line-en with the accent on the first syllable, was one of these people. Since Finnish is very different from the other Scandinavian languages, my Finnish daughter-in-law, Rebecca Wuorinen Fiske, helped me with this pronunciation.

Ruotsalainen was born north of Helsinki at Iisalmi and spent most of his life living on a little farm at Nilsia. He lived his entire life in poverty and had no formal education. Having learned to read but never to write, he didn't leave a single written word from his own hand. The major source of what we know about him is from a collection of 80 letters which he dictated, plus a few pamphlets for which he is said to have been responsible. This was when Swedish, not Finnish, was the official language of the land.

What Ruotsalainen lacked in academic training he made up for in courage towards people and humility before God. He has been called the "outstanding layman in the history of the Church of Finland." Dr. G. Everett Arden, former professor at Augustana Seminary in Rock Island, IL, wrote "no other man in the history of the Church of Finland occupies a more commanding position."

Those were difficult times for Finland. For over 500 years, the Finns had been under the rule of the Swedish kings and were a buffer zone in Sweden's border disputes with Russia. There was also a struggle going on in Sweden between the king and the nobles, as well as between two factions of nobles. It was called the war of the "Caps" and the "Hats." The Caps formed conspiracies with Russian agents to force Sweden to reduce the number of troops stationed in Finland. The Hats were ready to go to war against their powerful neighbor to the east to protect Swedish interest.

After much diplomatic sparring and political maneuvering, the Russians occupied Finland in 1742, forcing the surrender of 16,000 Swedish troops. Fortunately, the Russians returned Finland to Swedish rule except an area near St. Petersburg (Leningrad), which became a point of contention in the 1939-1940 Winter War. It had not been the intention of the Russian Empress, Elizabeth, permanently to annex Finland.

This situation kept see-sawing back and forth mainly at the expense of the Finns who were uneasy about their situation. As much as they distrusted the Russians, many Finns weren't sure they could trust their Swedish overlords either. The Russians expoited this situation by encouraging a Finnish independence movement. But the older loyalties of the people remained firmly attached to the Swedish crown.

This was the Finland in which Paavo Ruotsalainen, driven by an inner religious quest, became the spokesman to the troubled souls of his country. The oldest of seven children, the greatest influence on his life was the pietistic religious revival which swept across the land. There was also a spontaneous reaction against the state church which seemed to the people to be more concerned with maintaining its status than with their spiritual condition.

Some pastors were leaders in the revival movement, but more often it was laymen, who were well-read in the Bible and in the teachings of the church, that led the movements. But as you would expect, the revival movement attracted as leaders those who had little or no training and who often substituted enthusiasm and emotionalism for pastoral care based on reliable information.

Religion was the central issue of Paavo in his young days. When he was 22 years old, yearning for inner peace and understanding, he sought out the advice of a blacksmith, Jacob Hogman, who had a reputation for giving good spiritual counsel. After listening to the young man's fears, hopes and doubts, the blacksmith gave him this simple advice: "One thing you lack, and therewith you lack all else; the inner awareness of Christ." He was then led to understand that his need was for the gift of "inner light."

Paavo returned home and spent many hours in diligent prayer and Bible study. It wasn't long before his neighbors saw a dfference in his life and began turning to him for religious counsel. Within a few years, he became the leader of a religious revival and developed into a powerful preacher. He travelled by foot, skis and horseback, covering almost the entire nation, like Hans Nielsen Hauge in Norway.

Ruotsalainen soon became the recognized religious leader for all of Finland. But unlike some of the other leaders, he remained loyal to the national church, guiding the movement away from emotionalism, ecstatic excesses and self-centered mysticism. By the time of his death, Ruotsalainen had become the "chief architect" of a religious tradition that influenced the immigrants from Finland to America.

We generally think of the real influence molders of society as politicians, writers, military leaders and other people who grab the headlines. This is not always true. Sometimes, like a small fire that lies smoldering for hours and then breaks out into bright flame, there are leaders who are being trained without their own knowledge for service to a nation that no one could anticipate. It's only after the fact that people recognize their genius and the worth of what they have done.

The deep burning questions of the soul drive many people to drink. Ruotsalainen, like St. Augustine, St. Francis and Martin Luther, did not stop until his soul found rest. Naturally, these people are controversial. Though he did not have the benefit of an academic education, this Finnish farmer challenged the prevailing pietism of the day which said you had to "feel" saved in order to have salvation. Ruotsalainen claimed this impatience with God was a form of unbelief. He rejected both religious ecstasy and sensuality as evidence of God's presence, and regarded these as an invitation to disaster for the weak in faith.

Instead, Ruotsalainen preached that being a Christian required the same kind of patience, tenacity, realism, and hopefulness that's needed to survive in the climate of the Northlands. The winters of Finland, with their cold temperatures, deep snow and frigid winds, were his analogy to living the life of faith. He counseled people that life is not only summertime. He also warned people not to love God for selfish reasons, not even to escape judgment, but rather for God's own sake.

THE SCANDINAVIAN SPIRIT

During his last illness, Ruotsalainen suffered from intense physical pain and weakness. He did not consider these sufferings to be a punishment from God but as part of what is to be endured in this life. He called this the "school of the cross." When his wife urged him to believe more strongly in God to overcome his sufferings, Ruotsalainen is reported to have said, "Be quiet, woman! Let God's will be done." I've known a few people who face life with this kind of stark realism. They're not always easy to live with, but they don't wallow in self-pity.

The serious conversation between this farmer and a blacksmith was the spark that ignited a fire which warmed the soul of a nation and shaped the piety of thousands of its people, including the Finnish immigrants who have become Americans. Never underestimate the power of a few selected words. They can change a nation. The influence of this simple farmer has lived long beyond the conspiracies of nobles which drained the energies of government in his day. Ruotsalainen was living embodiment of The Scandinavian Spirit.

*Paavo Ruotsalainen —
religious leader.*

You will also enjoy
reading these other
Scandinavian-interest
books
published by

**North
American
Heritage
Press**

These are available at
your local book store
or Scandinavian gift shop
or may be ordered from
North American Heritage Press

P.O. Box 1 • Minot, ND 58702

(Please add $2.00 per book for shipping.)

The Scandinavian Heritage

By Arland O. Fiske

This hard-to-put-down book of 100 interestingly-told stories is about the people, places, traditions and history of Denmark, Finland, Iceland, Norway and of course Sweden. Well-known Scandinavian-American syndicated newspaper columnist Arland O. Fiske offers well-written and researched vignettes on topics which vary from Viking burial customs to the Scandinavian Royal Families.

Here's some excerpts from the book's foreword by Dr. Sidney A. Rand, former president of St. Olaf College and United States Ambassador to Norway:

"Arland Fiske is a good story teller. In these vignettes he has taken events in Scandinavian history and made them live and breathe. Some of them deal with well-known historical figures; others tell us of persons and places that do not dominate the pages of history. But there is a human warmth and interest in each one.

One virtue of this collection of articles is its breadth. So often we read about the Norwegians or the Swedes or the Danes or the Finns, they are presented almost as competitors for places in history. Here is an author who is attracted to and

NOW... The Scandinavian Heritage Book. Based on the popular syndicated column by well-known Scandinavian-American author Arland O. Fiske.

The Scandinavian Heritage

Arland O. Fiske

Foreword by Sidney A. Rand

100 interestingly told stories about the people, places, traditions and history of Denmark, Finland, Iceland, Norway and Sweden.

charmed by the exploits and accomplishments of all the Scandinavians. The reader may make comparisons or draw contrasts; the author does not.

Fiske's collection of "little stories" is easily read and can be taken a bit at a time if preferred. Each story has its own attraction."

A best seller, now in its fourth printing!

---

248 pages, 6"x9", softbound   **No. HP-120 $9.95**

Contents of The Scandinavian Heritage

Who Are The Scandinavians?
General L. J. Sverdrup—"Engineer Soldier
　At His Best"
Queen Margaret I—Ruler Of All Scandinavia
April 9, 1940—The "Bitter Years" Begin
"Prillar-Guri:" The Country Girl Who
　Saved Norway
The Vikings In Ireland
The Scandinavian "Oscars" And
　The "French Connection"
"Syttende Mai"—Norway's Constitution Day
"Call Her Nettie Olson"—
　An Immigrant Family's Story
Snorri Sturluson: Iceland's "Royal Storyteller"
The Norse Gods—Where Have They Gone?
Leif Erikson Discovers America!
Ole, The Cotter's Son—A Story Of Courage
　And Love
Vikings Attack Lindisfarne, Britain's
　"Holy Island"
The Vikings In Russia
"Fourth Of July" Celebrated In Denmark
Norwegian Folk Tales—Retold
John Ericsson And The Civil War's Great
　Naval Battle
"St. Olaf"—Norway's Best Remembered King
The Saarinens: Finland's Architectural
　Gift To America
Danes Solve 2000 Year Old Murder Mystery
"Black Death" Strikes Europe
John Hanson—America's First President
The Day The Nazis Lost Denmark
Where Did The Greenlanders Go?
Hans Heg—Hero Of Chickamauga
The Vikings In France
Norway's Royal Family
"Høstfest"—A Time For Celebration
Carl Ben Eielson: "Viking In The Sky"
Knut—The Dane Who Ruled England
Thor Heyerdahl—Discoverer Of
　"Old Worlds"
The Stave Churches Of Norway
Oslo—"Friendly City Of The North"
Akershus—Fortress Of Old Norway
Jean Sibelius And The Music Of Finland
Sweden—Its People And Royalty
H. C. Andersen—Denmark's Beloved
　Storyteller
How Scandinavia Became Christian
Oscar Overby—"He Taught Us To Sing"
The "Resistance Museum" In Oslo
Ole Rolvaag—A "Giant In The Earth"
T. F. Gullixson—As I Remember Him
Rjukan—Norway's Heavy Water Plant
　Attacked
Viking Burial Customs
Soren Kierkegaard—A Dane Whose
　Ideas Outlived Him

The Scandinavians In North Dakota
"Munkholmen" In The Trondheim Harbor
Hans Nielsen Hauge—Norway's Greatest
　Folk Hero
Grundtvig—The Most Danish Of The Danes
Dag Hammarskjold: Sweden's "Apostle
　Of Peace"
Herman Wedel Jarlsberg—A Statesman
　To Be Remembered
Gustavus Adolphus—"Lion Of The North"
Mannerheim—A Name The Finns Trust
Journey To Surnadal
Visit To Storen
Discoveries In Trondheim
A Surprise In Hattfjeldal
A Short Stop In Oppdal
At The "Presthus" In Orkdal
Travelling With "Holger Danske"
By The Sands Of The North Sea
"Legoland"—A Playland For All Ages
A Birthday Party In Denmark
First Stop—Ellis Island
A "Halling" Who Showed No Fear
The Korens Come To America
A Swedish Immigrant Writes Home
The Mystery Of The "Runes"
The "Varangians" In The Emperor's Court
Harald "Hardrada" Returns
The Normans In England
The Normans In Italy And Sicily
Knut Hamsun—Norway's Vagrant Novelist
Finland—Land Of Surprises
The Swedish Spirit
A Visit To Tivoli
"Wonderful Copenhagen"
The "Hanse" In Bergen
Journey Through The "Vestlands"—Part I
Journey Through The "Vestlands"—Part II
Henrik Ibsen—"Shakespeare Of The North"
Edvard Grieg And "Troldhaugen"
Selma Lagerlof And "The Adventures Of Nils"
Discovering The "Wasa Ship"
Who Are The "Lapps?"
"Maihaugen" In Lillehammer
Linka Comes To America
Going To Church In Scandinavia
The Lighthouse At Lindesnes
Hans Egede—"Apostle To Greenland"
Harald "Haarfagre"—The King Who United
　Norway
"Up In The Seters"
Stockholm's "Storkyrkan"
Prince Eugen's Island
The Wild Adventures Of Knute
Georg Sverdrup—"Apostle Of Freedom"
The "Resistance Museum" In Copenhagen
King Olaf Tryggvason
Celebration On Moster Island

Prairie Wind, Blow Me Back

By Evelyn Dale Iverson

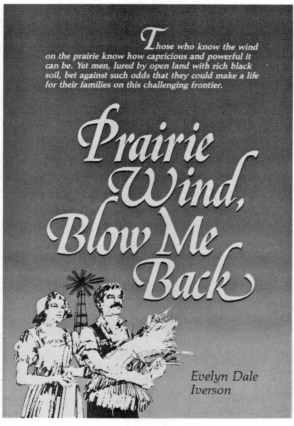

Those who know the wind on the prairie know how capricious and powerful it can be. Yet men, lured by open land with rich black soil, bet against such odds that they could make a life for their families on this challenging frontier.

Evelyn Dale Iverson

Rakel: *"How can Renhild be so devious? I think she is the most evil person I have ever met!"*

"Nils thought of the prairie wind as a sparring partner. How could he beat this fellow?"

PRAIRIE WIND, BLOW ME BACK.

But where? It depends who and where you are.

For Nils, when he was homesick and struggling, it was his childhood home. But later it was other things.

For most of us, it is a glimpse of a different world a hundred years ago, and what life was like "in those days."

And like Nils, before we leave it, a look at desires, priorities, and values.

—*Evelyn Dale Iverson*

About The Author...

Evelyn Dale Iverson is a granddaughter of Nils A. Dale in this story, and a daughter of Hans M. Dale, the infant who came in a covered wagon to Dakota Territory over a hundred years ago.

The author is a native of Canton, SD, where her father was a professor and later the president of Augustana Academy. She graduated from Concordia College, Moorhead, MN, when her father was treasurer of that college. He also owned a part of the homestead in Miner County, which he felt close to, and his family visited often.

Almost all the names in this book are real places and real people, with the exception of Arne and Renhild, who are composites of others who lived "in those days."

---

158 pages, 6"x9", softbound   No. HP-122 $7.95

The Scandinavian World

By Arland O. Fiske

CONTENTS

Well-known Scandinavian-American author and syndicated columnist Arland O. Fiske delights us, in his unique story-telling way, with stories and tales of the Scandinavian World.

100 interestingly told stories about the people, places, traditions and history of Sweden, Norway, Iceland, Finland and Denmark.

The Scandinavian World

Arland O. Fiske

Foreword by Alvin N. Rogness

The Swedes Of Jamestown, New York
Gutzon Borglum - Sculptor Of Presidents
Sigurd The Crusader
Carl Milles - Swedish Artistic Genius
Raoul Wallenberg - "Righteous Gentile"
Norway Honors General Jones
The "Ola And Per" Comics
Halvdan The Black
The Scandinavians Of Detroit
The American Swedish Institute
"News From Norway"
Church Life In Norway
The Oslo Cathedral
The Town Hall In Oslo
A.M. Andersen - Pathfinder For Dana College
Knute Nelson - Champion Of Children's Rights
Orion Samueslon - The Voice Of American Agriculture
The Scandinavians Are Coming
An Evening With Victor Borge
My Unforgettable Swedish Friend
T.G. Mandt - "Wagonmaker"
"Hap" Lerwick - From Lumberjack To Surgeon
"Snowshoe" Thompson Carries The Mail
Rasmus B. Anderson And King Frederick's Pipe
Jens Hanson And The Vatican Library
Knute Reindahl - Violin Maker
Anna The Immigrant Girl
Skansen - Sweden In Miniature
Knut Haukelid - Resistance Hero
The Cathedral In Trondheim
Denmark's "Jelling Stone"
Helsinki's "Rock Church"
Hans Hyldbakk - "King Of The Cliff"
Lindholm Hoje - Viking Winter Camp In Denmark
The "Primstav" - Old Norse Calendar
"Flying With The Scandinavian Airline System"
"Scoop" Jackson - Counselor To Presidents
Norwegian Deaconesses Build Hospital In Chicago
Discovering Numedal
Trolls And Mountain Roads
Homecoming To Hemsedal
The Viking World
Night Voyage To Helsinki
The American Church In Oslo
Kaare Of Gryting
The Icebreaker "Fram"
The Promise Of America
The Hans Christian Andersen House
Stockholm's "Gamla Stan"
Bindslev - A Small Town In Denmark
Cleng Peerson's Boyhood In Norway
Cleng Peerson Sails The "Restauration"
Cleng Peerson's Adventures In America
The "Great Church" In Helsinki
Molde - The "City Of Roses"
The "Independent Order Of Vikings"
Tracing A Family Name
Myron Floren Goes To Norway
The Tales Of Askeladden
The Prime Minister Who Saved The King
The Anatomy Of A Story
A Visit To The Bergen Aquarium
Alfred Nobel And The "Prizes"

Impressions Of "Native Americans" By Swedish Immigrants
The Historic Tingvoll Church
The Scandinavian Colleges In America
The Norwegians Of Lake Wobegon
Johan Falkenberget - The "Copper Mine" Novelist
Scandinavian Immigrant Worship Traditions
The Fritjof Saga
Lady Inger Of Austraat
Erik The Red
Where Is Vinland?
The Tale Of Thorfin Karlsefni
The Vinland Map
Norse Rune Stones In America
Immigrants From Voss To America
Scandinavia And The Northern Crusades
Jon Wefald - Kansas State Prexy
Slaves And Free Men In The Viking World
Political Views Of Norwegian Immigrants
The Norwegian Immigrant Press
Family Life In The Viking World

Chiefs, Earls And Kings In The Viking World
Everyday Life In The Viking World
Erling Rolfsrud And The "Tiger Lily Years"
Folke Bernadotte - Sweden's Humanitarian Diplomat
Trade And Commerce In The Viking World
Warfare In The Viking World
Christmas In Scandinavia
The Saga Of Torger Skaaden
George Reishus Remembers
Vikings In The Turtle Mountains?
The Enigma Of Vikdun Quisling
When The Vikings Came To Troyes
"Gamle Norge - Old Norway"
Who Are The "Sons Of Norway?"
The "Bygelag" Movement In America
The Norwegian-American Historical Association
Geir Botnen - Norway's World-Class Pianist

---

248 pages, 6"x9", softbound   **No. HP-121**   **$9.95**

Skis Against The Atom

By Lt. Colonel Knut Haukelid

The outcome of World War II could very possibly have been much different if Knut Haukelid and his small, but courageous band of Norwegian soldiers had not been successful in sabotaging the Nazi's supply of "heavy water." The "heavy water" produced at a facility in occupied Norway was vital to Hitler's race with the United States to develop the atomic bomb. Knut Haukelid's "Skis Against The Atom" gives the reader an intimate account of the valiant and self-sacrificing service that the not-to-be-subdued Norwegians performed for the whole free world.

The exciting, first-hand account of heroism and daring sabotage during the Nazi occupation of Norway.

KNUT HAUKELID

Excerpted from the Introduction of Skis Against The Atom by General Major Sir Collin Gubbins, CO of Special Operation Executive

I am glad to write for my friend Knut Haukelid an introduction to this enthralling story of high adventure on military duty so as to give the background to the operations which this book so vividly describes, and to show how they fitted into the wider picture of "Resistance." I hope, too, it will enable the reader to have a fuller appreciation and understanding of the remarkable exploits of a small and devoted group of Norwegian soldiers.

---

252 pages, 6"x9", softbound   No. HP-123 $9.95